BEYOND URBAN BIAS

BEYOND URBAN BIAS

Edited by

ASHUTOSH VARSHNEY

FRANK CASS

First published 1993 in Great Britain by
FRANK CASS AND COMPANY LIMITED
Gainsborough House, 11 Gainsborough Road,
London E11 1RS, England

and in the United States by
FRANK CASS
c/o International Specialised Book Services Inc.
5804 N.E. Hassalo Street
Portland, OR 97213-3644

Copyright © 1993 Frank Cass & Co. Ltd

British Library Cataloging in Publication data

Beyond Urban Bias
I. Varshney, Ashutosh
338.9

ISBN 0–7146–4511–7

Library of Congress Cataloging-in-Publication Data

Beyond urban bias / edited by Ashutosh Varshney.
    p.   cm.
    Includes bibliographical references.
    ISBN 0–7146–4511–7 (hard)
    1. Poor—Developing countries—Case studies.   2. Rural poor-
-Developing countries—Case studies.   I. Varshney, Ashutosh, 1957–

    HC57.72.P6B48   1993
    305.5′6′091724—dc20   93–24138
                                                                         CIP

This group of studies first appeared in a Special Issue:
'Beyond Urban Bias' of *The Journal of Development Studies*, Vol. 29, No. 4
published by Frank Cass & Co. Ltd.

Typeset by Florencetype Ltd, Kewstoke, Avon

Contents

Preface

The idea for this volume came from a panel on 'State-building, Industrialisation and the Peasantry in the Third World', organised at the 1991 annual meeting of the American Political Science Association (APSA) in Washington, DC. Having read parts of my work, David Laitin, in his capacity as Program Chair for the Comparative Politics of Developing Countries, invited me to organise the panel. When I looked around for contributors who could add to what we already knew about the impact 'late industrialisation' has on the countryside and vice versa, a list of scholars quickly emerged. A thoughtful commentary by Robert Bates at the meetings and revisions suggested by various readers gave our first version much greater coherence.

To the panel contributions, two papers – Peter Timmer and Jean Oi – were finally added. In addition to Robert Bates, a participant on the panel, Michael Lipton also agreed to write a detailed commentary on our papers. We hope that the new research and debate presented in this volume sheds greater light on 'urban bias' in Asia, Africa and Latin America.

For initiating this collaborative project, I am especially thankful to David Laitin and Mick Moore. Through their invitations, they conspired to generate this volume.

Ashutosh Varshney   June 1993
London, England

I. INTRODUCTION

Introduction:
Urban Bias in Perspective

ASHUTOSH VARSHNEY

Under what conditions might urban bias erode? Are those conditions entirely uncommon? Or is it that our customary understanding was wrong in several key respects? These are the questions underlying this volume. To express our vantage point clearly, the papers focus on the conditions under which the countryside is not 'squeezed'. Four critiques of the urban bias theory emerge, three of which are new. First, the urban bias theory neglects political institutions. The urban bias outcome is not true across political systems (democracy versus authoritarianism), or across ideological orientations of the ruling elite (pro-rural or pro-industrial). Second, the urban bias theory did not anticipate how technical change over time could begin to make the rural sector powerful. Third, the conception of how rural interests are expressed in politics is limited in urban bias theory to the strictly economic issues. Ethnic (and religious) identities may cut across the rural and urban sectors, and may obstruct an economic expression of rural interests more than the power of the city. Finally, as pointed out earlier a special issue of this journal on urban bias, the urban–rural boundaries may at times be hard to detect.

The 'urban bias' theory has long been influential in development studies. Associated primarily with the works of Michael Lipton [*1977*] and Robert Bates [*1981*], it has contributed a great deal to our knowledge of the grim realities of rural life in the developing world. Political economy research of a more recent vintage, however, suggests that it is time to redefine the problem of urban bias.

Viewed as a collective engagement with the urban bias theory, this volume presents the new research along with the responses of Bates and

Ashutosh Varshney is Associate Professor of Government at Harvard University. He thankfully acknowledges Mick Moore's helpful comments on an earlier draft. Some of the arguments in this essay draw upon the author's forthcoming book, *Democracy, Development and the Countryside: Urban–Rural Struggles in India*, New York: Cambridge University Press (Cambridge Studies in Comparative Politics).

Lipton. Our studies do not add up to an alternative theory of why the state behaves the way it does towards the countryside. They do, however, point to the factors that need careful attention in future research. These papers can be seen as building blocks for the construction of an alternative theory of 'the state and agriculture'.

Reduced to its bare essentials, the urban bias theory puts forth two propositions: (i) that the development process in the third world is systematically biased against the countryside; and (ii) that this bias is deeply embedded in the political structure of these countries, dominated as they are by the urban groups. In other words, the countryside is *economically* poor because it is *politically* powerless. If it were more powerful, it would be taxed less, it would get more public investment, and it would get better prices for its products. In the polemical but influential words of Michael Lipton:

> . . . the most important class conflict in the poor countries of the world today is not between labor and capital. Nor is it between foreign and national interests. It is between rural classes and urban classes. The rural sector contains most of the poverty and most of the low-cost sources of potential advance; but the urban sector contains most of the articulateness, organisation and power. So the urban classes have been able to win most of the rounds of the struggle with the countryside . . . [*Lipton, 1977: 13*].

Theories of collective action have led to a further development of this argument. Lipton's argument did not allow for distinct state treatment of different crops, nor was it clear what elements of his analytical structure would explain the overvaluation of agriculture in the developed world. Responding to these concerns in his work on African agriculture, Robert Bates [*1981*] advanced our analytic understanding of the urban–rural relationships in economic development. It was, he argued, not enough to say that the urban sector was powerful and the countryside powerless. It was necessary to understand why that was so, and whether a change in the urban–rural equation was possible. Using the rational choice methodology, Bates gave us *microfoundations* of the observed outcomes.

Bates' nuanced reformulation opened the way for an increasing academic acceptance of the theory. The acceptance went beyond the universities. Over the 1980s the urban bias view neatly dovetailed into the 'getting prices right' paradigm of thinking, promoted by the international development agencies. Indeed, it would be no exaggeration to say that on the agricultural sector the urban bias theory became 'hegemonic' in the 1980s. 'Rational price regimes', as the World Bank put it, 'are essential to the success of development strategies'. [*World Bank, 1982; 1986; 1988*]. But agricultural prices, the World Bank argued, were highly 'distorted' in the Third World, principally because of the urban-dominated politics in these countries. A series of World Bank studies sought to document the claim about price distortions against agriculture,[1] and inferred that these biases were embedded in the power structure.

Under what conditions might urban bias erode? Are those conditions entirely uncommon? Or is it that our customary understanding was wrong in several key respects? These are the questions underlying this volume. To express our vantage point clearly, the papers focus on the conditions under which the countryside is *not* 'squeezed'. In the industrialisation of a primarily agricultural society, some resources are bound to be transferred from the rural sector. *Transferring* a surplus, therefore, should be distinguished from *squeezing* a surplus out of agriculture. The former may facilitate industrialisation as well as help agriculture [*Lewis, 1954; Timmer, 1992*]; the latter may hurt both, as the urban bias theorists have reminded us. The belief that industrialisation in the developing world is often at the cost of agriculture is, of course, not confined to the urban bias theorists. They have simply been some of its most widely read exponents.

The criticisms of urban bias theory made by these papers can be grouped under four headings, three of which are new. First, the theory neglects political *institutions*. The urban bias outcome is not true across political systems (for example, democracy versus authoritarianism), or across ideological orientations of the ruling elite (pro-rural or pro-industrial). How the polity and political institutions are organised, what objectives the political elites have, and how those objectives are expressed in the policy process may have varying implications not only for the power of the rural sector but also for its economic well-being. Second, the urban bias theory did not anticipate how *technical change* over time, especially of the green revolution variety, could begin to make the rural sector powerful. Third, the conception of how rural interests are expressed in politics is limited in urban bias theory to the strictly economic issues. That would not be such an omission, were it not damaging to the argument. Ethnic (and religious) identities may cut across the rural and urban sectors. When they begin to dominant the political agenda of a country, they can obstruct a sectoral construction of rural interests in politics. The cross-cutting nature of rural identities and interests may thus weaken the countryside more than the power of the city. Finally, as pointed out in the first special issue of this journal on urban bias [*Harriss and Moore, 1984*], the *urban–rural boundaries* may at times be hard to detect. Evidence from Ivory Coast and China presented in this volume adds further to the earlier critique.

To put the contributions in perspective, this essay starts with a brief review of theories and ideas about town–country relations in the process of development. The relationship of urban bias theory with this literature will be made clear. The next section will elaborate on the four criticisms summarised above, also indicating the directions in which the new research takes us. Finally, I deal with an important issue raised by Lipton.

I. TOWN–COUNTRY STRUGGLES IN DEVELOPMENT: A BRIEF OVERVIEW OF IDEAS

A history of ideas on town–country struggles[2] must start with the obvious fact that as economies develop and societies modernise, agriculture declines. Before the rise of industrial society, all societies were rural. If we look at the most industrialised societies of today, their agricultural sectors constitute less than five per cent of gross domestic product (GDP). Contrariwise, in the poorest economies of the world, agriculture still accounts for anywhere between 30 to 65 per cent of GDP [*World Bank, 1991: 208–9*]. The notion of agricultural development in the poor economies is thus imbued with an inescapable irony. Without agricultural development food may not be forthcoming. Agriculture must, therefore, develop but it develops sectorally only to decline inter-sectorally. It is a rare idealist, or a utopian, who believes in keeping agriculture and rural communities as they always were.[3] Whether one likes it or not, industrialisation requires the eclipse of agriculture.

This irony has given birth to the central question of town–country debates: on what *terms* should agriculture decline, for decline it must. The question has both economic and political implications. Focusing on the role of agriculture in industrialisation, the economic literature deals with how to industrialise and the implications industrial development has for agriculture. The political economy literature examines the conflicts and coalitions that emerge as industrialisation proceeds, and investigates how the rural people deal with the 'imperatives' of industrialisation. The urban bias view belongs to the political economy genre. It entails both an economic and political view of development.

Agriculture and Industrialisation

The agricultural sector is intimately tied up with the question of how to raise resources for industrialisation. Particular significance is attached to three kinds of resources: (i) food for the increasing urban population, (ii) labour to man the expanding industrial workforce, and (iii) savings to finance industrial investment.[4] All three resources may not be simultaneously forthcoming. Worse, maximising one may minimise the other, which is especially true of food and savings. If, to raise savings for industrialisation, agricultural prices are kept low and industrial prices are artificially increased, food production may decline. If, to ensure steadily increasing supplies of food, agricultural prices are raised, enough savings for industrial investment may not be forthcoming. These dilemmas essentially have led to two kinds of analytical exercises: how should agriculture be *developed* and how should agricultural resources be *transferred*. Broadly speaking, thinking about the first issue is associated with the micro views of agriculture, and thinking about the second, with the various macro views. Agricultural production must go up. This requires an understanding of what makes farmers produce. At the same time, agricultural resources should be transferred, so the transfer should be of a kind that does not hurt agricultural production. Balancing the micro and the macro has been a nagging problem in the economic literature.

The first economists were pessimistic about agriculture. The 'classical pessimism' of the eithteenth and nineteenth century (mainly Adam Smith and David Ricardo) stemmed from the belief that, in contrast to industry, agriculture suffered from decreasing returns to scale. This fact itself led to, as well as called for, a transfer of resources to industry. Later, marginalists like Marshall believed that technical progress was inevitably slower in agriculture – hence, the inevitability and desirability of transferring resources from agriculture, given the critical role of technology in economic development.

Ricardo and Malthus: The first famous terms of trade debate took place between two classical economists, Malthus and Ricardo, concerning the Corn Laws in nineteenth-century England. The issue was whether laws limiting grain imports into England should be repealed. If higher imports were allowed, food prices would come down; if they continued to be restricted, food prices would remain high. How would all this affect industrialisation in England? Malthus defended the Corn Laws on the following lines. If food imports were increased, terms of trade would turn against agriculture as a result of the lowering of food prices and, faced thus with a drop in real incomes, the landlords would cut spending. This cut would in turn retard industrial growth since the agricultural sector accounted for a large part of the demand for industrial goods. Ricardo disagreed. To realise gains from trade, he favoured repealing the Corn Laws. He also argued that aggregate demand was retarded, not stimulated, by landlords' rents. Land rents ought to come down, not increase. Repeal of the Corn Laws, by cheapening food and therefore turning the terms of trade against agriculture, would facilitate this process. Modern treatments of this debate suggest that the answer as to whether aggregate demand will go up or come down as a result of food imports and the consequent lowering of food prices depends essentially on how wage-earners spend their incomes between goods produced by the two sectors [*Taylor, 1983: 38–48; Rao, 1986*].

In the twentieth century, the issue of agriculture–industry linkages was confronted in a more elaborate and dramatic manner than ever before. The reason was simple. The late developers of the world were unwilling to industrialise in the manner of England and France. Economic processes that took two to three centuries in England and France were now to be telescoped into a few decades. The late developers' desire to industrialise quickly required clarity on the agriculture–industry relationships in the process of industrialisation. Dealing with the new drive for industrialisation, the Soviet industrialisation debate and W. Arthur Lewis's work on economic development became the economic classics of the twentieth century.

The Soviet industrialisation debate: The Soviet debate of the 1920s continues to be intellectually important for understanding late industrialisation.[5] Communism may have collapsed in the 1990s, but for the first communist country in the world, whether or not a communist country could modernise its economy faster than its capitalist predecessors was clearly a matter of historic proportions. The issue was how to finance industrialisation in the newly-born socialist state. The protagonists were Evgeny Preobrazhensky and Nikolai Bukharin and the debate formed the basis of the socialist economic policy.

Preobrazhensky argued that the state should turn the terms of trade against agriculture: it should offer the lowest possible prices for farm products and sell the industrial products to the country at the highest possible price. The surplus thus gained would finance industrialisation. Supported by Lenin, Bukharin argued in favour of 'equilibrium prices', not 'non-equivalent exchange' for agriculture. Preobrazhensky's prescriptions, he thought, were self-defeating for they would drastically cut food supply. The kulaks were the dominant class in the countryside, and they would respond to unfavourable terms of trade by producing and/or marketing less. Rural demand for industrial output would also contract, as the kulaks, with incomes falling, cut their spending. Bukharin advocated market forces in agriculture, along with a state policy encouraging co-operatives for inputs, credit and farm sales, whose resources and facilities would, however, be especially earmarked for the small pea-santry. Co-operatives would reduce unit costs of small peasants, and the scale economies, so obtained, would make small peasants much more competitive than the kulaks in the market. Economic rationality would thus liquidate the kulaks as a class and collectivisation would dominate the countryside. State-directed market forces would lead to socialism.

Making the argument that parallel lines never met (the parallel lines being the socialist urban sector and an unyielding, uncollectivised rural sector), Stalin finally embraced Preobrazhensky's model for state policy. He solved its intrinsic economic problem – the possibility of the kulaks not providing food supplies – by physically liquidating the kulaks (and also eliminating a mass of peasants resisting collectivisation). Stalin argued that if the state liquidated those who did not provide food for socialist industrialisation at reasonable prices, it would end up getting food from the agricultural sector as well as savings (that is, food at low prices). If both savings *and* food from agriculture were required, vio-lence, in Stalin's reasoning, was absolutely necessary.

It turns out that, due to unanticipated economic reasons understood later by economists, Stalin was wrong. So was Preobrazhensky. Even though the investment rate in the USSR went up from a mere 14.8 per cent of GDP in 1928 to 44.1 per cent by the end of the First Plan in 1932, this increase in investment was not *primarily* financed by agricultural surpluses. A large part was actually financed by the 'forced savings' of the industrial working class [*Ellman, 1975*]. Collectivisation did not increase the net agricultural *surplus*, nor did it increase the total agricultural *output*; only the *state procurement* of *wage goods* (especially food) increased. Even more important, the terms of trade did not turn in favour of industry. Rather, the food that could not be procured went into the free ('black') market and food prices in the free market shot up so much that the overall terms of trade for agriculture in fact improved during the plan period.[6] Inflation was the result. Inflation decreased the real value of the wages paid to the industrial workers. *Both* the savings thus forced on the urban sector (fall in real wages) and an agrarian surplus, therefore, financed Soviet industrialisation under the First Plan (1928–32).

W. Arthur Lewis and after: Writing in the middle of the twentieth century, W. Arthur Lewis [*1954*][7] had no doubt that a price-squeeze on a stagnant agriculture (à la Stalin) would only choke off food supplies, thereby hurting industrialisation. He argued that 'industrial and agricul-tural revolutions always go together' and 'economies in which agricul-ture is stagnant do not show industrial development' [*Lewis, 1954: 433*]. At one level, this position is a re-statement of Bukharin. Lewis, however, did not stop there. Bukharin's conclusion was unsatisfactory, in that he could not see the profound dilemma inherent in his prescription. If the agriculture sector became more productive, 'we escape', argued Lewis, 'the Scylla of adverse terms of trade' but 'we may be caught by the Charybdis of real wages rising because the subsistence sector is more productive' [*ibid*.]. Since poor economies did not have a high level of savings, low wages, by increasing profits, could finance industrial investment. Industrialisation was not only dependent on steady food supplies but also on low wages, which would be transformed into high wages by a productive agricultural sector. Thus, both stagnating and prospering agriculture could hurt industrialisation.

How should one, then, solve the problem? Taxing *prospering* farmers was Lewis' solution:

> the capitalists' next best move is to prevent the farmer from getting all his extra production. In Japan this was achieved by raising rents against the farmers, and by taxing them more heavily, so that a large part of the rapid increase in productivity which occurred (between 1880 and 1910 . . .) was taken away from the farmers and used for capital formation . . . [*Lewis, 1954: 433–4*].

The abiding value of Lewis' model remains precisely in forcefully stating the dilemma and proposing a solution that seemed to correspond with a historical case (Japan).

Starting with Theodore Schultz [*1964*], a *micro*economic orientation, focused more on peasant behaviour and raising agricultural production than on viewing agriculture as a means to industrial development, came to dominate the economic thinking about agriculture in developing economies. Like Lewis, Schultz argued that, for an agricultural revolution to take place, technological investments in agriculture were essential. Unlike Lewis, however, he also argued for price incentives for farmers, because such incentives would be necessary for the adoption by farmers of new technology. Both price incentives and technological upgrading were essential.

Politically speaking, a microeconomic view, reliant as it is on price incentives for farmers, is perhaps the most favourable to the countryside. But a purely microeconomic view leaves a serious economic problem unresolved: how should one raise resources for industrialisation? Schultz did not engage with this question.

In principle, two non-agricultural sources of savings do exist. Minerals or 'foreign savings' (loans or direct investment) can step in to provide resources. Not all countries, however, have rich deposits of minerals. And some can use the income from minerals or oil so recklessly that they end up hurting agriculture through what is known as the 'Dutch disease'. The examples of Mexico and Nigeria after the oil price hike of the 1970s have often been cited to illustrate the point. Foreign aid (or foreign loans and investment) can rarely provide all the resources needed. In the early stages of development, countries typically aim at a 15 per cent investment rate but save only 5 per cent of their income. Only in exceptional cases does foreign aid make up such a large shortfall (American aid to Israel and South Korea in the 1950s comes to mind). A slow pace of industrialisation, if chosen, may also reduce the burden on agriculture, but very few poor countries choose to be slow industrialisers.

It is not surprising, therefore, that a microeconomic view alone would not be feasible. Realising this, later developments in economic theory recast the micro position, by linking it with the macro problem of the extraction of agricultural resources for industrialisation. In this reconstructed vein, Peter Timmer argues that a Schultz-induced productivity in agriculture 'creates a surplus, which . . . can (then) be tapped directly through taxation . . ., or indirectly, through government intervention into the urban–rural term of trade' [*Timmer, 1988; 1992*]. This position is a marriage of Lewis and Schultz.

Recent empirical research has thrown further light on how the resources are generated and transferred in the process of industrialisation. It turns out that the *extent* of agricultural contribution has generally been overestimated, though agriculture does provide resources – in some cases a very large part [*Quisumbing and Taylor, 1990*]. The contribution of agricultural sector has been overwhelmingly large typically in countries with a large export agriculture sector, which makes it easier for the government to tap agricultural resources. This argument does not amount to saying that Third World leaders have not tried to force the price scissors on the countryside; rather, even when they have done so, the objective economic consequences of their actions have been that inflation and a fall in urban wages have financed *part* of the investment. Only in the presence of cheap food imports in adequate quantities could this result – squeezing of food sector leading to inflationary consequences – be avoided. An export-oriented agricultural sector is typically more readily exploitable. In much of Africa and also South-east Asia, therefore, agricultural exports may have contributed heavily to the modernisation of economies.

These works help us categorise the various ways in which agriculture has intertwined with the process of industrialisation. Late developers seem to have followed one of the following four paths to industrialisa-

tion: (i) squeeze agriculture (à la Stalin); (ii) extract a surplus from the
export agriculture sector but do not squeeze the entire agricultural
sector; (iii) extract a surplus from minerals or rely on foreign resources
for funding industrialisation; (iv) make agriculture productive (via technological investments) but transfer resources through taxation or terms
of trade.

By now, it is clear that route (i) is self-defeating (much of Africa
seems to have followed this option). Options (ii) and (iii) are not
available to all countries since not all of them have large export agriculture sectors or great mineral deposits, and aid (or foreign resources)
do not easily come in such large magnitudes. Option (iv) remains the
best option for low income countries still in the early phases of industrialisation. One may also add that the urban bias view essentially
focuses on options (i) and (ii).

The Political Issues

Economic theories may suggest the obvious truth that agriculture declines in the process of modernisation. The political tangles, however,
remain. Why should the rural sector accept a plummeting fate? What
helps society at large may not benefit the villages. At any rate, the social
benefit at time T, which may improve the lot of the rural folk in the end,
may not help them at time T-1. Does not the peasantry fight the march
of history? If not, why not? If yes, why does it not succeed? The
economic view, in other words, requires political *microfoundations*. We
ought to be able to explain why the rural sector is powerless in the face
of industrialisation

In *The Eighteenth Brumaire of Louis Bonaparte*, Karl Marx provided
the initial formulation on why the peasantry is powerless when confronted with the larger forces of history:

> . . . (T)he great mass of the French nation is formed by simple
> additions of homologous magnitudes, much as potatoes in a sack
> form a sack of potatoes . . . In so far as there is merely a local
> interconnection among these smallholding peasants, and the ident-
> ity of their interests begets no community, no national bond and
> no political organisation among them, they do not form a class.
> They are consequently incapable of enforcing their class interest in
> their own name, whether through a parliament, or through a
> convention [*Shanin, 1987: 332*].

Barrington Moore's well-known classic [*1966*] carried the argument
further. Moore identified three political routes to a modern (that is,
industrial) society: democratic (England, USA, France), fascist (Ger-

many and Japan) and communist (Russia and China). In all cases, the peasantry is sooner or later subdued.

Peasant revolutions of the twentieth century were the only cases, according to Moore, when peasants were not an object but a subject of history. But a peasant-based revolution, he added, did not lead to a consolidation of peasant power after the revolutions. 'Twentieth century peasant revolutions have had their mass support among the peasants, who have then been the principal victims of modernisation put through by communist governments' [*Moore, 428*]. Peasants thus suffer no matter how the political system is constructed.

For Moore, whether or not peasants would revolt depended on three factors: (i) whether peasants had strong links with the lords, (ii) whether peasants had a strong tradition of solidarity; and (iii) whether links with urban classes against the lords were established. Investigating conditions under which peasants revolted, Scott [*1976*] further developed the first two insights. Popkin's work [*1979*] emerged as a counter to Scott, and developed the third insight fully.

Theories of urban bias: About the same time, the urban bias argument emerged. All of the above arguments were about the powerlessness of the peasantry, not about the entire rural sector. The urban bias view sought to explain why the lords would not speak for the rural sector, and even if they did, why that would not matter. The power structure of the third world, this view held, is marked by an 'urban bias'. Urban power subdues rural interests with disastrous results. According to Michael Lipton:

> The rural sector contains most of the poverty and most of the low-cost sources of potential advance; but the urban sector contains most of the articulateness, organisation and power. So the urban classes have been able to win most of the rounds of the struggle with the countryside but in so doing they have made the development process needlessly slow and unfair. Scarce land which might grow millets and beansprouts for hungry villagers, instead produces a trickle of costly calories from meat and milk, which few except the urban rich (who have ample protein anyway) can afford. Scarce investment, instead of going into water pumps to grow rice, is wasted on urban motorways. Scarce human skills design and administer, not clean village wells and agricultural extension services, but world boxing championships in showpiece stadia. Resource allocations, within the city and the villages as well as between them, reflect urban priorities rather than equity or efficiency. The damage has been increased by misguided ideologi-

cal imports, liberal and marxian, and by the town's success in buying off part of the rural elite, thus transferring most of the costs of the process to the rural poor [*Lipton, 1977: 13*].

The overriding concern of the city is cheap food. Artificially low food prices result from this concern, amounting to a tax on the countryside. There are of course many consequences of urban bias that would reflect in many policy areas – investment, taxation and not simply prices – but food prices are absolutely critical. Whatever else might happen, food must remain cheap. Indeed, the 'basic conflict' in the third world boils down to a conflict, says Lipton, between 'gainers from dear food and gainers from cheap food'. All urban classes are interested in cheap food: the industrialist because that will keep wages low, the worker because that 'makes whatever wages he can extract from the boss go further' [*Lipton, 1977: 67*]. And the salaried middle classes, too, would benefit from lower allocations for food in their relatively tight household budgets.

Conversely, 'the whole interest of the rural community is against cheap food' [*ibid.*]. The surplus farmer gains from dear food because he can get more for what he sells; the deficit farmer because he can supplement his income from greater employment and/or higher wages that would result from the surplus farmer hiring more when food is dearer; rural craftsmen because rural carpenters and ropemakers get more work when their patrons are rich; and the same is true of the landless agricultural labourers – starved of work generally, they also get employment if patrons are richer. The surplus farmer, however, is bought off by the city, says Lipton, through agricultural subsidies. In the end, the surplus farmer thus does not lose out. His acquiescence to cheap food, however, is purchased to urban advantage and to the great detriment of the countryside.

Using theories of collective action, Bates [*1981*], as briefly stated earlier, reformulated this argument. One can identify three steps in his argument. First, to extract resources for the treasury, city and industry, African states set prices that hurt the countryside. Second, by selectively distributing state largesse (subsidies and projects), African states divide up the countryside into supporters that benefit from state action and opponents who are deprived of state generosity, and are frequently punished. Such policy-induced splits pre-empt a united rural front. Third, independently of the divisive tactics of the state, rural collective action is difficult because (a) the agriculture sector is very large with each peasant having a small share of the product, and (b) it is dispersed, making communication difficult. The customary free-rider problem in such situations impedes collective action. Industry, on the other hand, is small and concentrated in the city, and the share of each producer in the market is large, making it worthwhile for each producer to organise.[8]

II. HOW URBAN BIAS IS REVERSED, NEUTRALISED OR REDUCED

Lipton sought to explain the biases of development by providing an argument about the relative weight of urban or rural groups in the power structure. While his view identified political power as a key force shaping industrialisation, he did not address the dynamics of power. Whether the power of groups could change over time was not a question he asked. Lipton concentrated on the economic outcomes for the countryside, and then *inferred* that the unfavorable economic outcomes were due to rural powerlessness. Lipton still maintains that 'urban bias is defined upon outcomes, not causes and processes' (this volume).

To put it methodologically, the dependent and independent variables get somewhat mixed up in Lipton's analysis. The dependent variable (the urban bias of economic outcomes) is analysed in detail, and on that basis the independent variable (the urban bias of power structure) is assumed, not demonstrated, to exist. Can the causation be specified independent of the outcome? How does one know that the urban bias of the economic outcome is due to the urban bias of the power structure? Does Lipton not need to explore the intricacies of the power structure to make his claims? Lipton does not engage in such an exercise, even though methodologically it would appear to be necessary for his argument. Whether the power structure is static or has possibilities of change is a matter left unattended.

In his work on Africa, Bates supplied the missing link. He connected the large size, dispersion and communication difficulties of rural groups to their lack of political organisation in general. Needless to add, such difficulties could be surmounted if the rural sector were small, or if a small number of producers accounted for a very large proportion of some crops. Bates was thus not only able to explain why the African states deployed their anti-rural strategies but also (i) why they could get away with it, (ii) why some crops were able to escape the predation of the state but others were not, and (iii) why in the industrialised countries the agriculture sector was subsidised but in the developing world it was taxed. Urban bias was dependent on the landholding structure of a given crop, on whether it was a food crop or an export crop, and on the level of development.

Bates' argument – emerging from a theoretical tradition different from that of Lipton (Moore in this volume) – thus dealt with the proverbial 'black box': why does the state behave the way it does? The papers in the volumes are also, on the whole, more comfortable with Bates' explanations. Bates' framework has greater room for political and economic contingencies in accounting for urban bias (Moore and Varshney in this volume; also see Lipton's response). Politics being a relatively open-ended process, these contingencies matter.

Despite such welcome nuancing, however, the urban bias argument, according to the contributors here, did not go far enough. The papers make four critiques. The urban bias theory does not pay attention to institutional factors. Different political institutions may have varying economic implications for the countryside. It is also *temporally under-specified*, in that it does not recognise the political implications of technical change. Its *urban–rural boundaries* may at times be hard to detect. And finally, its conception of how rural interests are expressed in politics is limited to the strictly economic issues. *Cross-cutting rural identities and interests* may weaken the countryside independently in politics. Let us briefly see the implications of each claim.

The neglect of political institutions in the urban bias theories is perhaps the single most important theme of these contributions. It can take two forms: society-centred and state-centred. Single or competitive party systems, single candidate or multiple-candidate electoral systems have implications for how – and how well – rural interests can be organised. Varshney and Colburn document the role of a competitive party system in making the government responsive to rural interests.[9] In India especially, all political parties have been ruralised over time. And in Costa Rica, a vigorous democracy makes it easier for the rural sector to defend its interests. Widner in this volume and Bates in an earlier work [*1989*] show that even in single party systems rural interests can be reflected in politics, *if* candidates are allowed to compete.

Some state-centred institutional parameters can also be decisive. The models of Bates and Lipton were society-centred. They inferred the biases of public policies from the power of interest/pressure groups. They did not 'go inside the state' to examine how actually economic policy is formed. As a result, the possibility that some state organs themselves may promote rural interests went unexplored. State agricultural agencies in Taiwan (Moore, this volume), local governments in China (Oi, this volume), powerful pro-rural leaderships (Colburn, Timmer, Widner; this volume) have contributed to rural well-being. The continuation, or even the existence, of urban bias may thus depend on the nature of political institutions.

A state-centric focus leads to two other insights. First, while some state agencies may become spokesmen for farm interests in the policy process, other agencies may seek to constrain the power of pro-agriculture bureaucracies. This process can be called *inter-bureaucratic politics*, a relatively unexplored factor in the studies of economic policy in Third World. Varshney [*1989*; this volume; *forthcoming*] reports how Finance, Agriculture and Planning Ministries viewed the agriculture sector very differently in India, and how even though the power and advocacy of rural interests went up in the policy-making organs of the state, the Finance Ministry did not let pro-rural pressures progress beyond a point, managing thereby to restrain 'the onward march of rural, sectoral power'.

Second, some states may consciously emulate the successful models of economic development (Moore and Timmer, this volume). Moore demonstrates how Taiwan and South Korea emulated the Japanese model of agricultural development. Timmer points to the independent role of some key policy objectives of the state. International rice prices typically fluctuate a great deal. To protect their economies from the destabilising effects of these fluctuations, the governments of East and Southeast Asia have attached tremendous importance to price stability as a policy goal. According to his measurement, this policy goal in and of itself explains as much as 90 per cent of the variation in rice prices in these economies, in relation to world prices. In his response, Bates argues that this result, as well as the power of the Finance Ministry in India, still needs a political explanation. Why are the technocrats of Indonesia and the bureaucrats of India's Finance Ministry so powerful? They are not powerful elsewhere, surely in the African cases he studies. For future research, this exchange underlines the necessity of (i) taking inter-bureaucratic politics seriously in the making of economic policy, and (ii) locating, as Bates puts it, 'sources of the power of public bureaucracies'.

Technical change, over time, can have implications for government action. Agro-industries, engaged in the production of seeds, fertilisers and agricultural machinery, may begin to lobby on behalf of agriculture (Moore and Widner, this volume). By lowering costs and thereby exerting moderation on food prices, technical change may also blunt the town–country contradiction, making it possible for the government to please both farmers and city-dwellers. Further, commercialisation may make it less difficult for farmers to organise.

The difficulty of maintaining urban–rural boundaries at times was noted at some length in an earlier special issue of this journal on urban bias [*Moore, 1984*]. It appears here in two forms. In Ivory Coast, urban-based associations lobby for rural projects due to pre-existing linkages (Widner, and Moore, this volume), and in China, local governments, for fiscal reasons, have undertaken economic programs that are beginning to blur the urban–rural boundary (Oi, this volume). Rural industries are transforming Chinese countryside beyond all prior expectations. Whether or not rural migration to the city can significantly alter rural fortunes, however, remains as debatable as before (Widner and Lipton, this volume).

Finally, the cross-cutting nature of rural identities and interests and their political implications are ignored by the urban bias theorists. For the rural sector to push the state and economic policy in its favour, it helps if it can present itself as a cohesive force. As a critique of the urban bias theory, much has been said about *intra*-rural class differences in the past [*Harris and Moore, 1984*]. That such internal class differences can sometimes create problems for rural unity is beyond doubt. Intra-rural class differences, however, do not destroy the case for urban bias, as Lipton argued [*1977*]. Higher producer prices, larger agricultural subsidies and greater rural investment can benefit some classes more, others less, but benefit all classes none the less. Lipton's argument about how these policies benefit the entire sector was economic; the criticisms against a sectoral benefit have also been economic [*Mitra, 1977; de Janvry and Subbarao, 1984*]. As anticipated by Taylor and Lysy [*1979*] and later demonstrated by Tyagi [*1986*], it is very hard to settle conclusively the distributional consequences of higher agricultural prices or subsidies. The results of the models depend on how the model is closed and what the starting assumptions are.

Politically, however, the case is less ambiguous. First of all, it is neither theoretically nor empirically clear that economic classes would also be political actors. Vertical patron–client ties have often come in the way of horizontal class mobilisations. Second, and more important, a potential rural unity on economic interests transcending internal class differences is possible. Sectorally based rural mobilisation flourished in India in the 1980s [*Varshney, forthcoming*].

The most serious obstacles to sectoral mobilisation lie not in internal class differences, as often assumed in political economy, but in ethnic and religious identities. Sectoral politics seeking higher agricultural prices, subsidies and investment may run up against politics based on other cleavages – caste, tribe, ethnicity, religion. Politics based on these latter identities makes sectoral politics difficult, for typically caste, ethnicity and religion cut across the urban and the rural. In India, there are Hindu villagers and Hindu urbanites, just as there are 'backward castes' in both cities and villages [*Varshney, this volume; forthcoming*]. Examples along these lines from other countries can also be cited [*Moore, 1985*]. In situations where an entire ethnic group is rural and another group urban, this cross-cutting dimension may not hold. Otherwise, until an economic construction of interests completely overpowers identities and non-economic interests, rural power – even if it exists – is likely to remain self-limited.

The ultimate constraint on rural power, thus, may not be the 'urban bias' of the power structure. At the deepest level, it may well stem from how farmers, like other human beings, perceive themselves – as people having multiple selves. A preponderance of the economic over the non-economic self is not how this multiplicity is necessarily resolved. That is what the urban bias argument assumes.

III. CONCLUDING REMARKS

These studies were conceived in the cumulative spirit of research. We have learned from the urban bias theories, but recognising some difficulties we wished to go further. In his response, Bates agrees with a number of arguments made by these studies and points to future directions of research. While accepting some of the points, Lipton (this volume) is on the whole less convinced. One of his principal contentions is that these contributions concentrate more on the price-based interventions of the state, less on the expenditures-based interventions. And that, to his mind, reduces the force of our arguments.

In a basic conceptual sense, Lipton is right. It is only the vector sum of all state interventions in the countryside that will clinch whether an urban bias exists or not. Price-based interventions of the state may have become favourable to the countryside in several parts of the developing world, but non-price interventions, he says, may well have gone in the other direction.

After all is said and done, this problem is easier stated theoretically than investigated empirically. Imagine the empirical difficulties of not only working out the implications of price-based interventions for rural welfare, but also of factoring in the direct and indirect implications of government expenditures. We will need data over time and across countries. It is not clear when – if ever – we will be able to get a time-series on all of these dimensions for a large enough number of countries. Seen in this sense, the urban bias theory is unfalsifiable.

Ironically, however, if such empirically demanding standards of theorisation and testing are employed, Lipton himself may have been wrong in his initial argument about urban bias. For, lacking complete data sets on both price and non-price interventions, he could not have *definitively* proved or disproved the existence of urban bias for as many countries as he covered in 1977. Much of his argumentation was based on drawing reasonable inferences from data, even when the existing data, in and of themselves, did not fully support the conclusions.[10]

In a realistic theoretical sense, which allows the analyst to combine inductive and deductive reasoning and permits reasonable inferences on issues on which conclusive data may not be available, we can both debate and learn from the urban bias theory. In a more demanding sense, urban bias threatens to become an image, not a theory.

NOTES

1. See Krueger *et al.* [*1991*; *1992*], Singh, Squire and Kirchner [*1985*]; Tolley, Thomas and Wong) [*1982*]; Bale and Lutz [*1981*].
2. Given the amount written on town–country struggles in development, all attempts at reconstructing a history of ideas are necessarily selective. For other surveys, see Lipton [*1977: 89–144*]; Moore [*1984*], and Timmer [*1992*].
3. Gandhi, Ruskin, Tolstoy belong to this category. Also, writing at the time of the industrial revolution, romantic poets such as William Wordsworth lamented the coming decline of rural life and its simplicities.
4. Some more linkages should be noted. Agriculture can supply raw materials to industries. Moreover, the rural sector can also serve as a market for industrial goods. See Mellor [*1966*] and Timmer [*1992*].
5. One of the best reviews of the debate is Mitra [*1977*].
6. In 1930, 1931 and the first half of 1932, the free market was a black market. The benefits of free market prices accrued to the peasants and regions that had not yet been collectivised (Central Asia in particular).
7. Lewis won the Nobel Prize for his insight.
8. Also see Lindert [*1991*], and Hopkins [*1991*].
9. Though that response may still not be enough for a variety of reasons (Varshney, this volume).
10. Consider the various examples of Lipton's reasoning on India. On pro-urban expenditure-bias, Lipton's account was based on public investments, not on the fact that agricultural incomes were, and are, not taxed in India. His case on pro-urban price-bias, for example, was based on procurement price-fertiliser cost ratios and on the differential between the procurement price given by the state and the free market price for foodgrains. Putting together a fuller set of data incorporating not simply fertiliser costs but also other costs, Varshney (this volume, and forthcoming) demonstrates that plausible as they may have appeared at the time, Lipton's measures were partial and can be revised in the light of new data. In his response in this volume, Lipton argues that if price-bias has come down in India, expenditure-bias has not. Increasing gap between rural and urban infant mortality rate is the measure he primarily chooses. One can argue back and say: how about the waiver of agricultural loans by the Indian government? How about the continuing absence of a tax on agricultural incomes? How about the fact that just two subsidies (food and fertiliser) constitute a third of the total defense expenditure of the country? See Varshney (this volume). How do we incorporate them all and come up with a vector sum of all *and* over time? If such problems exist with respect to India where agricultural data are quite good, consider the difficulties in Africa (Widner, this volume). A combination of deductive and inductive reasoning, and reliance on inferences (as opposed to fully empirically established conclusions) are thus inevitable in empirical research. Lipton uses these measures as much as we or others do. Until he himself can provide a

complete accounting of all factors and show how to formulate their net effect on rural welfare, he cannot claim empirical validity for his criticisms.

REFERENCES

Bale, Malcolm and Ernst Lutz, 1981, 'Price Distortions in Agriculture and Their Effects: An International Comparison', *American Journal of Agricultural Economics*, Vol.63, No.1.

Bates, Robert, 1981, *Markets and States in Tropical Africa*, Berkeley, CA: University of California Press.

Bates, Robert, 1989, *Beyond the Miracle of the Market*, Cambridge: Cambridge University Press.

de Janvry, Alain, and K. Subbarao, 1984, 'Farm Prices and Income Distribution in India', *Economic and Political Weekly*, Review of Agriculture, Dec. 22–29.

Ellman, Michael, 1975, 'Did the Agricultural Surplus Provide the Resources for the Increase in Investment in the USSR During the First Five Year Plan?', *Economic Journal*, Dec.

Harriss, John and Mick Moore (eds.), 1984, 'Development and the Rural–Urban Division' *The Journal of Development Studies*, Vol.20, No.3, April (Special Issue).

Hopkins, Raymond, 1991, 'Notes on Agriculture and the State', in Peter Timmer (ed.), *Agriculture and the State*, Ithaca, NY: Cornell University Press.

Krueger, Anne O. (ed.), 1991; 1992, *The Political Economy of Agricultural Pricing Policy*, 5 vols., Baltimore, MD: The Johns Hopkins University Press for the World Bank.

Lewis, W. Arthur, 1954, 'Economic Development With Unlimited Supplies of Labour', *Manchester School of Social and Economic Studies*, Vol.22, No.2, pp.139–91.

Lindert, Peter, 1991, 'Historical Patterns of Agricultural Policy', in Peter Timmer (ed.), *Agriculture and the State*, Ithaca, NY: Cornell University Press.

Lipton, Michael, 1977, *Why Poor People Stay Poor: Urban Bias in World Development*, Cambridge, MA: Harvard University Press.

Mellor, John, 1966, 'Towards a Theory of Agricultural Development', in Bruce Johnston and Herman Southworth (eds.), *Agriculture and Economic Development*, Ithaca, NY: Cornell University Press.

Mitra, Ashok, 1977, *Terms of Trade and Class Relations*, London: Frank Cass.

Moore, Barrington, Jr., 1966, *Social Origins of Democracy and Dictatorship: Lord and Peasant in the Making of the Modern World*, Boston, MA: Beacon Press.

Moore, Mick, 1984, 'Political Economy and the Urban–Rural Divide', *Journal of Development Studies*, Vol.20, No.3, April (Special Issue).

Moore, Mick, 1985, *The State and Peasant Politics in Sri Lanka*, Cambridge: Cambridge University Press.

Popkin, Samuel, 1979, *The Rational Peasant*, Berkeley, CA: University of California Press.

Quisumbing, M.A.R. and Lance Taylor, 1990, 'Resource Transfers from Agriculture', in Kenneth Arrow (ed.), *The Balance Between Industry and Agriculture in Economic Development*, London: Macmillan.

Rao, Mohan, 1986, 'Agriculture in Recent Development Theory', *Journal of Development Economics*, June.

Schultz, Theodore, 1964, *Transforming Traditional Agriculture*, Chicago, IL: University of Chicago Press, 1964.

Schultz, Theodore, 1981, *Distortion of Agricultural Incentives*, Bloomington, IN: Indiana University Press.

Scott, James, 1976, *The Moral Economy of the Peasant*, New Haven, CT: Yale University Press.

Scott, James, 1985, *Weapons of the Weak: Everyday Forms of Peasant Resistance*, New Haven, CT: Yale University Press.

Shanin, Teodore, 1987 (ed.), *Peasants and Peasant Societies*, New York: Basil Blackwell.

Singh, I.J., Squire, Lyn and James Kirchner, 1985, *Agricultural Pricing and Marketing Policies in African Context: A Framework for Analysis*, World Bank Staff Working Papers, No.743, Washington, DC: World Bank.

Taylor, Lance, 1983, *Structuralist Macroeconomics*, New York: Basic Books.

Taylor, Lance and Frank Lysy, 1979, 'Vanishing Income Distributions', *Journal of Development Economics*, Vol.6.

Tolley, George, Thomas, Vinod and C.M. Wong, 1982, *Agricultural Price Policies and the Developing Countries*, Baltimore, MD: Johns Hopkins University Press.

Timmer, Peter, 1992, 'Agriculture and Economic Development Revisited', in Paul Teng and F.P. De Vries, (eds.), *Agricultural Systems*, London: Elsevier Science Publishers.

Timmer, Peter, 1988, 'The Agricultural Transformation', in Hollis Chenery and T.N. Srinivasan, *The Handbook of Development Economics*, Amsterdam and New York: North Holland Press.

Tyagi, D.S., 1986, 'On the Relevance on Farm Prices', *Economic and Political Weekly*, 1 March.

Varshney, Ashutosh, forthcoming, *Democracy, Development and the Countryside: Urban–Rural Struggles in India*, New York: Cambridge University Press.

Varshney, Ashutosh, 1989, 'Ideas, Interests and Institutions in Policy Change: Transformation of India's Agricultural Strategy in the mid-1960s', *Policy Sciences*, Vol.22, pp.289–323.

World Bank, 1982, 1986, 1988, 1991, *World Development Report*, New York: Oxford University Press for The World Bank.

II. CASES

The Origins of Agricultural Policy in Ivory Coast 1960–86

JENNIFER A. WIDNER

There is a more limited degree of 'urban bias' in Côte d'Ivoire than in most other African countries. Different explanations for relatively high producer price shares, reliable extension services, etc. are required for the periods 1960–70 and 1970–86. The arguments offered focus on the composition of the income portfolios of senior political elites and on the rise of special kinds of urban, informal associations that have acted as lobbying organisations on behalf of rural household members. The article seeks to dispel the notion that differences in opportunities for political participation alone can account for the variations in the outcomes observed in the African cases.

Africa specialists usually classify the Ivory Coast (henceforth Côte d'Ivoire), along with Kenya and Zimbabwe, as a country whose government has created a policy environment favourable to producers of export crops and exhibited less 'urban bias' than others. That is, it has (1) allocated a higher proportion of the world price of export commodities to the producer than most others, (2) until recently, kept its exchange rate in line with the market rate, limiting indirect taxation of farmers, and (3) provided generally reliable extension services and infrastructure to rural areas without which high farmgate prices may mean little. It has performed less well with respect to a fourth criterion: level of productive investment in agriculture, where it has provided funds both for projects that have reduced costs of production, such as roads, as well as for programmes of sugar development, port facilities and hydropower that promised very low or negative returns on investment even under the most optimistic scenarios. None the less, despite a number of misdirected agricultural development projects and transfer of resources from agriculture to less productive uses, such as the construc-

Jennifer Widner is Associate Professor of Government, Harvard University. She wishes to thank the McNamara Fellowship Program of the World Bank, the Harvard Center for International Affairs, and the Centre Ivoirien de Recherche Economique et Sociale for assistance provided during this research.

tion of Notre Dame de La Paix, the enormous basilica at Yamous-soukro, agriculturalists have fared better in Côte d'Ivoire than in most countries of sub-Saharan Africa.

In the period between 1960 and the mid-1980s, farmers saw producer prices for major export crops grow gradually, keeping pace with infla-tion so that real prices were relatively stable [Hecht, 1983: 26]. Thus, despite a net outflow of financial resources from agriculture for much of the post-independence period, agriculture long remained remunerative relative to the kinds of urban alternatives available to most low-skill people. In a World Bank study published almost 20 years after the country gained independence, Bastiaan den Tuinder noted that unlike many sub-Saharan countries, Côte d'Ivoire

> continued to encourage its export-oriented agricultural sector. At first this encouragement was mainly through public investment in infrastructure, but later it was broadened to a host of direct incentives to production, particularly high and stable producer prices for the main agricultural products. Recognizing the econ-omic vulnerability of too much dependence on three export com-modities (unprocessed cocoa, coffee, and timber), the government diversified agriculture by introducing or expanding the cultivation of oil palm, coconut, pineapple, rice, rubber, cotton, and later sugarcane . . . [Tuinder, 1978: 5].

Although the policies or their management failed to generate sus-tained economic expansion and indeed sometimes proved quite dele-terious to the country's general economic condition over the long term, it is none the less correct to suggest that they have favoured export-crop producers and that through the early 1970s, they fuelled the seven per cent average annual rates of growth that so astonished observers.

At a time when multilateral development agencies are pondering the kinds of political arrangements that can support development of African agriculture, the case of Côte d'Ivoire is especially instructive. The government of long-time president Félix Houphouët-Boigny chose to emphasise export agriculture as a key source of economic growth at Independence and has maintained this focus over a 30-year period, with some variation depending on crop. Although several attempts to explain this kind of pattern in other countries suggest that favourable policy environments for agriculture are associated with more open political systems in which regular, competitive elections take place, the case of Côte d'Ivoire shows that 'democratic political processes' are neither necessary nor sufficient to produce the outcomes desired. Côte d'Ivoire's policy-makers enacted and implemented a favourable policy environment in a single-party system which limited electoral choice to approval or disapproval of a party list, until 1980. Even after 1980, debate within the National Assembly was rare, as reflected in the request of one deputy after a special session in 1986. 'Until now, the National Assembly had always waited for legislative bills to arrive from the government or for ministers of the government to present their views here', he said. 'This is the first time that we have presented and developed our own views. I like that idea. Following this example, perhaps the *députés* could interrupt and express themselves freely, before being divided into committees' [*Assemblée Nationale, 1 July 1986: 16*]. Major diversions of funds from agriculture to non-productive, urban uses took place after 1980, when multi-candidate single-party elections on the model of Kenya were held.

No single account of the maintenance of a policy environment favourable to agriculture has explanatory power for the full period of Côte d'Ivoire's post-Independence history. Robert Bates, Michael Lofchie, and others have argued that collective action on the part of rural producers to protect their economic status occurs when a few large landholders, who bear a disproportionate stake in the character of the policy environment, organise to influence decision-making. If the chief of state himself derives private income from farming, a country is also more likely to pursue policies favourable to agriculture. This argument sheds considerable light on the early independence period. Not only did many key political elites farm considerable acreage, they also shared beliefs about market structure and behaviour that led them to favour high producer prices for export crops. Houphouët-Boigny himself was the model, the owner of large plantations of cocoa, coffee, coconut palms, oil palms, and other crops who once told his compatriots, 'If you don't want to vegetate in bamboo huts, concentrate your efforts on growing good cocoa and good coffee. They will fetch a good price, and you will become rich' [*Zolberg, 1964: 151*]. As president, he defended the '*bon prix*' [high price], arguing that it was also a '*prix juste*' [fair price] and struggled constantly to improve his country's leverage against '*les speculateurs*'.

With time, the rationale for maintaining the policy environment changed, and the influence of elites with private agricultural interests diminished, although their role in decision-making did not disappear entirely. Economic strategy fostered the rise of a new interest group, a small but influential coterie of Ivorian and French managers whose firms dealt primarily with processing of agricultural commodities. These men had a stake in a continued, reliable supply of high-quality agricultural inputs. Because the president's own background prejudiced him against extraction of farm surpluses through use of force (he had built his political career through the fight against forced agricultural labour), the only way to sustain the new agri-businesses was to offer comparatively high prices and hope either to secure subsidies for other aspects of operation or to boost efficiency in order to turn a profit.

Further, institutional choices made a difference in the bargaining power of the parties to this convergence of interest. In the early years of Independence, Ivorian law had prevented the formation of independent associations outside of the ethnic units that provided a base for the *Parti Démocratique de Côte d'Ivoire* (PDCI). Pressure from younger elites resulted in a loosening of restrictions in 1969–70, however, and provided the impetus for a new and unusual form of political exchange: the dialogue, a convocation of Ivorians from different walks of life, or *couches sociales*, who came to Abidjan to express their views directly to the President and his advisors, bypassing the ministries. Although a farmers' union or syndicat did not emerge until 1991, the anticipation of periodic '*jours de dialogue*' was a spur to formation of new kinds of interest groups and to articulation of demands for higher producer prices.

This study assesses and rejects the argument that favourable policy environments for agriculture are associated with the existence of competitive elections by way of a careful examination of the Côte d'Ivoire case. It first explores the dependent variable, asking the question, 'in what respects did the government in Abidjan favour rural producers?' It briefly considers alternative explanations for the patterns observed, then discusses the roots of agricultural policy in Côte d'Ivoire, 1960–69 and 1970 through the present. Finally, it assesses the significance of the Côte d'Ivoire case for understanding the political economy of agricultural policy in other developing countries.

THE POLICY ENVIRONMENT IN COMPARATIVE PERSPECTIVE

Distinguishing the degree of urban bias in agricultural policy, or whether a country has a 'favourable' and 'unfavourable' agricultural policy environment, is more easily said than done. The ideal measure would adjust the proportion of the world market price a farmer received for a crop for the costs of transport under open-economy conditions, input subsidies, direct taxes and indirect taxation created by currency overvaluation and import licensing. As Anne Krueger *et al.* have pointed out, however, 'While international trade theorists have long known that protection of some activities discriminates against the re-

mainder, that knowledge has not been transformed into usable estimates of the extent of total discrimination against agriculture' [*Krueger
et al., 1989: 256*]. Although the comparative project on the political
economy of agricultural pricing Krueger launched was designed to
produce such estimates, participants were often hard-pressed to obtain
the data required.

The elaborate comparison of actual producer prices to what prices
would have been had there been a free trade regime is beyond the scope
of this research. Partially-adjusted comparative data on producer price
shares, parallel market to official exchange rate ratios, and transport
costs can provide rough estimates of the degree of urban bias in Côte
d'Ivoire, compared to other African countries, however. Because most
food crops, except rice, are traded in Côte d'Ivoire without government
intervention, the measures are used to assess policy toward export crops
only. For these crops, evaluation according to *multiple* criteria, as
accuracy would dictate, suggests that although the policy environment
in Côte d'Ivoire is not as unambiguously favourable as it is in Kenya or
Zimbabwe, it none the less displays less urban bias than other African
producers of the same major export crops: cocoa, coffee, oil palms, and
cotton.

Producer–Price Shares

A simple, although limited measure of urban bias is the producer–price
ratio, the ratio of the farm-gate price to the international price of a
commodity. In a world without government intervention, the ratio
would approach unity, with transport costs accounting for the remaining
divergence from the world price. Where governments extract tax revenues from exports, where marketing is inefficient, or where some
portion of the difference between prices goes to a stabilisation fund, to
be paid out in the form of subsidies when world prices drop, the
producer–price ratio may be quite low. The degree to which a low ratio
indicates strong urban bias depends on the reason for the difference in
prices and the ultimate destination of the government's share of the
funds extracted, the degree to which government subsidises inputs, and
the extent of the divergence between the real exchange rate and the
official exchange rate, which is used to convert producer–prices in local
currency to dollars in the computation of the ratio.

At first glance, Côte d'Ivoire appears to offer producers of its major
export crops only about 50 per cent of the international reference price,
on average, while several other countries have offered producers higher
shares (see Table 1). By this rough approximation, Cameroon also
appears to perform on a par with Côte d'Ivoire, and Zaire is not nearly

TABLE 1

PRODUCER–PRICE SHARES FOR MAJOR EXPORT COMMODITIES

(RATIO OF THE NOMINAL PRODUCER PRICE TO THE INTERNATIONAL REFERENCE PRICE)

(USING OFFICAL EXCHANGE RATES)

	1975	1976	1977	1978	1979	1980	1981	1982	1983	1984	1985	1986	1987
Cameroon													
coffee	0.53	0.33	0.74	0.77	0.95	1.21	0.93	0.74	0.65	0.78	0.77	1.38	1.27
cocoa	0.29	0.16	0.27	0.36	0.51	0.57	0.53	0.43	0.34	0.39	0.54	0.66	0.80
cotton	0.39	0.37	0.45	0.46	0.53	0.51	0.54	0.47	0.43	0.59	1.11	0.85	0.94
Côte d'Ivoire													
coffee	0.56	0.31	0.53	0.65	0.92	1.14	0.86	0.64	0.58	0.69	0.70	1.28	1.48
cocoa	0.37	0.19	0.31	0.34	0.52	0.57	0.52	0.39	0.32	0.36	0.53	0.64	0.77
palm oil	0.45	0.34	0.41	0.40	0.45	0.35	0.56	0.43	0.32	0.52	1.24	1.15	0.93
Ghana													
cocoa	0.26	0.15	0.20	0.27	0.49	0.66	2.30	1.62	0.22	0.22	0.28	0.25	0.41
Kenya													
coffee	0.96	0.73	0.82	0.84	0.80	0.66	0.70	0.78	0.72	0.77	0.69	0.72	*
tea	0.74	0.89	0.82	0.75	0.83	0.89	0.86	0.68	0.99	0.91	1.08	0.85	*
Nigeria													
cocoa	0.53	0.25	0.44	0.47	0.74	0.98	1.03	0.85	0.71	0.67	0.52	1.16	*
palm oil	1.14	0.85	0.85	0.99	1.55	1.54	1.82	1.50	1.18	3.75	6.35	3.43	1.29
cotton	0.93	0.86	0.97	0.98	0.96	1.12	1.36	1.20	1.18	1.60	1.74	0.90	0.53
Zaire													
coffee	0.26	0.14	0.25	0.13	0.43	0.99	0.72	0.34	0.17	0.78	0.35	0.45	0.40
palm oil	0.67	0.89	1.17	0.76	1.43	0.85	1.10	0.70	0.30	*	*	*	0.53
Zambia													
tobacco	0.98	0.74	0.95	0.89	0.87	0.77	1.07	0.96	0.78	0.58	0.35	0.35	0.86
cotton	0.95	0.97	1.15	1.01	0.86	0.84	0.97	0.72	0.54	0.48	0.34	0.32	0.72
Zimbabwe													
tobacco	0.78	0.68	0.71	0.68	0.56	0.49	1.00	0.74	0.76	0.62	1.02	0.81	0.94

Source: World Bank, *African Economic and Financial Data*, Washington, DC: The World Bank, 1980, pp.146–50.

the policy disaster it is so often considered. Careful examination of the time series data suggests that the relatively low shares accorded producers during the mid to late 1970s in Côte d'Ivoire correspond with the boom in beverage crop prices, however. A government that seeks to offer stable producer prices, protecting farmers against the income instability that potentially accompanies volatile world prices by taxing export crops at a higher rate during boom periods and subsidising them during price collapses, would create the pattern observed. In 1955, before Independence, Côte d'Ivoire created a stabilisation fund, the *Caisse de stabilisation*, or Caistab. It has maintained this arrangement, limiting the exposure of farmers to the short-term effects of commodity booms and busts, in contrast to Kenya, which has passed on to producers a major part of price increases and declines. Theoretically, then, it is more appropriate to examine average producer–price shares for periods that include strong fluctuations, in order to assess the extent of urban bias, on the grounds that some part of the funds extracted during commodity booms returns to farmers in the form of subsidies when world prices decline. Using this measure, for the period 1974–82, Côte d'Ivoire accorded its coffee farmers 70 per cent of the world price, and cocoa farmers, about 50 per cent of the world price, on average.

Also not reflected in the producer–price ratio is the degree to which the government subsidised inputs and the degree to which farmers have used fertiliser, pesticides, and other products. Subsidy programmes for coffee, cocoa, and palm oil varied within Côte d'Ivoire and between countries during the period covered by the table of producer–price ratios. The *Société d'Assistance Technique pour le Modernisation Agricole de la Côte d'Ivoire* (SATMACI) has responsibility for promoting cocoa and coffee production. Until 1984, SATMACI and the CIDT subsidised several important inputs. For example, just before the 1984–85 removal of fertiliser subsidies, cotton growers received a subsidy of about 7.5 CFAF per kilogram of complex fertiliser (which cost about 73.9 CFAF per kilogram) and a subsidy of about 11 CFAF per kilogram of urea (which cost about 119 CFAF). For a farmer using these fertilisers in the correct proportions for a hectare of land, subsidies were equivalent to a little under one-sixth of average returns. In the case of cocoa and coffee production, such subsidies have played less of a role. Studies have suggested that fertiliser and pesticide use in the mid-1980s was minimal. Only 7.6 per cent of cocoa farmers and 15 per cent of the coffee farmers used chemical fertilisers; 22 per cent of the cocoa farmers and 15 per cent of the coffee farmers used insecticides [*Deaton, 1988: 22*]. If it is possible to extrapolate from that information (relatively constant yield levels suggest that it may be appropriate to do so) and to

TABLE 2

PRODUCER–PRICE SHARES FOR MAJOR EXPORT COMMODITIES, USING PARALLEL MARKET EXCHANGE RATE

(RATIO OF THE NOMINAL PRODUCER PRICE TO THE INTERNATIONAL REFERENCE PRICE)

(USING PARALLEL MARKET RATES)

	1975	1976	1977	1978	1979	1980	1981	1982	1983	1984	1985	1986	1987
Cameroon													
coffee	na	0.29	0.21	0.38	0.39	0.47	0.53	0.43	0.36	0.31	0.37	0.39	0.66
cocoa	na	0.31	0.24	0.34	0.41	0.55	0.54	0.57	0.43	0.37	0.42	0.59	0.70
cotton	na	0.12	0.13	0.15	0.19	0.19	0.18	0.19	0.16	0.16	0.23	0.38	0.28
Côte d'Ivoire													
coffee	na	0.23	0.15	0.24	0.32	0.44	0.48	0.37	0.32	0.27	0.33	0.36	0.60
cocoa	na	0.37	0.27	0.32	0.42	0.55	0.53	0.52	0.41	0.34	0.39	0.56	0.67
palm oil	na	0.83	0.77	0.73	0.71	0.82	0.95	1.01	0.94	0.69	0.89	2.38	2.04
Ghana													
cocoa	0.12	0.04	0.08	0.08	0.09	0.22	0.11	0.12	0.13	0.19	0.22	0.32	0.41
Kenya													
coffee	1.51	0.66	1.03	0.84	0.80	1.12	0.99	0.83	0.93	1.18	0.65	na	na
tea	1.48	0.68	0.74	0.87	0.97	0.88	0.78	1.37	0.59	0.98	0.76	0.90	*
Nigeria													
cocoa	0.38	0.26	0.27	0.34	0.55	0.67	0.61	0.36	0.19	0.19	0.40	na	na
palm oil	*	*	*	*	*	*	*	*	*	*	*	*	*
cotton	0.22	0.19	0.18	0.18	0.22	0.28	0.26	0.17	0.12	0.17	0.22	*	*
Zaire													
coffee	*	0.04	0.03	0.04	0.09	0.19	0.18	0.16	0.11	*	*	*	*
palm oil	*	0.48	0.46	0.43	0.69	0.56	0.47	0.76	0.56	*	*	*	*
Zambia													
tobacco	*	*	*	*	*	*	*	*	*	*	*	*	*
cotton	*	0.13	0.13	0.14	0.19	0.17	0.18	0.24	0.19	0.17	0.16	0.15	0.72
Zimbabwe													
tobacco	0.60	0.24	0.22	0.34	0.11	0.35	0.71	0.57	0.29	0.35	0.52	0.81	0.94

Source: Computed from producer price series in World Bank, *African Economic Financial Data,* Washington, DC: The World Bank, 1989, pp.146–50 and world price data in World Bank, *Commodity Trade and Price Trends* and *world Commodity Outlook,* using parallel market rates from *Pick's World Currency Yearbook.*

suggest that few farmers were affected either by the subsidies or the high prices of these inputs after subsidies were removed, then the producer price ratio is a fairly accurate gauge of the proportion of the world price the farmer received. Similarly, input subsidies for cotton were removed in 1984, increasing production costs for those who used these.

Finally, adjustment of producer–price shares for overvalued official exchange rates casts Côte d'Ivoire's pricing policies in a more favourable light. Until the late 1980s, the CFA was not significantly overvalued, in contrast to the currencies of many other African countries. Other producers of comparable export crops, except Kenya and Zimbabwe, had seriously overvalued exchange rates. To adjust for exchange rate overvaluation in estimation of share of income received by farmers, the real effective exchange rate replaces the official rate in computation of the producer price shares in economists' calculations. Because lack of adequate data has hampered estimation of real effective exchange rates for most African countries, the adjustments in Table 2 use parallel market rates, however. The adequacy of the parallel market rates as proxies for real effective rates varies, but the adjustments give some sense of the direction and magnitude of the changes in producer–price shares that would occur, using the more appropriate measure. The adjusted calculations, accounting for indirect taxation, suggest that Côte d'Ivoire has offered its farmers a better deal than most other African countries (see Table 3).

Indirect Taxation: Exchange Rate Regimes

For most African countries, indirect taxation of agriculture through maintenance of an overvalued currency overwhelms the effects of input subsidies. For most of the post-Independence period, Côte d'Ivoire has performed relatively better than other producers of comparable export crops in Africa, according to this measure. The CFA Franc is tied directly to the French Franc at the rate of 50 CFAF to 1 FF. Parity adjustment requires unanimous agreement among the member countries and is, therefore, outside the control of the Ivorian government. Within these institutions, it is none the less possible for the real exchange rate, the price of tradables compared to the price of nontradables, to increase or diminish, depending on the fiscal policies a government chooses. In the aftermath of the coffee and cocoa boom of the mid-1970s, Côte d'Ivoire did experience an appreciation of the real exchange rate [*Devarajan and De Melo, 1987: 459*].

Which method of assessment the researcher chooses makes a significant difference in the relative ranking of Côte d'Ivoire against other countries with respect to indirect taxation through currency overvalua-

TABLE 3

REAL PROTECTION COEFFICIENTS FOR MAJOR EXPORT COMMODITIES
(1971=100 FOR REAL EXCHANGE RATE)

	1970	1971	1972	1973	1974	1975	1976	1977	1978	1979	1980	1981	1982	1983	1984	1985
Cameroon coffee	1.28	1.23	1.17	1.03	1.15	0.58	0.34	0.72	0.76	0.96	1.40	1.10	0.84	0.72	0.84	0.75
Côte d'Ivoire coffee	1.11	1.13	1.07	1.04	1.37	0.64	0.30	0.51	0.56	0.78	1.19	0.96	0.76	0.71	0.84	0.72
Ghana cocoa	0.64	0.59	0.37	0.22	0.38	0.18	0.09	0.12	0.19	0.28	0.18	0.51	0.53	0.19	0.25	0.55
Kenya coffee	0.93	1.11	1.11	1.08	1.08	1.25	0.89	0.96	1.05	1.02	0.92	0.92	1.09	0.96	1.00	1.02
Zaire coffee	na	0.82	0.91	0.75	1.11	0.22	0.09	0.14	0.08	0.29	0.71	0.50	0.20	0.26	1.15	0.53
Zambia tobacco	1.10	1.29	1.55	1.58	1.17	1.35	1.05	1.35	1.28	1.27	1.13	1.37	1.33	1.32	1.04	1.30
Zimbabwe tobacco	0.87	1.04	1.18	1.06	1.20	1.07	0.93	1.18	1.10	0.94	0.78	1.36	1.16	1.25	1.13	1.60

Source: William Jaeger, 'The Impact of Policy in African Agriculture', Policy, Research, and external Affairs Working Paper 640, Washington, DC: World Bank, March 1991, pp.55–6.

tion. Approximations of the real effective exchange rate by Jaeger and Kreuger show that significant indirect taxation of agricultural producers occurred during and after the beverage boom (see Tables 4 and 5). Jaeger suggests that using this measure, Côte d'Ivoire's exchange rate policies produced overvaluation at the margin of acceptability – that is, at the cut-off used to distinguish countries with policy environments favourable to agriculture from those with unfavourable policies [*Jaeger, 1991*]. The Krueger study produces a slightly different ranking, indicating substantial indirect taxation in Côte d'Ivoire but at levels half of those in Ghana 1975–79 and a third those of Ghana in 1980–84 [*Krueger et al., 1989: 262*]. Officials of the IMF have rejected attempts to calculate real effective exchange rates for Côte d'Ivoire on the grounds that the data are too inadequate to derive accurate approximations. A simpler measure of the ratio of the parallel market rate to the official rate suggests that Côte d'Ivoire has suffered from less serious levels of indirect taxation. In this case, Côte d'Ivoire falls squarely into the group of countries with 'favorable policy environments'.

TABLE 4

REAL EFFECTIVE EXCHANGE RATE
(1970–=100)
(CRITERION FOR FAVOURABLE POLICY ENVIRONMENT BELOW 120)

Country	Average 1984-86	1987
Cameroon	114	139
Côte d'Ivoire	105	127
Ghana	112	50
Kenya	90	74
Nigeria	249	50
Zaire	79	66
Zambia	62	37
Zimbabwe	72	63

Source: William Jaeger, 'The Impact of Policy in African Agriculture', Policy, Research, and External Affairs Working Paper 640, Washington, DC: World Bank, March 1991, p.52.

Recently, the FCFA has appreciated substantially and indirect taxation has increased (not indicated in the table). Because Côte d'Ivoire is part of the West African Monetary Union, with a common central bank, the BCEAO, that governs its monetary policy, it has little control over its exchange rate, and it cannot devalue without convincing other mem-

TABLE 5

RATIO OF PARALLEL MARKET RATE TO OFFICIAL EXCHANGE RATE
(1970-=100)
(CRITERION FOR FAVOURABLE POLICY ENVIRONMENT BELOW 1.3)

Country	Average 1984-86	1987
Cameroon	1.02	1.01
Côte d'Ivoire	1.02	1.01
Ghana	2.41	1.37
Kenya	1.06	1.06
Nigeria	3.94	3.32
Zaire	1.04	0.80
Zambia	1.51	1.89
Zimbabwe	1.70	1.59

Source: William Jaeger, 'The Impact of Policy in African Agriculture', Policy, Research, and External Affairs Working Paper 640, Washington, DC: World Bank, March 1991, p.52.

ber states to go along. Previously, these arrangements created some limits on the power of individual leaders to use exchange rate policy to favour urban industries. Now, the system imposes some burdens on farmers.

Extension Services and Marketing

In some countries, the producer price-ratio is a meaningless statistic because the delivery of plants or seeds, collection of crops, and payment of farmers are unreliable, at best. In the relatively better standards of operation of their extension and marketing services, Kenya, Zimbabwe, and Côte d'Ivoire stand out from most of their neighbours in Africa. One can speak of these as 'production subsidies' offered by government in lieu of their provision by private farmers. 'Reliability' is difficult to measure, of course, and the assessment is to some degree reputational and qualitative.

Until the 'cocoa crisis' began in 1987, payment of farmers for their export crops in Côte d'Ivoire was fairly reliable for the major export crops. For example, extension services for oil palm production and cotton kept careful records through a network of field agents and regional buying centers. In none of the author's extensive interviews with farmers did non-payment or under-payment by Palmindustrie, which has taken over these functions from SODEPALM, or the CIDT, the cotton parastatal, feature in discussions of individual or local eco-

nomic problems, although cotton growers did complain about the parastatal's practice of assigning one price to all cotton produced in a village,
regardless of the quality of an individual farmer's production [*Widner,
1992b*]. Marketing of cocoa and coffee in Côte d'Ivoire takes place
through a system of competitive private trading, instead of through the
parastatal charged with extension responsibilities, SATMACI. Reports
of unscrupulous traders who received stocks on credit from farmers and
never remitted the sums fixed by the government were relatively uncommon until the late 1980s, when banks found it increasingly difficult to
finance the traders up front, awaiting later reimbursement of traders by
the government, and when buyers sometimes refused to purchase harvests at the price fixed by the government, on the grounds that a
reduction in the producer price was imminent.

The reliability of the marketing system is to some degree a function of
the level of infrastructure development and the existence of an extensive
private-sector trucking industry. Kilometres of passable road, whether
graded dirt access roads or paved roads, are an important measure of
the ability to deliver inputs and pick up harvests on time; most inputs
must arrive as rains start or during the rainy season, making well-
maintained roads essential. In effect, a poor road system significantly
increases the risks associated with crop production. Certainly, by this
measure a country such as Zaire, with fewer kilometres of passable road
now than it had at independence, lies at one end of a spectrum, while
Zimbabwe, Côte d'Ivoire, and Kenya, with their more extensive and
better-maintained networks, lie at the other. In 1985, estimated road
transport costs measured in US dollars per ton-kilometre at purchasing
power parity exchange rates were 0.11 for Côte d'Ivoire, compared to
0.13 for Zambia, 0.14 for Zimbabwe, 0.20 for Cameroon, and a high of
0.39 for Kenya [*Jaeger, 1991: 59*].

Re-Investment of Tax Revenues in Agriculture

A favourable policy environment ultimately includes not only maintenance of relatively high producer prices, a stable exchange rate regime,
and reliable extension services, but also investment in ways to increase
productivity over the long run. In competitive world markets, prices for
primary agricultural commodities have diminished as new producers,
operating at lower costs, have entered the market. If African governments are to maintain their ability to generate revenues by taxing
agricultural production, they must ensure that yields improve, as prices
drop, so that household revenues remain stable and farmers have
incentive to continue to produce. Failure to do so means that governments will have to 'squeeze' farmer incomes, decreasing still further the

ratio of the producer price to the world market price, and quite likely
triggering retreats to subsistence production, shifts out of agriculture to
other activities, and long-term erosion of the revenue base.

It is in this respect that the government in Abidjan has failed most
conspicuously. The aim of the Caistab was to save revenues collected
from the agricultural sector in periods of high world prices in order to
maintain producer prices when world prices dropped and to invest in
productivity improvements, such as new varieties of seeds, irrigation
systems, and research. In reality, the monies collected during commodity booms dissipated quickly, as the government borrowed from the
Caisse to support projects unlikely to yield positive economic returns
and to finance expansion of industry.

During the period 1975–80, the period of the boom in commodity
prices, Caistab on average provided funds for about 57 per cent of
overall public investment, peaking at 78 per cent of public investment in
1976 [*Cooper, 1992: 5*]. The failure to sequester incremental revenues
had severe repercussions for the Ivorian economy, although farmers
were not immediately affected. Richard Cooper has summarised the
consequences of the government's policy, writing that,

> When prices fell, the government could not pay all of its bills,
> including its obligations to the farmers. Farmers and wholesalers
> had (collectively) large seasonal loans which they were unable to
> pay, so total credit to the agricultural and commerce sectors rose
> substantially. Some of this could be discounted at the BCEAO,
> resulting in total credit creation, but banks ran up against their
> limits for credit and consequently had to deny credit to other
> borrowers, thereby contributing to the slump in economic activity
> [*Cooper, 1992, Ch.12: 4*].

Moreover, in the Ivorian case, the investments made using Caistab
funds did little to increase productivity in export agriculture.

A large proportion of the funds accumulated went to finance a
massive and poorly planned effort to bring development to the northern
part of the country, already under way at the time of the boom in coffee
and cocoa prices. In a recent defence of the use of funds from the
Caisse, President Houphouët-Boigny argued, quite accurately, that,

> It is thanks to the Caisse that without awaiting the promises of the
> World Bank we have been able to build the roads linking Katiola
> and Korhogo, Man and Odienne, by way of Touba; it is thanks to
> the Caisse that we have been able to expand electrification, that
> we have been able to organise 'fêtes tournantes' (independence

celebrations rotated among regions) . . . It is thanks to the Caisse that we have been able to wage war against regional disparities in development [*Marchés Tropicaux, 6 Oct. 1989: 2852*].

Beginning in 1974, the government embarked on investments in infrastructure and agricultural diversification with high unit costs and low potential to generate foreign exchange, which eventually totalled over CFAF 100 billion. For example, the government poured money into creation of irrigated sugar plantations and factories destined to produce sugar at costs above projected world market prices. Lavish expenditures on the SODESUCRE programme also encouraged mismanagement of money; in 1982 alone, 'over-billing' wiped out the entire value added of the company – about 10 billion CFAF [*Berthelemy and Bourguignon, 1987: 35 and 115–16*]. During this period, in the country's investment programme as a whole, finance of buildings dwarfed finance of machinery purchases or transportation improvements. On average, between 1975 and 1982, 59 per cent of investment funds went to buildings. [*Berthelemy and Bouguignon, 1987, Appendix: 6*].

Farmers' Incomes

Some analysts have suggested that the most appropriate measure of trends in farm incomes relative to urban incomes is to calculate a return index, defined as the ratio of crop prices to production costs, multiplied by yields [*Varshney, 1991: 29*]. Although this measure has strong intuitive appeal because it provides a notion of how various price changes affect farming households, it says nothing about relative shares of income between sectors and, in African settings, proves enormously difficult to calculate. The return index presupposes a model of production decision-making that takes account of the way techniques and input use vary with prices of inputs, including labour. That is very important. However, where farmers can shift between hired labour and family labour or various kinds of share contracts, labour costs are extremely difficult to compute. Further, yields can vary dramatically according to weather conditions and soil fertility, rendering meaningful averages difficult to obtain. Although the index has much merit, its use demands more data than is usually available in African cases.

Using a less specific but similar measure of farmer welfare, Robert Hecht has argued that 'Ivoirian small-holders have gained only limited benefits from economic growth, measured in terms of their assets, incomes, and living standards' [*Hecht, 1983: 26*]. Although farming households have generated the tax revenues that have spurred the country's economic development, the farmers' share in the incremental benefits has been relatively low (that assessment requires adjustment for the fact that more and more people live in urban areas, however). Until the recent cocoa crisis, farmers' incomes remained stable. Because nominal producer prices increased steadily to keep pace with inflation, most farmers none the less developed an 'image of positive price movements' [*Hecht, 1983: 31*], despite inflation and increasing costs of inputs to the relatively few who used these. Payment of producer bonuses to farmers who adopted new techniques or varieties also contributed to the government's image as a champion of the peasantry when, in fact, incomes were stagnant.

Hecht points correctly to the source of confusion in understanding the Ivorian case. Farmers' incomes were not 'squeezed' in the sense that households faced increasing levels of taxation and lower absolute incomes. Rather, they received a shrinking share of the pie. Hecht writes, correctly, that,

> . . . the Government has consistently followed a set of policies designed to encourage expansion of cocoa and coffee production, while at the same time taxing small-holders heavily for capital accumulation and reinvestment elsewhere in the economy. Other countries, including Sierra Leone, Ghana, and Nigeria, have also tried to finance public expenditure in similar fashion, but have ended up by either crippling or retarding this sector. The Ivory Coast, on the other hand, has successfully nurtured this golden goose, and exploited its precious eggs – without killing the animal [*Hecht, 1983: 26*].

THE ORIGINS OF A FAVOURABLE POLICY ENVIRONMENT FOR AGRICULTURE

In trying to understand policy decisions in the immediate post-independence period, an 'institutional analysis' that understands policy as the result of newly-empowered rural voters is of little use. Côte d'Ivoire became a single-party state in 1957. Unlike Kenya, which became a *de facto* one-party system in 1966, the constitution did not sanction multi-candidate elections. When voters went to the polls, they could either cast their ballots for the PDCI list or choose to abstain. Further, the government refused to tolerate associations other than the ethnic welfare societies that were part of the party's own structure. Under these conditions, interest group organisation was a risky business. The farmers' organisations that had provided the energy for the struggle with French power rapidly faded out of existence. Finally, even before acquiring presidential power, Houphouët-Boigny effectively abandoned the representative structures in the party and conducted government business without consulting senior party officials [*Morgenthau, 1964: 210*]. For the first ten years of Côte d'Ivoire's existence, a form of the analysis offered by Lipton and by Bates in *Markets and States* holds greatest explanatory power.

Formative Experiences

Although consistency of belief is rarely a hallmark of chiefs of state, the policy perspectives of the president at Independence were most surely shaped by personal experiences. Houphouët-Boigny's ascent to power took place largely through his pursuit of fair treatment and greater opportunity for Ivorian coffee and cocoa growers against the French. Before the Second World War, Côte d'Ivoire's cocoa and coffee farmers competed directly with about 200 French settlers, who grew the same crops. The French plantation owners secured workers through a system of impressed labour, from which the Ivorian farmers benefited too, but to a much lesser degree. Because of differential access to technology and crop research, the French yields were higher. And for a variety of reasons, some economic, some not, the French producers received higher prices for their crops. Although there were efforts to organise opposition to the settlers as early as the 1930s, action was relatively ineffective until the post-war period.

With the help of Governor André Latrille, who hoped to weaken the economic power of the pro-Vichy settlers, Houphouët-Boigny constituted the *Syndicat Agricole Africain* (SAA) in 1944. Early in his career, Houphouët-Boigny had served as a medic in the cocoa zones and observed first hand the labour conditions which prevailed on the plantations, as well as the benefits afforded the French. Shortly after its creation, the SAA became the base for the *Parti Démocratique de Côte d'Ivoire* (PDCI) and dedicated itself to securing, for Africans, the right to sell crops directly to trading houses, to liberating planters and 'cultivateurs' from middlemen [*Lawler, 1990: 99*] and to eliminating interference in farming by inspection teams, which had burned a number of African-owned fields, allegedly to eliminate diseased bushes. Over 20,000 farmers qualified for membership in the SAA.

Unlike many African nationalist movements then, the Côte d'Ivoire struggle had its roots in rural areas, among farmers, not among teachers or civil servants. Indeed, so suspicious was the later PDCI leadership of civil servants, who were subject to manipulation by the colonial government and were often the initiators of ethnically-based opposition parties, that the party banned *fonctionnaires* from holding office in the organisation. Further, the major opposition party which developed in the late 1940s and early 1950s, the *Parti Progressiste de Côte d'Ivoire*, represented not urban interests but rather planters from the south-east and the north, who felt outnumbered in the SAA/PDCI.

When coffee and cocoa prices collapsed in early 1954, the new political organisations set aside some of their differences with the European settlers and joined forces to lobby both for a lower tariff and for the creation of a stabilisation fund. By that time, African production far exceeded French, and increasing numbers of Europeans had moved into trade and processing of African harvests, which were more profitable than farming. According to Michael Watts and Thomas Bassett, these new French business interests decided that stabilisation of producer prices was in their interest as well [*Watts and Bassett, 1986: 116*]. It was a European, Georges Monnet, who argued the case for guaranteed producer prices on behalf of this coalition in France. Thus was Ivorian agricultural policy born.

Houphouët-Boigny's inaugural address and early policy statements echoed this experience. The lengthy 'discours d'investiture' or inaugural address emphasised the important role of agriculture in the country's development policy.

> The first duty of my government will be devote special and warm attention to the rural masses.
> I say that for two, related reasons:
>
> – first, because the rural masses represent the overwhelming majority of the population of this country;
>
> – further, because without doubt Côte d'Ivoire will remain, for a long time, an agricultural country [*Houphouët-Boigny, 1978: 258*].

Quoting a famous French phrase, Houphouët-Boigny later returned to this theme:

> It is often said that animal husbandry and grazing are the two breasts that have suckled France, but we think that this famous phrase can be adapted to us: 'agriculture and grazing are the two breasts that feed the young République de la Côte d'Ivoire', thanks to what we will accomplish together in the northern part of our country [*Houphouët-Boigny, 1978: 275*].

Formative experiences and concerns to maintain a rural political base at least partly accounted for the adoption of policies favourable to agriculture in the early 1960s.

Elite Landholdings

Even the strongest beliefs can give way to material interest, however. That Houphouët's early policy views continued to hold sway while so many neighbouring countries were constructing import-substitution industries and transforming the urban–rural terms of trade is a consequence of the continued interest of senior political elites in agriculture. The end of the 1950s saw a boom in the prices of coffee and cocoa and led many political leaders to invest in land. Only later did the earning potential of civil service positions and manufacturing overshadow, for some, the attractiveness of farming as a source of income.

Houphouët and many of the militants who held high office around him acquired individual agricultural interests which they continue to hold to this day. Houphouët inherited large amounts of land around Yamoussoukro upon the death of his maternal uncle in 1940. He later increased his family fields, which some say are now equivalent in size to a French *département* [*Africa Contemporary Record, 1972–73: B626*]. Although the 'President-Paysan', as he likes to be known, claims to have sold off his coffee holdings [*Fraternité Matin, 27 April 1983*] and has given some of his acreage to the state, it is certain that he maintains large plantations of cocoa. During the 1987–88 season, his share of the nation's production rose to 100,000 metric tons (about a fifth of the country's total exported output), sold separately through Intercafco, a Geneva-based company, which manages the marketing of other crops as well and peddled the President's harvests at below market prices to ensure sale [*Gombeau et al., 1990: 314*] Houphouët's public estimate of his pineapple production in 1983 was 3,000 tons per month – equivalent to roughly a third of the country's production at that time. He has diversified into coconut palms, rubber and other crops as well. Because of his large personal stake in cocoa, the president personally directs much of the international bargaining over the annual fate of the Ivorian crop. His direct ties to the sector have sparked a strong personal interest in other aspects of agricultural as well, and he has periodically assumed the responsibilities of a minister of agriculture.

Senior militants of the party and close advisers to the president are also major landholders, although the secrecy surrounding land ownership and economic opportunities make a systematic assessment of their holdings impossible. Among the old guard, Philippe Yacé, the former president of the National Assembly, Antoine Konan Kangu (former mayor of Abidjan, the capital), and Mathieu Ekra have large plantations. If the president's farms produce over 30 per cent of the national pineapple production, Yacé is rumoured to produce an additional ten per cent, leaving relatively little room for smallholder participation in the pineapple export trade [*Hecht, 1983: 51*]. Lambert Amon Tanoh, Yacé's brother-in-law and former minister of education, was patron of the *Sociétés de conserves d'ananas*. Other major landholders have included Abdoulaye Sawadogo, former minister for agriculture and university professor; Alphonse Boni, president of the Cour suprème; Outtara Thomas-Daquin, army general, and the families Laubhouet and Anoma, close confidants of the president [*Koffi Teya, 1985: 18–19*]. In 1972, in response to popular rumblings about the rise of a bureaucratic bourgeoisie, the president urged passage of laws encouraging land investment by high officials and civil servants, to ensure that they would maintain a stake in the future of the country's agriculture [*Africa Contemporary Record. 1972–73: B626*]. Many *fonctionnaires* acquired land during this period, usually within a short distance of regional centers, but relatively few appear to have cultivated their holdings. More recently, Marcel Amon-Tanoh, son of Lambert, and René Ekra, son of Mathieu, entered the rarified world of the international cocoa trade, thanks to the president's intercession, and acquired new stakes in the agricultural future of the country.

To argue that a few senior officials had personal interests in agriculture and used their positions to influence policy is not to say that an agricultural bourgeoisie, a self-conscious class of agricultural entrepreneurs dedicated to reinvesting their earnings in expansion of production, developed during this period in Côte d'Ivoire. There is 30-year-old argument among Côte d'Ivoire scholars about the existence of a '*bourgeoisie des planteurs*,' or an elite of large landholders capable of influencing policy to their advantage. On the one side stand Samir Amin, Bonnie Campbell and others, who argue that, indeed such a class exists. Amin contends that the 20,000 farmers eligible to participate in the SAA constituted an agricultural bourgeoisie because they generated a large surplus and were able to use the money acquired through its sale to reinforce their control over their communities and to invest, although most chose not to do so [*Amin, 1973: 61–2*]. Campbell claims that a commercial bourgeoisie is absent in Côte d'Ivoire and attributes its suppression to the existence of a dominant planter bourgeoisie which had successfully secured control over the state [*Campbell, 1985: 269*]. On the other side, Aristide Zolberg, Jean-Marc Gastellu, Affou Yapi, Marcel Amondji, and Robert Hecht have argued that there is no such class. Zolberg suggested that, at Independence, it was difficult to discern such a group; there was no 'intergenerational transmission of concentrated landholdings' and parcel size was most closely associated with the age of the household head, and, thus, indirectly, with the size of the family labour force [*Zolberg, 1964: 26–7*]. Gastellu and Affou Yapi have similarly argued that most of the country's wealthy planters remain 'peasants,' heavily dependent on the labour of their own households and not imbued with a spirit of investment to reproduce the capital they already own. [*Gastellu and Affou Yapi. 1982: 155*]. Hecht offers as evidence the fact that most of the expansion in export crop production has come from creation of plots by new producers, not through expansion of existing enterprises, which he suggests is difficult to accomplish within the current policy framework [*Hecht, 1983: 26*]. To the extent that there is a bourgeoisie in Côte d'Ivoire, it is an administrative or bureaucratic bourgeoisie, some of whose members have agricultural interests, usually acquired after entering the civil service or politics [*Bakary, 1984: 29*].

Whether such a *class* existed in the early post-Independence period is not particularly significant for the argument here. What is important is whether these men exerted influence on behalf of policies that benefited farmers, either through private actions or by inciting demonstrations in the countryside. Certainly, there were occasional rumblings from cultivators in the countryside when policies threatened to reduce rural incomes. Lack of credit with which to purchase inputs and the announcement of low cocoa and coffee producer prices for the 1964–65 season sparked discontent in 1964 (the one agricultural season in which the real producer price declined) [*Baulin, 1980: 95*]. The role of the large landholders in these disturbances remains unclear, however. In pineapple and banana production, where large landholders predominated, the state has gradually been forced out of the market, and returns to farmers have generally been much higher than for other crops, suggesting that the Bates and Lofchie hypothesis holds true for the Ivorian case in this period.

Agricultural Prices and Labour Demand

The existence of a political elite with direct, individual interests in agriculture may also account for the Ivorian government's unusual handling of a problem that brought fear to most African regimes: rapid expansion of the population of under-employed youth in urban areas. Throughout the continent, exceptionally high rates of urbanisation provoked fear in the ranks of governors, based on the belief that those who had come to the city looking for work would riot and undermine regime stability in reaction to increasing food prices, food shortages, or inadequate amenities. In Lipton's view, this fear lay at the root of urban bias in many areas. That is, governments kept producer prices low in an effort to provide cheap food to urban dwellers, and they taxed export crops heavily in order to finance construction of urban amenities. Typically, that is exactly what African governments did.

In Côte d'Ivoire, however, the government took a different approach to this problem. First, it chose not to intervene in the trade of food crops, except in the case of rice. Prices in these consumer markets rise and fall with market forces. Second, upon independence, it immediately began to promote a programme of 'retour à la terre', the 'relève paysanne', an effort to attract youth back to the farm. Relatively high producer prices figured importantly in the success of these efforts, which the government pursued with varying degrees of vigour over the years. Formal encadrement was another element of the programme. In 1961, a formal body under the Ministry of Defence and the Civil Service established camps, housing up to 1,000 people each, for returning youth at major regional centers [*Affou Yapi, 1990: 61*]. Third, during the late 1960s and periodically during the 1970s, the government took steps to limit expenditures in urban areas. In 1967, for example, the president announced:

> . . . our success depends in great part on the peasant masses.
> At the moment when we are going to ask for a redoubling of efforts to diversify export crops and to produce food, it is good, indeed, it is just that those who have been privileged by comparison with the peasant masses accept that they too must share the sacrifices.
> These are of two types.
> The one is perhaps temporary: a freeze on wages and salaries, accompanied by a tax . . . that will affect all salaried employees, in the public and private sectors.
> The other will be more permanent: abolition of housing allowances for civil servants [*Houphouët-Boigny, 1978: 432–3*].

The difference between the Ivorian approach to this problem and that of other African countries was most likely the consequence of two related phenomena. First, the proportion of the population living in Abidjan and other urban areas 25–30 years ago and at the end of the end of the 1960s was far higher than that of most other African countries whose economies were based on agriculture and equalled or exceeded the level of urbanisation in mining-based economies. Further, at independence, the rate of urbanisation was much higher in Côte d'Ivoire than in many other African countries (see Tables 6 and 7). Second, this phenomenon aggravated a significant and persistent shortage of cheap

labour with which to harvest crops in rural areas. The workforce in rural
Côte d'Ivoire was ageing thanks in part to migration and urbanisation
patterns, and there was a surplus of land in relation to labour. The
government either had to figure out how to lure young Ivorians back to
the land, or it had to ensure that household heads could pay sufficiently
high wages to foreign workers to attract and retain a salaried labour
force.

TABLE 6
PROPORTION OF POPULATION LIVING IN URBAN AREAS

Country	25-30 Years Ago	15-20 Years Ago	1988-89
Cameroon	16.4	26.7	45.9
Côte d'Ivoire	23.4	32.3	44.3
Ghana	26.2	29.8	32.2
Kenya	08.9	12.9	21.7
Nigeria	17.0	23.4	33.1
Zaire	26.3	32.3	38.1
Zambia	23.3	36.3	52.6
Zimbabwe	14.4	19.4	26.1

Source: World Bank, *Social Indicators of Development, 1989.*

TABLE 7
RATE OF GROWTH OF POPULATION IN URBAN AREAS

Country	25-30 Years Ago	15-20 Years Ago	1988-87
Cameroon	5.0	7.9	7.1
Côte d'Ivoire	7.4	7.2	6.7
Ghana	4.0	2.7	4.8
Kenya	6.5	7.8	8.7
Nigeria	7.2	5.3	6.6
Zaire	4.9	4.3	5.0
Zambia	8.1	6.3	6.7
Zimbabwe	6.6	5.4	6.1

Source: World Bank, *Social Indicators of Development, 1989.*

Discussions of the struggle to address this problem filled the president's speeches in the 1960s and remained high on the policy agenda during the 1970s and 1980s.

> In contact with modern life . . . traditional societies disintegrate little by little, engendering a disorder that causes an exodus of peasants and of youth from the countryside. This departure worsens the perceived gap between the possibilities for transforming their milieu and the real changes they observe there.
> It is illusory to think, in most of these cases, of the possibility of a return to the land (*retour à la terre*). In any case, it has become imperative to analyse the deep causes of this rural exodus in order to reduce its pace and its effects [*Houphouët-Boigny, 1978: 1272*].

The concern was palpable in discussions in the ministries. A planning document from the 1960s pushed the need to increase the returns to labour in rural areas in order to attract people back to the land. 'If one wants . . . to keep educated youth on the land, it is vital to increase returns to labor in the savanna zone: by extension of the area cultivated per planter and by reducing the labor time required to produce different crops' [*Affou Yapi, 1990: 30*].

Economic Thought

Added to the struggle to achieve equality with French settlers and the existence of real, individual interests in the success of farming ventures as motives to support favourable agricultural policies was a distinctive economic logic. Houphouët's early involvement in the French parliament and later flirtation with the French Communist Party instilled a highly distinctive way of understanding economic issues. The forces of supply and demand were, and remain, for him, social constructs that further the interest of foreign firms. In his view economic equilibria are instead the results of political bargains and deals. Low prices for Côte d'Ivoire's commodities issue from manipulation on the part of firms or countries. For a country to improve its economic standing, its leader must cultivate leverage over the chief executive officers of companies and even the presidents of countries so that, with a few telephone calls, it becomes possible to correct a price that has dropped too low.

Central to Houphouët's understanding of trade was and is the notion that prices are political artefacts. 'The prices of our agricultural products are fixed externally and against our interests by the "haves",' he once suggested [*Houphouët-Boigny, 1978: 16 Oct. 1975*]. This view was pervasive among members of the Ivorian elite. Said one député, for example, '. . . If the price of a brick of chocolate increases at the same time that the price of cocoa drops, it is in part to compensate for increasing costs of the manufacturers and in part to maintain their exceptional profits' [*Assemblé Nationale, 1 July 1986: 12*]. Ivorians were in effect assuming the burdens of the milk and sugar subsidy programme of France, Belgium, or other chocolate-manufacturing countries.

Why should Côte d'Ivoire not retain the benefit? A necessary corollary was the theory of the just price, for if prices were not the products of many individuals and firms interacting anonymously in a market-place but were in fact under the control of a small group, then someone could be held to account for fluctuations. Said the president before a group of American journalists, shortly after he assumed office, 'It is only just that because . . . we have countries whose economies depend on production of coffee, those countries secure decent prices that permit adequate profits' [*Houphouët-Boigny, 1978: 463*]. He continued to hold this view, in public, at least, through the 1980s. In an interview with *Le Monde* in 1981, he explained his economic views.

> I prefer [economic] liberalism, but I insist that it respect other people's interests; for instance, I will never stop condemning those who claim to follow economic liberalism yet, at the same time, systematically exploit the Third World by indulging in shameful speculation. The law of supply and demand only operates between countries whose level of development is more or less equal. There is constant trickery in the economic relations between developed and underdeveloped countries . . . It is shameful that we cannot even discuss the price of raw materials which we export [*Africa Contemporary Record, 1981–82: B450*].

In the quest for a just price which would permit the government to offer high levels of remuneration to farmers, Houphouët-Boigny dabbled in cartels and other forms of market manipulation. Again, these were logical consequences of his underlying assumptions about how markets worked, and he had considerable faith in his ability to play the game well. As one French journalist wrote, '. . . cocoa is more than an affair of the state. It is a personal concern of the head of state. In an agricultural country that has only its land as a resource, cocoa is a strategic interest' [*Gombeaud et al., 1990: 33*]. The government could maintain producer prices and contemplate increases because its chief of state believed he could exercise influence over the price at which commodities traders would buy Ivorian harvests. So powerful was this logic that Ivorian policy-makers believed that they could sustain the high prices of the later, 1975–76 boom period long enough for the country to achieve a level of development comparable to Portugal by 1990 [*Berthelemy and Bourguinon, 1987, Part 2: 52*].

INSTITUTIONS, AGRICULTURAL PRICES, AND PUBLIC
INVESTMENT: 1970–86

If a focus on the individual income portfolios of elites goes far in explaining the origin of a favourable policy environment for agriculture in Côte d'Ivoire, it fares less well as a way of understanding the maintenance of stable real producer prices and reliable extension services during the period 1970–86. Although the president and some senior militants still gained private income from farming ten years after Independence, the sources of individual income among the elite lay increasingly in urban activities, not in agriculture. Further, even the senior-most militants had diversified their sources of income to include participation in commerce, manufacturing and, especially, government. The farmers' unions that had existed before Independence and that had retained some power as underground, increasingly regional movements during the early 1960s, disappeared from the political scene. In what did the bargaining power of rural interests then consist?

The answer, in brief, lies in the rise of new kinds of urban–rural social linkages and the behavioural incentives that resulted, within the context of extremely high rates of internal population mobility and of a unique Ivorian political institution, the Dialogue. New regional development associations dominated by urban-based relatives of farming households sprang up rapidly, as they had in Kenya and many other African countries. Unlike their counterparts elsewhere, however, most of these groups were multi-ethnic in composition – the result of large-scale internal migration within the country during the 1950s and 1960s. Further, because of the relative ease of travel in Côte d'Ivoire, which had rapidly improved its road system, rural relatives found it easier to levy frequent demands upon urban kin, provoking urban association leaders to take unusual steps to use their organisational bases to protect their own limited ability to accumulate. Among these was indirect lobbying for high and stable producer prices, which the urban members promoted at their jobs in government and during occasional 'days of Dialogue' the president called. Without these, some association heads suggested, urban dwellers would confront a steady influx of rural relatives seeking economic harbour.

Agro-Industries and the Urban–Rural Alliance

As a strategy for explaining stable real producer prices and an otherwise favourable agricultural policy environment, the 'sociological argument' retains some power during this period. Although Ivorian elites increasingly drew their incomes from government service, commerce, or manufacturing, many of these positions lay in public sector companies or private firms that processed agricultural products. The country's industrialisation strategy included some import-substitution industries but was based much more heavily in agro-processing. Just as the French cocoa and coffee processors had joined forces with Ivorian farmers to secure lower tariffs and a stabilisation scheme in the late 1950s, the managers of agri-business in independent Côte d'Ivoire saw a reason to pay prices adequate to elicit steady, high-quality harvests of key commodities – but certainly no more. Their influence helps account for the lack of deterioration in real producer prices, for their own economic fortunes were linked to continued production of high-grade harvests. It can also explain the maintenance of unexceptional producer–price shares; the involvement of manufacturers and traders in the international market–place gave them a stake in keeping prices in line with international trends.

The extent of these relationships is still difficult to evaluate. Ivorian industrial purchases of domestically-produced agricultural products remain a low 12 per cent of total purchases by manufacturing, with 30 per cent of inputs imported, even in most of the food industry [*Riddell, 1990: 161–2*]. Agro-industries grew relatively more rapidly than other kinds of industries during the 1970s, however – most likely giving their managers and owners greater influence in policy circles. Food processing, the beverage and tobacco industries, and textile manufacture all grew during the 1970s, while the overall rate of growth of manufacturing slowed in Côte d'Ivoire. By the late 1980s, the first three categories accounted for almost half of the country's manufacturing value-added, from a base of 28 per cent in 1960 [*Riddell, 1990: 158*]. In addition to palm oil production, limited cocoa processing, and other kinds of food processing, Côte d'Ivoire has engaged in transformation of its cotton crop to a greater degree than other African countries. Between 1964 and 1970, four separate cotton textile mills were established with the intention of producing cloth both for the local market and for export.

Most of these enterprises had some private-sector involvement and had to pay attention to the bottom line – and hence to the volume and quality of product they received. The palm oil industry was a good example of industry behaviour during the 1970s, although it is one of the few industries in which there was local demand for consumption of a crop destined largely for export. Most African producers of palm oil, including Nigeria, Benin, and Zaire, had allowed palm oil producer prices and yields to deteriorate, and they rapidly moved from being the world's major sources of palm products to insignificance. Côte d'Ivoire maintained its industry, competing with Malaysia and Indonesia. Its 'Plan Palmier' included room for both public and private enterprise, smallholder and plantation production. By 1977, Palmindustrie was 'second in the Ivory Coast in terms of cumulated investments, fifth in terms of industrial turnover, fourth in export earnings, and number eight in the number of industrially employed workers' [*Marcussen et al., 1982: 79*].

To maintain their efficiency and competitiveness, both the private and public companies involved in processing had to ensure that the state set the producer price for palm fruit high enough to prevent smallholders from shifting to cultivation of other crops or selling their harvests to local, home-manufacturers of oil. The industry lobbied for a doubling of the producer price in 1974, when smallholders demonstrated their unhappiness with the existing official rate by selling their palm fruit in local markets, forcing factories to operate below capacity and threatening the marketing edge of these companies. Again in 1977, production dropped because farmers marketed their production elsewhere, protesting deterioration in the price.

New Urban–Rural Linkages

The interests of agri-business lay in adequate transportation facilities and producer prices high enough to elicit quality production but no higher. The decision to emphasise agro-processing in industrial development was probably an important factor in generating a favourable policy environment. It was not the only source of pressure for such policies, however. Indeed, for perennial crops such as coffee and cocoa for which there was no local market and for which abandonment meant long-term loss of opportunities to take advantage of price changes, the alliance between farmers and industry was much weaker. Attention to rural interests was communicated by other means.

During the 1970s, a different kind of urban–rural linkage emerged. By the end of the first decade of PDCI rule, urban dwellers had discovered the limits of vertical, ethnic organisation as a vehicle for problem solving and for securing policy changes and pushed both for a public airing of grievances by different *couches sociales* and for greater latitude in forming horizontal associations [*Cohen, 1974*]. They succeeded in winning both a presidential audience, in the form of a national

Dialogue, and a loosening of legal restrictions. At the same time, tension had built up in the rural areas, as the militants of the independence struggle blocked political participation by a younger, more highly educated, 'developmental' elite. Some of those excluded from power were able to secure bargaining leverage by stirring local conflict and using these signs of discontent to bid for sub-regional autonomy or for informal liaisons with communities in neighbouring countries. The Houphouët-Boigny government was sufficiently concerned about threats to national cohesion that it took these actions seriously, in some cases incorporating the 'opposition' elites, as in 1966, 1970, and 1978, and in others, staging military or police crackdowns.

More important for the character of the agricultural policy environment, many of these elites tried to build new vehicles to exercise policy influence and gain greater control over the economic circumstances of their households by organising *groupes de ressortissants*, or regional development associations led by the urban members of rural households, who contributed money to their home villages and acted on behalf of rural relatives in their efforts to win a hearing in town. In some cases, these groups paralleled lineage lines, as they tended to do in other African countries, to the extent that they did not fall prey to political repression. In Côte d'Ivoire, however, internal migration had produced ethnic diversity in many zones, spawning associations with heterogeneous memberships. Combined with the past ineffectiveness of ethnic societies as instruments of change, then, demographics provided the impetus for regional associations, often with clear sectoral interests. These included the Committee for the Improvement of the Cocoa Belt, Association for the Development of the Department of Odienné, the Mutual Aid Society for the Economic and Social Development of the Prefecture of Aboisso, and so on [*Cohen, 1974: 164*].

Although rural relatives were often eager for 'development projects', the incentive structure facing the *ressortissants* encouraged leaders to emphasise favourable policy. Rural relatives were sometimes a source of cheap food for urban dwellers during economic downturns, but in the Ivorian case, where there was steady, often spectacular economic growth until the 1980s, more often than not, rural folk sought assistance from city or town relations. The drain on accumulation was significant, especially because a network of well-maintained roads and competing transport companies made travel back and forth easier for the rural majority than it was in most African countries. In self defence, urban residents sought both to coordinate their own giving, managing development of small-scale projects such as wells or working to improve the efficiency of co-operatives, and also to champion measures that would

boost rural incomes and limit the extent of their obligations. Experience
in building even small-scale projects proved how costly these could be,
however, unless government officials could be convinced to take responsibility, which the Ivorian government refused to do. As elsewhere, as
soon as a *fonctionnaire* or a businessman set foot in his home village, he
could count on a deluge of individual demands on his resources–
obligations for funerals missed, loans for new agricultural ventures, etc.
The *ressortissants* thus preferred to keep contributions to family and to
projects at a minimum and to delegate supervisory responsibilities in the
village or region to one member of the association, while lobbying for
both high and stable producer prices and programmes to attract youth
back to the countryside. In this respect, they differed from the mainly
kin-based associations that flourished, often as employment networks,
during the colonial and early independence periods.

The effect of these new associations on policy was most often indirect.
Younger men and women with political ambitions built name recognition and bargaining power through their support and direction of
these associations. When the president or the party's political bureau
opted to incorporate them into the ranks of the militants, as they did in
1969–1970 and at several subsequent points, they brought with them the
interests they had developed as managers of these associations and they
maintained government interest in relatively high and stable producer
prices. Similarly, technocrats, often prominent leaders in these associations, also came to appreciate the rationale for high producer prices
and reliable extension services. Thus, although the actual determination
of producer price levels remained in the hands of a small group of men
at the top levels of government, the president and senior officials were
well aware of the views of their fellow politicians and staff and cognisant
of the local conflicts and calls for national debate the 'developmentalists'
could generate if policy began to 'squeeze' farmers' incomes more than
was already the case.

The Ressortissants *and Dialogue*

Although these groups were potentially in a better position than their
rural relatives to engage in collective action to prevent reduction in
producer price levels or to improve agricultural services, they have
picked their battles carefully. Certainly, they were fewer in number than
the farmers and in better positions, by virtue of location and often of
education, to lobby for change. Influence exerted within the halls of
government, or, informally, through friends, has been the more common form of political participation, however. Only when rural incomes
have threatened to deteriorate and the grumbling of rural relatives has

mounted, have the *ressortissants* escalated demands for national Dialogue.

Unlike multi-candidate single-party elections, which generally lead to communication of purely local demands (see below), Houphouët's semi-institutionalised Dialogue has provided incentive for the articulation of policy positions or broader issues whose benefits are not divisible. It has periodically accorded opportunities for horizontal associations and for members of occupations or broad social groups to express their concerns. Strict time limits and the near-absence of individual audiences with the president during these meetings has generally made lobbying for strictly local projects and benefits extremely difficult. Producer price policy and the reliability of extension services have been frequent themes at these sessions, even though no farmers, union has existed until recently. The leaders of *groupes de ressortissants*, with their prior, organisationally-generated interest in broad policy issues, have helped draw attention to rural demands at these sessions. With their ability to mobilise street demonstrations quickly, these Ivorians also possess a credible threat they can invoke in the absence of government responsiveness to their demands. Indeed, the government's inability to respond effectively to demands expressed during the 1986 exceptional '*grand débat*', which generated calls for improvement of rural incomes and an accounting of the waste and fraud that accompanied the creation of SODESUCRE and the *grand investissement du nord*, prompted street demonstrations in 1989, a new Dialogue, and ultimately pressures for political liberalisation and government restructuring. Said Député Brahima Wattara in the special debates of 1986, 'Monsieur le Président [de l'Assemblée], . . . the only way to resolve our crisis lies in eliminating the suffocation of our villages by our cities and towns' [*Assemblée Nationale, 2 July 1986: 11*]. Because of the kinds of resources commanded by these new associations of *ressortissants*, the government's failure to respond decisively to this demand was turned into a threat to the regime's survival.

CÔTE D'IVOIRE IN COMPARATIVE PERSEPCTIVE

Political scientists who have turned their attention to the task of explaining urban bias or its obverse have generally adopted one of two paradigms. Lipton, Bates, and Lofchie originally offered an interest group account of agricultural policy that focused on the composition of nationalist coalitions and on the ability of large farmers to marshall influence for higher producer prices, under some circumstances. They understood the problem of urban bias in terms of the limited political bargaining power of rural producers in countries where landholdings are small and of relatively equal size. Farmers face a collective action problem, occasionally resolved when a few large landholders agree to assume the costs of protest against taxation that reduces their incomes. Where heads of state or senior political elites gain personal income from farming, a government is more likely to create a favorable policy environment for agriculture. For example, Lofchie has sought to explain the difference in producer price and exchange rate policies between Kenya and Tanzania in terms of the degree to which political elites may invest in land and agriculture. 'The land policies of the Tanzanian government have been exactly opposite to those of Kenya, and intended to prevent politicians and administrators from investing in land' [*Lofchie, 1989: 191*]. Government elites were in consequence much more tolerant of policies that hurt farm production.

A second paradigm stresses the role of political institutions in empowering the rural sector. In his writing on Zimbabwe, Michael Bratton has argued this view. He has suggested that, from 'the period from political independence in April 1980 to the parliamentary elections of July 1985, farmers in Zimbabwe were able to speak out and to be heard. The government moved quickly to set prices and deliver services' [*Bratton, 1987: 175*].

Much recent writing on urban bias has similarly suggested that competitive political institutions can effectively empower rural groups and reduce discrimination against farmers. Where majorities are rural, the argument goes, the candidates in competitive elections have incentive to promise policies that favour agricultural producers and to act on these as means of getting into elective office and staying there. 'Democracy' should thus improve the lot of farmers.

When competitive elections take place within the framework of a single-party system, however, as they does in most of Africa, this kind of institutional argument carries less weight. Robert Bates has pointed out that in multi-party systems there is some rationale for choosing candidates on the basis of their stands on national issues. If elected, the candidate might join with others from the same party to forge a voting block. The expected value of a ballot cast for a 'national issue', such as producer price policy, is thus greater than it would be in a single-party competitive election [*Bates, 1989: 92*]. Where competitive multi-party systems exist, scholars would expect to see rural majorities select representatives who would defend policies favourable to agriculture. Where these systems are semi-competitive or where a single party exists, the policies promised and promoted are likely to be much more particularistic.

In my work on Kenya, I offer a different account of the same phenomenon. In multi-party competitive systems, where parties may alternate in power, as opposed to single-party systems with multi-candidate elections, political elites have incentive to defend positions on national issues and otherwise contest public policy, in addition to pursuing local benefits. First, competitive party systems help provide incentives for politicians to bear the costs of organising and supporting broad national policy changes that help them little in defending their legislative seats. They can promote a focus on the longer term. How? Parties are different from factions in that they have independent organisational bases and personnel to carry out administrative tasks. The party leadership can turn around and demand that candidates carrying the party banner contribute to the effort to pursue the watchdog and reform activities implied by that interest. That is, they can demand that each candidate claiming affiliation with the party take time out from the pursuit of purely local interests or even attenuate local demands.

Second, the factions that proliferate in most single-party systems provide a poor base for pursuit of national level policy changes in another respect as well. Where there is a high degree of factional competition and no clear and enduring organisational base for any sub-group, candidates are less likely to take a stand on a reform issue than they are simply to break with one *ad hoc* group and move to another. They have little incentive to demand changes in the positions held by other faction members. To do so would take investment of time if not of money and the creation from scratch of channels for articulating and discussing demands [*Widner, 1992a*].

One contribution of the Côte d'Ivoire case to understanding the political economy of argricultural policy is that it shows the weakness of explanations that emphasise the 'empowerment' of rural groups through semi-competitve elections. Even in the Kenyan case, where there has been a record of regular, multi-candidate single-party elections, parliament has never exerted a strong influence over policy decisions. With no record of competitive electtions between 1960 and 1980, and with extremely constrained opportunities for debate in parliament throughout the 1980s, the cae of Côte d'Ivoire shows that creation of a favourable policy environment most likely has other roots.

The experience of Côte d'Ivoire also contributes to understanding by directing attention to the incentives for varrious forms of collective action that *unofficial* institusions can create. Too often, political scientists focus their attention on the way formal systems of representation shape political behaviour and ignore the social organisations that govern the affairs of sub-groups and may provide the spur to collective action in 'official' arenas. Part of the explanation of the Côte d'Ivoire case lies with the rise of just such social organisations, the *groupes de ressortissants*, and specifically with (1) the political behaviour generated by their efforts to regulate rural demands on accumalattion while preserving the social safety nets provided by extended, diversified households, (2) the heightened ability of these interest groups to sustain demands for agricultural policy change, given the greater limits on free-riding their structures permitted, and (3) the gradually increasing capacity of the leaders of these groups to organise street demonstrattions on behalf of rural interests, forcing governmanet leaders to pay attention to their policy concerns.

Finally, the Côte d'Ivoire case points to the need for dynamic explanations. The income portfolios and interests of social groups can and do change. Institutions alter over time. There is no reason to expect a single root cause at the foundation of agricultural policy choices in Africa, or elsewhere. More interesting would be to try to determine whether sources of policy influence change in predictable ways, depending on patterns of economic growth and institutional character.

REFERENCES

Affou Yapi, Simplice, 1990, *La relève paysanne en Côte d'Ivoire*, Paris: Editions ORSTOM and Editions Karthala.
Amin, Samir, 1973, 'The Plantation Economy: Ghana and the Ivory Coast', in *Neo-Colonialism in West Africa*, Harmondsworth, Middlesex: Penguin Books, first published 1971.
Assemblée Nationale de Côte d'Ivoire, République de la Côte d'Ivoire, Septième legislature, Premier session ordinaire 1986.
Bakary, Tessilimi, 1984, 'Elite Transformation and Political Succession', I. Zartman William and Christopher L. Delgado, *The Political Economy of the Ivory Coast*, New York: Praeger.
Bates, Robert, 1981, *Markets and States in Tropical Africa*, Berkeley, CA: University of California Press.
Bates, Robert, 1989, *Beyond the Miracle of the Market*, Cambridge: Cambridge University Press.
Baulin, Jacques Baulin, 1980, *La Politique 'intérieure' d'Houphouët-Boigny*, Paris: Eurofor Press.
Berthelemy, J.C. and F. Bourguignon, 1987, 'Growth and Crisis in Ivory Coast', mimeo, Washington, DC: World Bank.
Bratton, Michael, 1987, 'The Comrades and the Countryside: The Politics of Agricultural Policy in Zimbabwe', *World Politics*, Vol.49, No.2.
Campbell, Bonnie, 1985, 'The Fiscal Crisis of the State: The Case of the Ivory Coast', in *Contradictions of Accumulation in Africa*, Bonnie Campbell and Henry Bernstein (eds.), London: Sage.
Cohen, Michael A., 1974, *Urban Policy and Political Conflict in Africa: A Study of the Ivory Coast*, Chicago, IL: University of Chicago Press.
Cooper, Richard, 1992, ' "The Coffee Boom, 1976–1979" and "Fiscal and Monetary Policy" ', unfinished manuscript.

Deaton, Angus and Dwayne Benjamin, 1988, 'The Living Standards Survey and Price Policy Reform: A Study of Cocoa and Coffee Production in Côte d'Ivoire', Living Standards Measurement Study Working Paper 44, Washington DC: World Bank.

Devarajan, Shantanyanan and Jaime De Melo, 1987, 'Adjustment with a Fixed Exchange Rate: Cameroon, Côte d'Ivoire, and Senegal', World Bank Economic Review, Vol.1.

Gastellu, Jean-Marc and Affou Yapi Simplice, 1982, 'Un mythe à décomposer: La bourgeoisie de planteurs', in Yves Fauré and Jean-François Médard (eds.), État et Bourgeoisie en Côte d'Ivoire, Paris: Karthala.

Gombeaud, Jean-Louis, Corinne Moutout, and Stephen Smith, 1990, La Guerre du Cacao: Histoire secrète d'un embargo, Paris: Calmann-Lévy.

Hecht, Robert, 1983, 'The Ivory Coast "Miracle": What Benefits for Peasant Farmers?' Journal of Modern African Studies, Vol.21, No.1.

Houphouët-Boigny, Félix, 1978, Anthologie des Discours 1946–1978, Abidjan: Edition CEDA, (author's translations).

Jaeger, William, 1991, 'The Impact of Policy in African Agriculture: An Empirical Investigation', Policy, Research, and External Affairs Working Paper 640, Washington, DC: The World Bank.

Koffi Teya, Pascal, 1985, Côte d'Ivoire: Le Roi est Nu, Paris: Editions l'Harmattan.

Krueger, Anne, Schiff Maurice, and Alberto Valdés, 1989, 'Agricultural Incentives in Developing Countries: Measuring the Effect of Sectoral and Economy-wide Policies', World Bank Economic Review, Vol.2, No.3, pp.255–71.

Lawler, Nancy, 1990, 'Reform and Repression Under the Free French: Economic and Political Transformation in the Côte d'Ivoire, 1942–45', Africa, Vol.60.

Lofchie, Michael F., 1989, The Policy Factor: Agricultural Performance in Kenya and Tanzania. Boulder, CO: Lynne Rienner.

Marcussen, Henrik Secher and Jens Erik Torp, 1982, Internationalization of Capital: Prospects for the Third World: A Re-Examination of Dependency Theory, London: Zed Press and the Scandinavian Institute of African Studies.

Morgenthau, Ruth Schachter, 1964, Political Parties in French-Speaking West Africa, Oxford: Clarendon Press.

Riddell, Roger C., 1990, 'Côte d'Ivoire', in R.C. Riddell (ed.) Manufacturing in Africa: Performance and Prospects of Seven Countries, Portsmouth, New Hampshire: Heinemann.

Tuinder, Bastiaan A. den, 1978, Ivory Coast: The Challenge of Success. Baltimore; HD: Johns Hopkins University Press for the World Bank.

Varshney, Ashutosh, 1991, 'Has Rural India Lost Out? Paradoxes of Power and the Intricacies of Economic Policy', Paper presented at the Center for South Asian Studies, University of Virginia, Conference on Public Policy and Social Change in Contemporary India; also see this volume.

Watts, Michael and Thomas J. Bassett, 1986, 'Politics, the State and Agrarian Development: A Comparative Study of Nigeria and the Ivory Coast', Political Geography Quarterly, Vol.5.

Widner, Jennifer, 1992a, The Rise of a Party-State in Kenya: From Harambee to Nyayo, Berkeley, CA: University of California Press.

Widner, Jennifer, 1992b, 'Economic Change and the Politics of Agricultural Policy in Africa, mimeo.

Zolberg, Aristide, 1964, One-Party Government in the Ivory Coast, Princeton, NJ: Princeton University Press.

Exceptions to Urban Bias in Latin America: Cuba and Costa Rica

FORREST D. COLBURN

This essay speculates on the structural conditions under which the peasantry in Latin America is able to prosper. Contemporary Latin American states invariably meddle in agricultural markets. Despite government affirmations to the contrary, peasants ordinarily do not benefit from state intervention in the agricultural sector. However, there are two exceptions to this pattern in Latin America, and surprisingly they are the cases which ideologically bracket the political spectrum in the region – Cuba and Costa Rica. These two cases suggest that the proclivity towards urban bias can be thwarted by the socialist ideology of a well-ensconced and politically invulnerable elite, such as in Cuba, or by a vigorous democratic regime, such as Costa Rica.

The Mexican poet Octavio Paz once remarked that there is an organic relationship between power and cities. If that posited relationship holds sway anywhere, it is in Latin America. Indeed, no other region boasts of countries where the name of the capital is the same as the nation-state itself: México and México, Guatemala and Guatemala, San Salvador and El Salvador, and Panamá and Panamá. And throughout Latin America capital cities are commonly home to between a fourth and a third of the country's population. Mexico City is now the largest city in the world. Even in Argentina, a country nearly the size of India (which has a population of 830 million), roughly a third of the nation's 32 million inhabitants live in the greater Buenos Aires metropolitan region. Moreover, government budgets invariably are disproportionately dispersed in the capital, sometimes grossly so. For decades the Duvalier regime spent 90 per cent of its government budget (what was not stolen) in Port-au-Prince despite the fact that 90 per cent of Haitians were peasants.

No one has more succinctly described the sway of cities in the poor countries of the world than Michael Lipton with his phrase 'urban bias'

Forrest D. Colburn is Assistant Professor of Politics at Princeton University.

[*Lipton, 1977*]. More importantly, his explanation for urban bias has been most influential. He persuasively argues that small, interlocking urban elites substantially control the distribution of resources. The power of the urban elite is tied to their leverage over economic resources and government but, more broadly, also to their capacity to organise, control, communicate, and engage in transactions. Rural people are much more dispersed, poor, inarticulate, and unorganised. Consequently, the prosaic working of personal and group self-interest in less developed countries has led to wide disparities between urban and rural standards of living.

Two acclaimed books which build upon Lipton's analysis are Robert Bates' *Markets and States in Tropical Africa: The Political Basis of Agricultural Policies* and Merilee Grindle's *State and Countryside: Development Policy and Agrarian Politics in Latin America*. Both books explore, in different settings, the political calculations that induce governments to intervene in agricultural markets in ways which are harmful to the interests of most farmers. The state perpetuates the interests of those to whom it is beholden, to urban elites. And if a choice is to be made between the poor, the urban poor are systematically favoured. Bates and Grindle's books can be said to belong, unwittingly, to the flurry of studies of the state described as the 'new institutionalism' [*March and Olsen, 1984: 734–737*]. Here state elites are shown to have a variable capacity for autonomous decision-making and often have specific interests in national development that cause the state to become active in shaping economic and social relationships with dominant-class interests in society.

Lipton's work and the studies of those who have tried to unravel the relationship between urban elites, the state, and agrarian policy have been most illuminating. I myself found Bates' book indispensable to understanding post-revolutionary Nicaragua's agrarian policies and outcomes. But every focus eclipses something. Focusing on the state, on its autonomy, on its capacity, on its perniciousness, has obscured the question of how rural folk have survived, and under what conditions – if any – they have prospered. If urban bias is common in Latin America, under what circumstances do the rural poor majority escape its clutches, tame it, or even profitably succumb to it? Every 'rule' has its 'exceptions'. More importantly, degrees of import are often significant, especially for those living so close to subsistence. Some factors that might modulate or even diminish the seeming ubiquitous squeezing of the rural poor might include: (1) a democratic polity, (2) local organisations, (3) availability of substantial foreign resources from a patron or rent producing asset, (4) socialist ideology of political leadership, (5) the stage of economic development, and (6) fragmentation of the urban elite. These hypotheses fruitfully cast doubt on the uniform pessimism behind such questions as the one posed by Barrington Moore: 'Just what does modernisation mean for the peasant beyond the simple and brutal fact that sooner or later they are its victims'? [*Moore, 1966: 467*].

This essay speculates on the structural conditions under which the peasantry in Latin America is able to prosper. A review of trends in agricultural development in Latin America suggests that a host of variables affect peasant welfare. Some of them, such as demographic pressure, fall outside of the realm of politics. But politics is none the less the central – and most easily manipulated – determinant of peasant status. And given the evolution of Latin America, it is the state and not the landlord which is at centre stage. Evidence demonstrates that contemporary Latin American states invariably meddle in agricultural markets and that despite government affirmations to the contrary, peasants ordinarily do not benefit from state intervention in the agricultural sector. The case of Panama shows that even an abundance of governmental resources does not ensure agricultural policies which benefit the rural poor majority. However, there are two exceptions to this pattern in Latin America, and surprisingly they are the cases which ideologically bracket the political spectrum in the region – Cuba and Costa Rica. These two cases suggest that the proclivity towards urban bias can be thwarted by the socialist ideology of a well ensconced and politically invulnerable elite, such as in Cuba, or by a vigorous democratic regime, such as Costa Rica.

After a review of agricultural trends in Latin America, this essay explores how two such different countries as Cuba and Costa Rica have been able to avoid 'squeezing' their peasantry. The conclusion underscores that politics alone does not determine peasant welfare and explores some paradoxes emerging from the discussion of Cuba and Costa Rica.

THE SETTING

Latin America's agricultural development has the following important characteristics:

(1) a relatively high rate of urbanisation and a continuing decline in the percentage of the occupied labour force which works in agriculture;
(2) an inequitable distribution of agricultural land and inputs;
(3) particularly in the 1960s and 1970s, an expansion of modern, capitalist agricultural exploitation;

(4) persistence of large numbers of marginalised peasants;
(5) expansion of agriculture into humid tropic lowlands.

All five characteristics can be observed in Africa and Asia, but in Latin America the characteristics seem most pronounced. Thus, Latin America is more urbanised than the developing countries of Africa and Asia and has the most inequitable distribution of income. Tropical rainforests are under assault all over the world, but the pace of deforestation appears most accelerated in Latin America.

The most consequential development in Latin America during the second half of this century is arguably not political or economic but instead demographic. There has been a rapid increase in population and a rapid growth in urbanisation. Tables 1 and 2 detail how rapid Latin America's population has grown within just 30 years and the extent to which people increasingly live in cities. Growth rates are stunning. Except for Argentina, Uruguay, Chile, and Cuba, every country more than doubled its population between 1960 and 1990. A demographic study of Guatemala is suggestive: 'In a half century the number of years required to double Guatemala's population has dropped from 145 years to about 20 years, because mortality plunged while fertility remained very high' [*Early, 1982: 48*]. Since Guatemala's growth rate of urbanisation is not high, there is inevitably heightened competition for land and other natural resources. But even in Mexico, where 73 per cent of the population is now urban, rapid population growth has meant that the rural population has increased from 18.6 million in 1960 to 23.9 million in 1990 [*CEPAL, 1991: 8 and 165*].

Increased urbanisation inevitably accompanies 'modernisation', but high population growth rates have prevented Latin America's rapid urbanisation from resulting in a decrease in the rural poor, the proverbial *campesinos*. As a percentage of the region's inhabitants, they are less than they were in the past. But in absolute numbers, they have grown. Statistics compiled by the Food and Agriculture Organisation (FAO) suggest that there is a close correlation between the proportion of the population which is rural and percentage of the population supported by agriculture. In some of the smaller and poorer countries, such as those of Central America, a share of the urban population too earns its livelihood in agriculture. So the problem of rural poverty is a problem of agriculture.

Throughout Latin America, capitalist agricultural exploitation has expanded rapidly. Impetuses (and indicators) are the widespread adoption of 'green revolution' innovations, increased investment in mechanisation, expanded production for export markets, greater penetration of

TABLE 1

LATIN AMERICA:
URBAN POPULATION*

Percentage of Total Population

County	1960	1970	1980	1990
Mexico	51	59	66	73
Guatemala	33	36	39	42
El Salvador	38	39	42	44
Honduras	23	29	36	44
Nicaragua	40	47	53	60
Costa Rica	37	40	46	54
Panama	41	48	51	55
Colombia	48	57	64	70
Venezuela	67	72	83	91
Ecuador	34	40	47	57
Peru	46	57	65	70
Brazil	45	56	68	77
Uruguay	80	82	84	86
Paraguay	36	39	44	48
Chile	70	75	81	86
Bolivia	39	41	44	51
Argentina	73	79	83	86
Cuba	55	60	68	75
Dominican Republic	30	40	51	60

* Urban is defined as it is used in each country.

Source: Economic Commission for Latin America and the Caribbean (CEPAL),
    Statistical Yearbook for Latin America and the Caribbean (Santiago, Chile:
    CEPAL, 1991), p.8.

multinational capital in agribusiness enterprises, and utilisation of wage
labour as the predominant form of labour relations. This 'modernisation' of agriculture has been based on the same inequitable distribution
of land that has characterised rural Latin America since the colonial era.
Indeed, scattered evidence suggests that despite some efforts at land
reform, in most countries agricultural land is concentrated in even fewer
hands than it was in the 1940s [Grindle, 1986: 2]. The concentration of
land undoubtedly facilities the modernisation of segments of agriculture
because it affords economies of scale and, equally important, enables a
small landholding elite to gain privileged access to state-provided
inputs, infrastructure, markets, and support services. But the concentration of land has meant, too, that the rural majority has seen few
benefits from the selected modernisation of agriculture.

For Latin America's peasants the modernisation of agriculture has
more often than not meant little more than that the best land is taken by
an enterprise instead of a hacienda, and that the land is more likely to be
sown with strawberries or soybeans than henequen or sugar cane. If

TABLE 2

LATIN AMERICA:
GROWTH OF URBANISATION AND TOTAL POPULATION

Percentage Growth Between 1960 and 1990

Country	Urbanisation	Population
Mexico	43	133
Guatemala	27	132
El Salvador	27	104
Honduras	91	166
Nicaragua	50	159
Costa Rica	46	144
Panama	34	119
Colombia	46	107
Venezuela	36	163
Ecuador	68	140
Peru	52	125
Brazil	71	107
Uruguay	8	22
Paraguay	33	141
Chile	23	73
Bolivia	31	109
Argentina	18	57
Cuba	36	52
Dominican Republic	100	122

Source: Computed from statistics presented in Economic Commission for Latin America and the Caribbean (CEPAL), *Statistical Yearbook for Latin America and the Caribbean* (Santiago, Chile: CEPAL, 1991, pp.8 and 165.

peasants have any relation to the estate, it is now more likely to be as wage earners and not as sharecroppers or tenants. Peasants are more likely to be landless and more likely to engage in two, three, or even more income-generating activities [*Grindle, 1986, 2*]. If they are fortunate enough to have their own plots, they may make intermittent use of commercial fertilisers and insecticides. Even so, unsystematic but persuasive evidence suggests the welfare of many rural Latin Americans continues to be as precarious as it has been for generations. In sum, the 'dualism' of Latin American agriculture that elicited much disdainful commentary on the heels of the Cuban Revolution in the early 1960s has only become more pronounced.

What has changed significantly as a result of population growth, increased urbanisation, incipient industrialisation, and a more integrated position in the world economy is the position of the peasantry in society and vis-à-vis the state. Here I must generalise and speculate, but there does seem to be a fundamental change: The peasantry is no longer an important generator, through wage labour and the production of cheap foodstuffs, of national development. With industrialisation and the exploitation of foreign aid and borrowing, agricultural exports are less important for nearly all countries in generating foreign exchange. And agricultural exports now often depend as much on the employment of technology as cheap labour. Furthermore, cheap food can be – and increasingly is – imported.

There is little indication that Latin American regimes have historically concerned themselves with the political disposition and behaviour of peasants. That indifference has not changed, but whereas governments also did not have to contend themselves with the urban poor, the explosive growth of cities, especially of capital cities, has meant that regimes do have to pay attention to the urban poor. A demonstration in Muy Muy does not cause consternation, but one in Managua is alarming. Thus the evolution of Latin America has left the rural poor more marginal both economically and politically.

The evolution of Latin America has also led to the state playing a much more complex role in agriculture. It is certainly more complex than the pattern Bates deftly describes as prevailing in Africa where states intervene in the markets of export commodities to skim off foreign exchange and in the markets of foodstuffs to protect urban consumers (and, by extension, urban employers). Latin America does not have Africa's colonial legacy of state marketing boards, although leaders as diverse as Perón and the Sandinistas have employed the gambit. But there are more cases, especially recently, of governments taxing agricultural exports modestly. And, especially with non-traditional agricultural commodities, there are sometimes even incentives to export. Similarly, while there are cases of food staples being controlled to protect urban consumers to the detriment of food producers, normally peasants, there are also many cases where food staples are at world prices or higher. For example, even during the economic crisis of the 1980s, the price for maize in Mexico was higher than world prices.

Latin America's more developed and diversified economies enable the region's governments to have sources of revenue other than agriculture, including taxes on imports, consumption, income, foreign borrowing, rent producing assets (such as oil wells), and so forth. Where the state gives agriculture a drubbing is on the expenditure side and in the use of an invisible source of revenue – the printing press. Whatever else they may be, government expenditures on the armed forces, elephantine bureaucracies, and the like are an expensive and inefficient form of subsidy for the urban middle class. The subsidy is large enough to attract hoards to the cities who seek to get in on the subsidy, catch part of the multiplier effect, or just live off the crumbs. Deficit financing, nearly ubiquitous in the region, stems from the lack of political resources – and will – to say no to all those powerful interests clamouring for a share of state revenue. Inflation is part and parcel of the process, posing a threat to all, including the rural poor. So the rural poor suffer not just from a possible direct tax on their labours, but also through not participating in subsidies that they none the less help finance by suffering the ravages of inflation and devaluation.

The evolution of Latin America has meant that the determinant of peasant welfare is no longer the hegemony of landlords and whether there are 'cracks' in that hegemony that peasants can exploit. Increasingly, the determinant of peasant welfare is, aside from demographics, the state. Grindle argues persuasively that the various agrarian reform initiatives of the 1960s and 1970s had a consistent outcome: the increased influence of the state on economic and political conditions in rural areas [Grindle, 1986: 8].

Not discussed by Grindle, but perhaps as consequential, increased state intervention throughout the economy has a significant impact on peasant welfare. This latter form of influence is not only indirect but often not guided by a rationality. As ineffectual, and at times farcical, as many agrarian reforms were, they at least had a rationality that made it possible to predict the range of possible outcomes. With more general state macroeconomic policies, virtually anything can happen and often does: inflation, hyperinflation, over-valuation of the national currency, under-valuation of the currency, rampant speculation, stagnation, and every other potential outcome. Furthermore, economic management by government teams increasingly assumes the form of fiscal and monetary coups, such as the sudden suspension of foreign exchange transactions [Corradi, 1990: 11]. Typical characteristics of these coups include secrecy, surprise, and exceptionalism. The population may find from one day to the next that the banks are closed and their deposits frozen, or that the currency has changed names, and so forth. It is a mistake to conclude that the peasantry, no matter how isolated and impoverished, is immune from the deleterious effects of the political and economic chaos that so often plagues Latin America. It is safer to conclude they have the most difficulty protecting themselves or profiting from the turmoil.

Not surprisingly, increased state intervention in society has led to the state becoming the primary target of agrarian protest, the principal mediator of rural social class relations, and the central actor in containing the effectiveness of agrarian protest. The state is also where claims are made for resources and, ironically, for relief from the pernicious effects of state policies.

A conceptualisation of the most significant variables that determine contemporary peasant welfare in Latin America would thus seemingly have to include some configuration of the following:

(1) demographic pressure;
(2) distribution of land and other resources;
(3) urban/rural terms of trade;
(4) presence, kind, and scope of government agricultural policies;
(5) impact of endogenous shocks to the economy because of political and economic turmoil;
(6) state sanctioned or controlled framework in which peasants can agitate to contest and possibly reverse assaults on their welfare.

The diversity among these six factors suggests that peasants' ills cannot be rectified solely by 'getting prices right', or finding a political coalition able to 'get prices right'. Neither will a straight redistribution of land end rural misery. Indeed, not only are all of the above factors important, but sometimes trying to address one set of issues causes problems elsewhere. For example, often an aggressive land reform results in political and economic turmoil which negates the benefits of more equitable land distribution.

In the end, the most decisive factor may be the state sanctioned or controlled framework in which peasants participate politically. This factor is more often a given and not one that can be manipulated. But the ability of peasants to voice their demands and make claims can best ensure that their disparate needs are met. Conversely, the absence of a political voice puts peasants at the whim of political actors who traditionally have not been responsive to the rural poor.

Examining the fate of peasants in different nation-states suggests the relative importance of the six factors enumerated above and an appreciation for the ways in which they interact. Arguably, the most suggestive paired comparison is of Cuba and Costa Rica, the two countries in Latin America that, notwithstanding their political differences, have practised the least urban bias in the region.

CUBA

Since its Revolution in 1959, Cuba has made major advances in education, health, social security, employment generation, and the elimination of absolute poverty. By 1985 infant mortality had been reduced to less than 15 deaths per 1,000 live births and average life expectancy had been increased to over 73 years [*Ghai et al., 1988: 123*]. By 1980 illiteracy had been reduced to two per cent [*Mesa-Lago and Díaz-Briquets, 1988: 17*]. These impressive gains have only been possible through sustained efforts to eliminate the pre-revolutionary disparity between urban and rural life. For example, the integration of urban and rural education has been powerfully promoted by the boarding school networks of 'schools in the countryside'. Their role in mingling children from urban and rural backgrounds has helped transform attitudes to rural life and work. Similarly, health programmes strongly emphasise rural areas. The campaign in the 1960s to provide universal access to health care led to the creation of many strategically situated cottage hospitals and rural clinics, and medical students are required to spend at least two years in rural service after graduating. Finally, virtually all Cubans, including private farmers, enjoy rights to some social security benefits.

Cuba's 'plantation style' agricultural system has facilitated the provision of these social services because of the ease of reaching labourers and their families which tend to be clustered instead of dispersed as is common in more peasant dominated economies. Indeed, roughly 75 per cent of the agricultural labour force works on state farms, with another 15 per cent working co-operatives [*Ghai et al., 1988: 103*]. Nowadays less than ten per cent of all agricultural workers are peasants. But reducing the traditional urban–rural dichotomy has involved more than an equitable distribution of social services. Equally important has been the priority accorded to the agricultural sector. With the exception of the first two years of the Revolution, this priority has been a constant of Cuban development policy and is manifested in allocation of investment funds and in wage policy. Thus, for example:

> Agricultural workers gained more than their urban counterparts in the 1981 wage reform, with those at the bottom of the scale receiving an increase of 30 per cent. Further, the rapid mechanisation of the sugar harvest and other agricultural processes has had the effect of upgrading workers to higher wage scales more rapidly and in greater numbers in agriculture than in industry. As a result, average agricultural wages increased by 51 per cent between 1977 and 1983, compared to 25 per cent for average industrial wages [*Ghai et al., 1988: 107*].

It is suggestive, too, that the performance of the farming sector over the first quarter century of the revolution roughly mirrors the performance of the economy as a whole, even if there is a lack of reliable data on which to base detailed year-by-year comparisons.

Critics of the Cuban regime suggest that the material gains in rural welfare are compromised by the lack of personal liberty which is resented and which has stymied personal initiative [*Cordova, 1989: 11–31*]. And a study of Cuban agricultural co-operatives published in Havana raises, in elliptical fashion, the question of whether or not the peasantry has been agreeable to the continued 'proletarianisation' of Cuban agriculture through which many benefits and social services have been tied [*Becerril et al., 1989: 187–9*]. Still, the extent to which Cuba has avoided the urban bias common elsewhere in Latin America is impressive. Its success raises the question, what conditions have made these gains possible?

The proclivity towards urban bias has been avoided in Cuba by a trio of factors: the socialist ideology of the governing elite, the regime's political-economic control, and Soviet aid. Socialist ideology has provided an impetus for broad-based economic development, where urban interests are not allowed to usurp rural needs. But it is political-economic control of state and society by the regime and international assistance which has made the ideal attainable. Political-economic control enables the regime to be single-minded and forceful in pursuing its objectives. It is free from both opposition and political crises which would derail its pursuit of socialism.

The relative importance of Soviet aid is difficult to measure. A precise calculation of Soviet assistance to Cuba would require the creation of an elaborate economic model for overall terms of trade, external balances, and derived exchange rates. A Yale economist, Richard Turtis, calculates that since 1976 (and until quite recently) total Soviet aid averaged about $2 billion a year, or roughly one-seventh of Cuba's GDP [*Turtis, 1987: 174*].

The case of Sandinista Nicaragua facilitates an appreciation of the relative importance of ideology, control, and foreign assistance in promoting egalitarianism. The Sandinistas shared with the Cuban elite a socialist ideology. But the Sandinistas never had political-economic control over Nicaragua. Soviet aid in the second half of the 1980s was significant, about $500 a year (excluding military assistance), lower in absolute terms than aid for Cuba, but higher in terms of percentage of GDP. On a per capita basis, though, aid from the Soviet Union to Nicaragua was about comparable to what Cuba received. Political-economic control thus appears to be a more decisive explanation for Cuba's success. The lack of Sandinista' control meant that the Nicaraguan Revolution was overwhelmed by the foot dragging of the private sector, by a counter-revolution that was able to recruit followers, and by the incapacity of the Nicaraguan state itself [*Colburn, 1986; 1990*].

In conclusion, the Cuban case shows that rural welfare can be dramatically enhanced if there is political leadership, absolute control of state and society, and a fountain of foreign exchange.

COSTA RICA

Costa Rica's cultivated image of yeoman farmers is misleading, but none the less rural folk have fared well [*Gudmandson, 1986*]. Indeed, a comparative study of Costa Rica and Cuba found that Costa Rica matched Cuba's impressive accomplishment in income distribution, health care, social security, and employment [*Mesa-Lago and Díaz-Briquets, 1988: 5–23*]. With some specific indicators, such as income distribution, Cuba performed better, but with other indicators, such as life expectancy, Costa Rica excelled. However, on the whole, performance was comparable. Costa Rica's indicators of 'growth' were more impressive: higher economic growth, expansion of the industrial share of the GDP, smaller balance of trade deficits, higher investment rates, and smaller external debt. Furthermore, Costa Rica received decidedly less foreign aid than Cuba.

Costa Rica's performance on such standard social indicators as infant mortality, literacy, and life expectancy could only be achieved by attending to the needs of all citizens, rural and urban. However, other indicators, also suggest that, while Costa Rica has not been entirely free of urban bias, it has consistently striven for broad-based development. For example, the most rural provinces have the highest rates of highway construction [*Salís, 1984: 127*]. The percentage of wage earners in the agricultural sector remained stable at 59 per cent between 1950 and 1973 (the year of the last census). Moreover, the percentage of the agricultural labour force which is self-employed actually increased from nine to 26 per cent during this period [*Vega, 1982: 241*]. These figures suggest that small and medium-sized farms continue to be important in Costa Rica. Although wages for agricultural labour do lag behind those of other sectors [*Schifter, 1983: 228*], between 1957 and 1983 agricultural salaries did rise appreciably in real terms [*FAO, 1985: 5*].

The Costa Rican state has intervened in agricultural markets in ways that significantly shape rural welfare. The production of coffee is the single most important activity in the country's economy. More specifically, it is the largest source of rural employment. The production structure is dominated by holders of small and medium-sized farms, leading one analyst to suggest that the income generated by the activity is the most equitably distributed income source in the country [*Salazar, 1984: 52*]. The production and export tax on coffee is computed to be 18 per cent of the international price [Salazar, 1984: 222]. This tax is significant but it is hardly the predatory tax common in Africa [*Bates, 1981: 136–145*].

State intervention in the markets for basic grain has been common. Somewhat surprisingly, the principal impetus has not been to reward urban consumers with low prices or to boost the incomes of poor peasants. Instead, the impetus has been a desire for national self-sufficiency of basic foodstuffs. Government price supports for maize and rice have consistently been higher than world prices. The domestic price of maize has sometimes been double the world price while the domestic price of rice is often only 15 per cent higher than the international prices [*Salazar, 1984: 220–21*]. Support prices for beans, however, have traditionally been lower than international prices.

Rice, not maize, is now the most important staple in the Costa Rican diet. The production of rice, though, is dominated by a relatively small group of producers with large farms. Maize is an important crop for animal feed, so high prices for maize adversely affect consumers of animal products. An exhaustive analysis of the impact of government intervention in the markets for basic grains concluded that in the end consumers paid slightly higher prices as a result of implicit income transfers to producers [*González, 1991: 173*]. Given that the maize crop is relatively small, that beans are produced largely by peasants, and that rice is produced by well endowed farmers, it none the less may be true that peasants suffer a net loss from government intervention in basic grain markets. Still, government intervention seems to be relatively benign. And there does not seem to be any question that the government has stimulated the production of maize and rice.

In sum, the Costa Rican state has provided comprehensive social services to the rural poor and has avoided economic policies which weaken the agricultural sector. Public investments in social services and infrastructure, peace, and the country's natural resources enable rural folk to live not so differently from their urban brethren.

If Cuba's success can be traced to the socialist ideology of the country's leadership, Stalinist control of state and society, and generous foreign aid, what factor or set of factors explains Costa Rica's success? There does not appear to be a simple answer. Costa Rica's liberal democracy, the most stable in Latin America, surely deserves credit. But even before the establishment of the country's liberal democracy (in

1948) Costa Rica had a more equitable distribution of income and more political stability than its neighbours.

In the last three decades, Costa Rica's democracy had clearly served to protect the rural poor, to provide them with social services, and to give them a political voice, but apparently the first two aspects are not necessarily part and parcel of a liberal democracy. Democracy does involve the granting of a political voice to all, but the Costa Rican elite seems to have made a commitment to equitable development that cannot be explained by political pressure or fear of political retribution. For example, it is argued that elected and appointed elites initiated social security programmes 'virtually free of significant pressure from present or future beneficiaries' [*Brumbaugh, 1985: 440*]. All that can be suggested is that perhaps democracy, like socialism, can promote an ethos of equality that is strong enough to influence political choices.

Given the important role played by the political elite in anticipating – and meeting – demands from the middle and lower classes, the results of a survey of 80 prominent politicians is illuminating. Respondents were asked what factors accounted for Costa Rica's democracy. The factors and the frequency in which they were mentioned are: political culture (66 per cent); education, literacy (60 per cent); democratic leadership (46 per cent); land tenure (41 per cent); racial homogeneity (39 per cent); no military (36 per cent); poverty (19 per cent); geographic isolation (19 per cent); and size of country (14 per cent) [*Stetson, 1969: 99*]. Seligson also mentions racial homogeneity as being important in explaining the lack of peasant exploitation and repression. The 'lower economic status of the peasant population is not compounded by inferior ethnic status' [*Seligson, 1980: 156*].

Yet while it is evident that political elites have taken initiatives to aid the rural poor, gains have come too from the political power democracy has conferred upon peasants and rural labourers. Costa Rica's two intensely competitive political parties (and the smaller parties, including the Communist Party) do seek to marshal support in rural areas. Voting turnout consistently exceeds 80 per cent of registered voters, ensured in part by a 1959 constitutional amendment making voting mandatory [*Brumbaugh, 1985: 29*].

Besides voting, Costa Ricans participate in other political activities. Common are: party membership, attendance at political rallies, and interaction with government officials. A majority of heads of households are members of at least one voluntary organisation and have taken part in community improvement projects [*Brumbaugh, 1985: 30–31*]. In a study of agrarian reform, Seligson found that the peasantry is more distrustful of government than are non-agriculturalists. But Seligson discovered that 83 per cent of the reform beneficiaries interviewed did state that they would try to do something about a law being proposed that they thought was harmful to their interest [*Seligson, 1982: 197 and 213*].

Perhaps surprisingly, then, labour is not well organised and is a weak participant in politics. Prior to 1968, for example, there was only one collective bargaining contract in the entire country, making Costa Rica the country with the lowest number of collective bargaining contracts in Central America [*Brumbaugh, 1985: 301*]. Less than 12 per cent of the wage-earning labour force was organised in 1977, well below the average in most of Latin America [*Brumbaugh, 1985: 301*].

None the less it is important to note that democracy provides an environment in which violence cannot be used to repress political organisations and agitations, including strikes. Rural Costa Rica is politicised and there are occasionally demonstrations, strikes, blockages of highways, and the like. Elsewhere in Latin America these confrontations would be violently repressed, but in Costa Rica confrontation leads to negotiation.

An anecdote drawn from a study of rural Costa Rica by Seligson is illuminating and so worth recounting despite its length:

> A group of peasants were working on a large estate under deplorable conditions. They began to surreptitiously cultivate plots on an unused part of land. When discovered the police were summoned. The peasants refused to abandon their fields. They moved into hastily built shacks set amongst the fields. When the police returned they could no longer burn the fields because of the threat to women and children living in the shacks. The police vowed to return in greater numbers to evict the peasants. The peasants then built a school on the squatted lands and put up a big sign saying, 'School Zone – Respect!' There was no teacher, of course, but in Costa Rica the Ministry of Education readily responds to petitions for new schools, even in remote areas, so long as the minimum number of children are in the area. When the police returned the implied threat of the squatters was evident; if the police burned down the school, they would be destroying public property and would consequently become involved in a serious conflict with the Ministry of Education. The police left never to return. The squatters won [*Seligson, 1980: 111–13*].

Such an incident – and outcome – would not be possible in, say, Guatemala or almost any other country in Latin America. The rule of law diffuses power. And a functioning liberal democracy provides a stable environment for economic development.

In summary, democracy has enabled Costa Rica to avoid the more perverse characteristics of urban bias. Disaggregating the country's liberal democracy suggests that, like Cuba, elite ideology is crucial. Also important in the Costa Rican case, though, is party competition and even the ability to engage in illegal forms of protest without fear of violent repression.

CONCLUSION

Reviewing the fate of the rural poor in Latin America reveals the diversity of ways in which politics has shaped agricultural development and so the welfare of the rural poor. Governments of every ilk have attempted to improve the provision of social services to the rural poor and have met with some success, especially with education. But access to land and remunerative employment remain as elusive as ever, in part because of the self-perpetuating legacy of income inequality and urban bias and in part because of population growth.

Among Latin American intellectuals and their North American and European colleagues there has long been a belief that progress towards social and economic equality can only result from profound political transformation – through revolution. That faith is questionable. On the one hand, the experience of Bolivia and Nicaragua suggests that the cost of social and economic disruption and government mismanagement can overwhelm the very real benefits to the poor of a revolution. On the other hand, Costa Rica suggest that real gains can come in the absence of profound political transformations.

But where students of Latin America seem to be prescient is in their sustained conviction that the only viable solution to rural misery in the region is a political solution. The touted solution in the 1960s – land reform – proved impossible without political reform. In the 1970s 'green revolution' technology was in vogue, but its benefits were usurped by the well heeled. In the 1980s the professed solution was 'getting prices right', but on the whole, prices have not been the serious problem in Latin America that they have been in Africa. Suggestively, in a number of Latin American countries, including Panama and Costa Rica, recent IMF and World Bank stabilisation and adjustment policies designed to remove 'price distortions' have led to lower prices for the peasants' crops.

There is an irony in that the two regimes in Latin America that provide the most for the rural poor are at opposite ends of the political spectrum – Cuba and Costa Rica. This suggests that rigid socialism (albeit with generous foreign aid) and uncompromised liberal democracy can fulfil the disparate needs of the poor. The difficulty is that most of Latin America is neither sufficiently socialist nor sufficiently democratic. It is perhaps also revealing that the two hopeful models are small countries. What would it take to match either Cuba's socialism or Costa Rica's democracy in one of Latin America's larger countries? Nevertheless, what Cuba and Costa Rica have in common is that in both countries the rural poor have a voice; and they have political power. In Cuba the voice of the rural poor is not their own, but that of the political leadership. There are contradictions and shortcomings in that relationship, but the poor do have a voice. In Costa Rica the voice of the rural poor is their own, but their historical antagonist, the landed elite, has a voice too – one that has been silenced in Cuba. The shared success of Cuba and Costa Rica therefore supports the argument for the rural poor having political power.

For most of its recent history, Latin America has been under authoritatian rule. However, the threat of another Cuba, where the fate of Batista's armed forces and the country's economic elite was never entirely forgotten, has always engendered a powerful reaction to any suggestion of socialism. But democracy too, with its implied limits on the monopolisation of power, has been circumspectly viewed. Authoritarian regimes have fallen recently and most Latin American regimes are now headed by a popularly elected civilian.

As an ideology, socialism has lost its currency. The electoral defeat of the Sandinistas, Cuba's political ossification and mounting economic problems, the collapse of the eastern European regimes, and the difficulties besetting what was the Soviet Union have undermined both the concept and the potential practice of socialism. It is sometimes quipped in Latin America that hope for the poor comes in the form of a lottery, a religious miracle, and revolution. Since 1989 the latter seems increasingly unlikely. An economic windfall (the national equivalent of the lottery?) also seems unlikely. Panama's good fortune to be the site of a trans-isthmus canal and pipeline is not to be duplicated. And even prodigious quantities of oil, such as those in Venezuela, Ecuador and Mexico have not reversed the status of the rural poor.

If democracy does take root in Latin America it may provide some assistance to the rural poor, but for that to happen democracy would have to mean more than undemocratic, urban-based political parties fielding candidates for an election every six years. Rural folk need the opportunity to organise their own parties or exercise influence proportionate to their votes within established parties. Just as important, they need a genuine rule of law so that they can organise, agitate, and demonstrate to protect their rights and have their needs met. It is timely to ask: if democracy does take root in Latin America, will it be extended even to isolated rural areas? [*Fox, 1990*]. For the last 45 years the political choices of the region have been decisively influenced by the cold war. Now that the cold war is over, it is more unclear than ever what the course of Latin American politics will be. A strong impetus for radical change is gone and so is a model of egalitarianism; gone too is a great bugaboo and a rallying cry of reactionary inertness.

Apart from elite defensiveness and hesitation, there are two challenges for promoters of rural democracy. To return to Tables 1 and 2, the first challenge is urbanisation. If democracy takes root at a time in which a country is, for example, 70 per cent urban, what assurance is there that the rural minority will not be trampled? Urban bias could continue with democratic blessings. Second, the electoral pliability of the rural poor is legendary. The PRI (the ruling party) in Mexico, for example, routinely gets its highest percentage of votes from the segment of Mexican society for whom the PRI has done the least – the peasantry. These obstacles are perhaps not insurmountable, but they are formidable. It is suggestive that not only in Cuba, but also in Costa Rica, elite commitment to rural welfare has been crucial in avoiding urban bias.

In the absence of a vigorous democracy, the potential gains of a republican government can be more than offset by the prosaic working of urban bias and individual and group self-interest. Further, as the cases of Bolivia and Nicaragua so sadly illustrate, the rural poor are particularly vulnerable to prolonged political and economic crises. If the urban elites refuse to give a greater voice to the rural poor and if political differences cannot be settled amicably, the rural poor are likely to continue depending overwhelmingly on migration to urban areas or those unsettled areas that are left in Latin America. The prospect is disturbing. It is hard to believe that, for example, Mexico City can grow much larger or that the countryside of El Salvador can absorb still more peasants. Yet, the most sobering statistic of all perhaps is that Latin America's population density is still only a fifth that of Asia's.

REFERENCES

Bates, Robert, 1981, *Markets and States in Tropical Africa*, Berkeley, CA: University of California Press.
Becerril, Lilia Nahela and Mariana Ravenet, 1989, *Revolución agraria y cooperativismo en Cuba*, Havana: Editorial de Ciencias Sociales.
Brumbaugh, Chalmers, 1985, 'Costa Rica: The Making of a Livable Society', Ph.D. thesis, University of Wisconsin.
CEPAL (Economic Commission for Latin America and the Caribbean), 1991, *Statistical Yearbook for Latin America and the Caribbean*, Santiago: CEPAL.

Colburn, Forrest, 1986, *Post-Revolutionary Nicaragua: State, Class and the Dilemmas of Agrarian Policy*, Berkeley, CA: University of California Press.

Colburn, Forrest, 1990, *Managing the Commanding Heights: Nicaragua's State Enterprises*, Berkeley, CA: University of California Press.

Cordova, Efren, 1989, *El trabajador cubano en el estado de obreros y campesinos*, Miami, FL: Ediciones Universal.

Corradi, Juan, 1990, 'Argentina', in Forrest Colburn (ed.), *Prospects for Democracy in Latin America*, Princeton, NJ: Center of International Studies, Princeton University.

Early, John, 1982, *The Demographic Structure and Evolution of a Peasant System*, Boca Raton, FL: University Presses of Florida.

FAO (Food and Agriculture Organisation), 1985, 'Examen de las políticas y estrategias para el desarrollo rural en Costa Rica', Rome, mimeo.

Fox, Jonathan (ed.), 1990, *The Challenge of Rural Democratisation: Perspectives from Latin American and the Philippines*, London: Frank Cass.

Ghai, Dharam, Kay, Cristóbal and Peter Peek, 1988, *Labour and Development in Rural Cuba*, London: Macmillan.

González, Claudio, 1991, 'Costa Rica: Evaluación de los mercados de granos básicos y el papel del Consejo Nacional de Producción', in Rigoberto Stewart (ed.), *La comercialización de granos básicos en Costa Rica*, San Jose: R. Stewart.

Grindle, Merilee, 1986, *State and Countryside: Development Policy and Agrarian Politics in Latin America*, Baltimore, MD: Johns Hopkins University Press.

Gudmundson, Lowell, 1986, *Costa Rica Before Coffee*, Baton Rouge, CA: Louisiana State University Press.

Lipton, Michael, 1977, *Why Poor People Stay Poor: Urban Bias in World Development*, Cambridge, MA: Harvard University Press.

March, James and Johan Olsen, 1984, 'The New Institutionalism: Organisational Factors in Political Life', *American Political Science Review*, Vol.78, No.3, pp.734–49.

Mesa-Lago, Carmelo and Sergio Díaz-Briquets, 1988, 'Estrategias diferentes, paises similares: las consecuencias para el crecimiento y la equidad en Costa Rica y Cuba', *Anuario de Estudios Centroamericanos*, Vol.14, Nos.1 and 2, pp.5–23.

Moore, Barrington, 1966, *Social Origins of Dictatorship and Democracy*, Boston, MA: Beacon Press.

Salazar, Mario, 1984, 'A Multicommodity Equilibrium Approach to Welfare Analysis of Market Interventions in the Costa Rican Agricultural Sector', Ph.D. thesis, Iowa State University.

Salís, Manuel, 1984, *Desarrollo rural*, San Jose: Editorial Universidad Estatal a Distancia.

Schifter, Jacobo, 1983, 'La democracia en Costa Rica como producto de la neutralización de clases', in Chester Zelaya et al. (eds.), *Democracia en Costa Rica*, San Jose: Editorial Universidad Estatal a Distancia.

Seligson, Mitchell, 1980, *Peasants of Costa Rica and the Development of Agrarian Capitalism*, Madison, WI: University of Wisconsin Press.

Seligson, Mitchell, 1982, *Peasant Participation in Costa Rica's Agrarian Reform*, Ithaca, NY: Rural Development Committee, Center for International Studies, Cornell University.

Stetson, Dorothy, 1969, 'Elite Political Culture in Costa Rica,' Ph.D. thesis, Vanderbilt University.

Turtis, Richard, 1987, 'Trade, Debt, and the Cuban Economy,' *World Development*, Vol.15, No.1, pp.163–80.

Vega, José Luis, 1982, *Poder político y democracia en Costa Rica*, San Jose: Editorial Porvenir.

Economic Structure and the Politics of Sectoral Bias: East Asian and Other Cases

MICK MOORE

Governments of poor countries generally practise 'urban biased' policies that penalise the agricultural sector to the advantage of non-agriculture. Conversely, governments of rich countries generally practise 'rural bias'. As South Korea and Taiwan have become relatively wealthy over recent decades, they have also shifted from urban biased to rural biased policies. Adherents of the rational choice approach to political analysis claim to provide an explanation of the causes of this pattern. This explanation is based on changing patterns of political interests and coalition-forming possibilities induced by the changes in economic structure characteristically associated with economic growth. An evaluation of this claim in the light of the South Korean and Taiwanese cases suggests that: (a) it has considerable validity, although its explanatory power is easily exaggerated; (b) a satisfactory rational choice approach would encompass a wider range of political actors than has been incorporated in existing analyses; and (c) that some important causes of the shift from urban to rural bias in South Korea and Taiwan lie in factors that are not illuminated by the rational choice paradigm – notably emulatory action between states.

I. INTRODUCTION

Why Poor People Stay Poor: Urban Bias in World Development by Michael Lipton [*1977*] and *Markets and States in Tropical Africa: The Political Basis of Agricultural Policies* by Robert Bates [*1981*] – at the

The author, a Fellow of the Institute of Development Studies at the University of Sussex, is indebted to the following people for useful comments on an earlier version of this study: David Leonard; Michael Lipton; Ashutosh Varshney; Robert Wade; and to Robert Bates and other participants in the Workshop of the 1991 Annual Meeting of the American Political Science Association at which the papers on which the contributions in this volume are based were discussed.

policy-making level, these two books about 'urban bias' in developing countries have generally been understood to be making very similar arguments: that urban bias is prevalent, an important drag on overall economic performance, and a cause of economic inequality. They are widely cited and have had a major impact on our understanding of development policy issues.

The agenda for this volume is to go beyond the landmark works of Lipton and Bates: to explore further the issues to which they (in particular) have alerted us, and to see whether we cannot build on their work to develop a more refined understanding of these issues. This study pursues that agenda by dealing with what might appear initially to be two distinct concerns. They are however so closely intertwined that there is little tension between them. One concern is more concrete and location-specific: the politics behind the major shift from urban to rural bias that has taken place in South Korea (henceforth, Korea) and Taiwan over recent decades as they have become relatively wealthy (mainly sections V to VII). The other concern is more theoretical: the adequacy of alternative analytical approaches for explaining the politics of sectoral bias. The prime objective here is to find an analytic framework that can satisfactorily explain the close association which exists between type of sectoral bias and income levels: governments of poor countries tend to practise urban bias, and those of rich countries to practise rural bias [*Anderson and Hayami, 1986*].

To those concerned with economic policy implications, the similarities between the work of Bates and Lipton are evident. If one focuses rather on the analytic frameworks that they use to understand politics, major differences appear between them. Each can be taken to represent one of the major paradigms within political economy: Lipton the 'class-theoretic' approach; and Bates the 'choice-theoretic' approach. I deal briefly with the class theoretic approach in section II, explaining why it does not appear to be a useful analytic tool for present purposes, that is, to explain why cases of urban and rural bias are distributed around the world according to a clear pattern. By contrast, the choice theoretic (or 'rational choice') approach appears to have major explanatory power.

In the rational choice analysis of sectoral bias, changes in economic structure associated with economic growth are held to change (a) the material interests of occupants of various economic roles; (b) the incentives which various categories of actors face to allocate their attentions and energies between politics and non-politics and between different kinds of political objectives; and thus (c) the nature of predominant political coalitions and of the pattern of societally-based political pressures on governments in relation to sectoral bias. The bulk of the study is spent wrestling with explanations of sectoral bias based on rational choice analysis. My conclusion is ambivalent. On the one hand, I find that the method makes an important contribution to explaining why urban bias is prevalent in poor countries and rural bias in rich countries, and for this purpose has no serious rival. On the other hand, I find myself critical of the rational choice approach on a number of related grounds. It is vulnerable to misuse by analysts who are more concerned about (a) providing interpretations of political processes that are consistent with their own politico-economic doctrines than about (b) the empirical verification of those interpretations. My discussion of the East Asian material is structured around a critique of one such case of misuse.

In its weakest form, my critique suggests that the 'standard' rational choice explanation of the shift from urban to rural bias in Korea and Taiwan must be a gross simplification because it is very much at variance with the observed facts about the nature and content of the political process in these countries. I make two stronger claims, recognising however that the very secrecy of the policy-making process in Korea and Taiwan renders me unable to provide satisfactory confirming evidence. These claims are therefore presented in tentative terms. One is that a satisfactory rational choice explanation of the distribution of urban and rural biased policies between countries and over time would have to take into account a wider range of categories of political interests and actors ('stakeholders in the agricultural economy') than have been incorporated into existing analyses. The other claim concerns 'the state' as a political actor. The shift from urban to rural bias in Korea and Taiwan owed a great deal to a factor lying outside the scope of the rational choice analytic framework: the conscious emulation of Japanese economic policies by the Korean and Taiwanese governments. The rational choice approach is at best able to illuminate how *societal* interests succeed or fail in coalescing and allying to influence government policy. It can rarely be used to explain the actions of 'the *state*' itself without running up against serious theoretical dilemmas (and/or moral hazards of an intellectual nature).

For those readers more interested in direct implications for the 'real world' than in sharpening the political scientists' tool-kit, this contribution has a clear message: the question of whether a country adopts urban or rural biased policies is less tightly determined by (the pattern of political pressures stemming from) the economic structure than the more mechanistic proponents of the rational choice interpretation have argued. In particular, it seems far from inevitable that, as poor countries become wealthier, they will emulate Western Europe and East Asia in financing the production of unwanted stocks of cereals, beef, wine or milk.[1]

In section II, I sketch out the major similarities and differences between the class-theoretic and the rational choice approaches to explaining sectoral bias, and briefly explain why I find the former unconvincing. The existing rational choice literature is summarised and evaluated in sections III to V. Sections VI to VIII are concerned with the East Asian cases; and the implications of the East Asian material for the rational choice analysis of sectoral bias are presented in section IX. Some broader, speculative points about relationship between agriculture and polity at different income levels are presented in section X.

II. CLASS AND CHOICE-THEORETIC APPROACHES

In some important respects, the intellectual paradigms shaping the work of Robert Bates and Michael Lipton's work were shared with other distinguished contemporary students of Third World rural issues.[2]

First, a major focus of concern was the paradox of numbers and political impotence: although rural people typically constituted a majority of the population, they seemed to have little political power, even in relatively democratic polities.

Second, the approach to explaining the actions of governments was heavily 'sociological', 'society-centric', or 'reductionist'. Government decisions were assumed to reflect the outcome of competition between organised socio-economic groups seeking to further their material interests. The state was essentially the instrument through which the victors implemented policies that advanced these interests. At most, a 'state class' might be recognised as a (privileged) interest group. But there was no evident recognition of either (a) institutionalist arguments that the state and political institutions can significantly filter and shape the way in which socio-economic interests are translated into policy, or vice versa [*March and Olsen, 1989*]; or (b) the autonomy which states sometimes enjoy (or achieve) to make policy independently of socioeconomic interests [*Evans et al., 1985*]. A characteristic feature of this work was therefore a concern with the processes through which powerful minorities appeared to be using the state to prevail over (typically rural) majorities.

Third, and less explicitly, these scholars shared the almost complete uninterest of Anglophone political economy in the political consequences of space and distance. Herein lies an irony, for the main societal process implicitly underlying much of this work is the way in which physical dispersal, when combined with poverty (illiteracy, poor communications, etc.), creates unusually potent obstacles to the political mobilisation of rural people. The political significance of distance is not denied. It is however recognised only implicitly and in a binary fashion: spatial dispersion is assumed to be an obstacle to rural political organisation to the same degree that concentration is fundamental to the power of urban (industrial) populations. *Intra-rural* differences in population density and communications facilities, which almost inevitably generate differences in political mobilisation capacity among different rural populations [*Moore, 1984b*], are ignored.

There are however three important differences between the work of Lipton and Bates on urban bias. One is that, while Bates is a political scientist, Lipton is an economist mainly concerned with the economic mechanisms and consequences of urban bias. Another difference lies in explanatory scope. Bates was concerned (only) to explain government intervention in three major categories of market affecting rural producers: those for agricultural commodities, factors of agricultural production, and consumer goods. The problem he set himself was why (in sub-Saharan Africa) governments typically intervened in these markets to the disadvantage of rural producers. Lipton, by contrast, operates with a broader concept of urban bias, which includes not only (a) market intervention (indirectly through tariffs and controlled exchange rates; directly through administered pricing, subsidies, etc.), but also (b) non-price interventions in the shape of the spatial and functional allocation of public revenue-raising responsibilities and public expenditure, both investment and public spending on recurrent resources such as high quality technical and administrative personnel. Lipton seeks to explain why agriculture and rural areas in the Third World generally get the rough end of the stick: no village roads while the urban areas get motorways; little agricultural research while urban industry is heavily subsidised; poor quality teachers, doctors and administrators while urban areas are relatively well supplied; as well as 'price twists' designed to extract resources from agriculture.

The third important difference between Lipton and Bates lies in the type of 'sociological' model of politics that they espouse. Lipton's model is class theoretic in origin, in the sense that the main political actors are assumed to be certain social aggregates which (a) exist temporally and analytically prior to, and for other reasons than, the existence of the political process; and (b) are formed in the sphere of the social organisation of production. It is however a rather heterodox variant of class theory, and one that has generated much criticism from orthodox adherents of that approach. For his central proposition about the politics of urban bias reads: 'The most important class conflict in the poor countries of the world today is not between labour and capital. Nor is it between foreign and national interests. It is between the rural classes and the urban classes' [*1977: 13*]. By substituting (economic-cum-spatial) sectors for the classes that form the building blocks of classical political economy, this formulation would at first sight appear to relegate rich-poor type distinctions to, at most, a minor role in the politics of rural bias. This is not however Lipton's intention: the differences of interest and affinity between rural rich and rural poor are central to his concerns and analysis. He and his readers and critics become engaged in extensive definitional diccussions about, for example, the sense in which the rural rich do or do not belong in the exploited rural class. The apparent ambiguity of this conceptual framework gives rise to colourful terms such as 'crypto-townsmen', 'crypto-countryfolk' and 'crypto-rural' [*Lipton, 1977: 149–50*]; to considerable debate [e.g., *Moore, 1984a; Lipton, 1984*]; and to rather little enlightenment.[3]

Bates' (sociological) model of politics is considered in detail in succeeding sections. He is fully orthodox in the context of the rational choice paradigm. He deals with contingent political collectivities that are formed through the interactions of socio-economic interests and the political process. He does not assume that the boundaries of those population categories that emerge from socio-economic analysis will necessarily correspond to the boundaries of political groups. Compared to the class theoretic approach, there is more flexibility in defining the boundaries of political collectivities. One problem, as is explained in section V, is that this flexibility may be abused.

My concerns about the adequacy of the concept of politics employed by Lipton (and other scholars also writing about inter-sectoral inequality and competition in class-theoretic vein) have been set out elsewhere [*Moore, 1984a*; also *Corbridge, 1982*]. They include: (a) the adequacy of the 'society-centric' approach to explaining politics; (b) the use of a deductive model to link assumed political interests with policy outcomes, without any supporting evidence from the political process itself;[4] and (c) doubts about whether Lipton's class categorisation could be operationalised in particular empirical contexts without generating more dispute and confusion than illumination. However, the major reason that I do not find in Lipton's work a basis for constructing a more satisfactory analysis of the politics of sectoral bias is that his framework only sets out to explain the prevalence of urban bias in the Third World; it contains no mechanism through which one could begin to explain the existence of rural bias in rich countries.

III. RATIONAL CHOICE THEORIES

Rational choice models of sectoral bias are built on two analytic bases. One is shared with other theories discussed above: the observation of the severe logistical constraints to political organisation inherent in (a) physical dispersion and (b) poverty. The other is a particular set of propositions about how the location of different economic actors in relation to particular markets affects their motivations to engage in political action to persuade governments to intervene in market processes on their behalf. These motivations change in response to the structural economic changes that are characteristically associated with economic growth.

It is useful to distinguish two versions of the rational choice explanation of sectoral bias: (a) that part of the work of Bates [1981] which parallels Lipton in providing an explanation for the prevalence of urban bias in the Third World, and deals with differences between Third World countries (this section); and (b) the more general rational choice model that attempts to explain patterns of sectoral bias worldwide, including the prevalence of rural bias in the advanced industrial nations (section IV).

Robert Bates' *Markets and States in Tropical Africa. The Political Basis of Agricultural Policies* [1981] relates to sub-Saharan Africa rather than to the Third World in general, but that is a distinction that has little relevance to present concerns. There are some ambiguities about the theoretical basis of Bates' model that are best highlighted by treating separately his analysis of the politics of (a) the food crop and (b) the cash crop economy.

Bates states that 'Farmers are seen as standing at the intersection of three major markets': 'the market for agricultural commodities'; 'the market for factors of production'; and 'the market for consumer goods' [1981: 3]. However, in the context of developing countries (especially sub-Saharan Africa), there are two major categories of agricultural commodity markets, with very different political implications: (a) markets for food and (b) markets for (export) cash crops such as tea, coffee, cocoa, tobacco and palm oil. It is best to follow Bates [1981: Chs.1 and 2] and treat each market separately.

Food Markets

The politics of the market for food derive from the fact that, in situations of underdevelopment, farmers tend to be both (a) unspecialised producers of a range of products and, perhaps more importantly, (b) producing mainly for auto-consumption, and therefore derive relatively little of their income from commodity (food) markets. By contrast, (urban) consumers tend to spend a high proportion of their income on one or two food staples. The benefit–cost ratio of engaging in politics to persuade governments to alter food prices tends to be much greater for urban consumers than for rural food producers. The characteristic differences in the ease with which rural and urban people can organise politically interact with the fact that a given amount of change in food prices will have more economic and political impact on the urban consumer than on the farmer. Not only will the proportionate change in real income, upwards or downwards, be greater for the urban consumer,[5] but the impact on political consciousness will also be greater because only a single commodity – the food staple – is involved from the consumer's point of view. Everything else being equal, political communication and mobilisation are more easily achieved around a single commodity than around several. The conclusion is that the societal interests that are organised politically in relation to food markets will be concerned mainly to pressure government to use the various policy instruments it has available to depress food prices.[6]

Markets for Factors of Production and Consumer Goods

Compared with this analysis of the politics of food markets, the treatment by Bates of the politics of markets for factors of agricultural production and (non-food) consumer goods is less rich and original. Urban-ness and involvement in producing (marketed) consumer and producer goods are assumed to coincide in large degree. Urban producer interests, both those of capital and of labour, use their privileged location near government and their superior capacity to mobilise politically to persuade governments to grant them favour and protection against imports, and thus by various means lever their prices up above market-determined levels. Farmers pay more for their fertiliser, tools, cloth, matches and tin sheets than they would in a free market regime. Although urban people may lose as a result of these high prices in their roles as consumers, they are more than compensated in their roles as producers [*Bates, 1981: Ch.4*].

Refinements to the Model

The model set out above makes explicit assumptions about the context that have not yet been spelled out here, but which can be modified as appropriate to particular situations. In particular, the model is posited on an agricultural sector dominated by smallholders. Once one has significant numbers of large farmers, the mechanics change. Large farmers (a) have much more interest than small farmers in commodity prices because they realise a larger proportion of their income on the market; and (b) have much greater capacity to engage in political action because of their superior access to the political resources of information, contacts and mobility. Bates accommodates the existence of larger African farmers into his model in two ways. Firstly, he demonstrates that countries where there are significant proportions of large farmers tend to be less urban-biased in pricing policies than those where small-holders predominate. Secondly, he argues, on a more impressionistic basis, that, in the more typical situation where large farmers are few, governments use development projects and public investments to direct benefits to them to 'compensate' them for price biases, purchase their support and that of their political clients, and thus strengthen the urban-biased coalition by undermining potential opposition [*1981: Ch.3*]. The latter point is especially significant from the methodological perspective. For it involves 'importing' the state into the model as a separate and distinct political actor, with its own motivations and objectives. This foreshadows wider concerns about the methodological basis of the rational choice approach that become more evident in relation to Bates' analysis of the politics of pricing in the cash crop sector, and which are discussed further in section V.

Cash Crop Markets

Since Bates' book is about sub-Saharan Africa, the pricing of cash (export) crops necessarily features prominently. However, his analysis of the comparative politics of food and cash crop pricing presents some problems:

(1) Since food consumers are not directly affected by pricing decisions affecting cash crops, they do not enter this particular arena as significant political actors.

(2) Since producers necessarily have a strong interest in the price realised for the cash crops they market, one can only assume that they will tend to be more militant over the pricing issue than are producers of food crops (who to some degree produce for auto-consumption).

(3) In consequence of the two previous points, the powerful societal-based pressures on government to intervene to depress producer prices, which operate in the case of food crops, do not operate to the same degree in the case of cash crops.

(4) Everything else being equal, an elementary rational choice model would predict a lesser degree of urban price bias in the case of cash crops than in the case of food crops.

(5) But this expectation is clearly violated in the case of sub-Saharan Africa, where price bias against agricultural producers has been greater in the cash crop case.

There are two ways of resolving this apparent anomaly without rejecting the rational choice framework. The first, which I find satisfactory, is to point to the typical institutional and logistic contrasts between food and cash crop markets. African cash crops are normally exported, while (marketed) food crops are sold domestically. It is possible for governments to extract 'surplus' from cash crop producers, despite the possible political costs enumerated above, because (a) excepting in cases where cross-border smuggling is prevalent, cash crops pass through physical channels – railways and ports – over which surveillance is relatively easy; (b) given the existence of tariff collection and foreign exchange control apparatuses, governments have virtually automatic access to opportunities to tax cash crop exporters, directly or through maintaining over-valued exchange rates; and (c) because of the 'mysteries' of foreign exchange rates and tariffs, governments have access to techniques to extract resources from the export of cash crops that are politically sustainable because they are obscure to the producers directly affected.[7]

These points sound like commonsense. One can dignify them theoretically by saying that adding them into the analysis is a matter of adequately specifying the particular institutional context before exploring the behaviour patterns likely to be exhibited by rationally self-interested political actors. The idea of 'rationality' cannot be made analytically operational without assumptions about the institutional context that will permit predictions about the consequences of particular actions.

The other possible way of resolving the anomaly is to do as Robert Bates does in his book, and talk of the 'revenue imperative' of states [1981: 12–19]. The implication is that governments focus on cash crops as a source of revenue because it is here that scarce foreign exchange is most easily obtained. The proposition at first appears unexceptionable. However, a little thought reveals that the notion that states are guided by a 'revenue imperative' has no analytic content, and indeed is introduced very much as *deus ex machina*. It is clearly false to suggest that revenue gathering is always the primary goal of state action in any context. Governments can be seen to pursue a wide variety of objectives, of which the most prevalent and most imperative is probably the maintenance of power. To call in the 'revenue imperative' on a discretionary basis to explain certain kinds of state action is, from the analytical perspective, suspicious behaviour.[8] As is explained in section V below, the rational choice approach provides considerable temptation to engage in such behaviour: this particular case merely illustrates a more general set of problems.

IV. THE SHIFT FROM RURAL TO URBAN BIAS

Had the rational choice contribution to the sectoral bias debate been limited to Bates' comparative statics analysis of contemporary sub-Saharan Africa, the analytic value of the paradigm would remain in serious dispute. Its real explanatory power becomes evident only when Bates and others [e.g. *Bates and Rogerson, 1981; Anderson and Hayami, 1986*] apply it in wider contexts to explain differences in sectoral bias between countries at different levels of income.

The analytic basis of the wider rational choice model lies in the extension of one element in the Bates' model set out above: the analysis of the politics of food markets. As is explained above, in situations of low incomes, food producers are posited to have little incentive or stimulus to engage in politics to persuade governments to raise food prices, while food consumers have strong incentives to do so. The more general model involves extending the analysis to a situation of relative societal wealth (see Figure 1).

Wealth implies industrialisation and structural economic change. There are three reasons why, in this 'wealth' scenario, farmers become more active politically in pursuit of high producer prices:

(1) They become more commercialised, depending more on the market for the acquisition of producer inputs and for the translation of production into income. They are thus more exposed to market prices, and correspondingly face potentially higher benefit–cost ratios from putting resources (time, money) into politics to try to persuade governments to alter prices in their favour.

(2) They tend to specialise in a narrower range of products, and thus, from the individuals' perspective, have greater stakes in the producer prices of particular commodities.[9]

(3) Improved transport and communications reduce the burden of high political transactions costs imposed by physical dispersal in the countryside.

One major change affects consumers: as they become wealthier, they spend a declining proportion of their income on food, with especially large relative reductions in expenditure on food staples. Food (or

FIGURE 1

THE 'CORE' MODEL OF THE EFFECT OF INCOME LEVELS ON THE POLITICS
OF SECTORAL BIAS

Actor	Poverty situation	Wealth situation
Farmers	Production for auto-consumption means low interest in commodity prices (in general)	Production largely for the market means high interest in high prices for commodity prices (in general)
"	Lack of specialisation means low interest in prices for specific commodities	Specialisation means high interest in high prices for specific commodities
"	Dependence on farm inputs produced at farm level means low interest in prices of industrially produced inputs	Dependence on purchased farm inputs means a relatively high interest in keeping prices low.
"	Poor transport and communication facilities impede political mobilisation	Improved transport and communication facilities reduce obstacles to political mobilisation
Consumers	Spending a high proportion of income on one or two staples generates high interest in keeping their prices low	Income is spent on a wide variety of different kinds of goods and services; there is no specific focus of concern on any one

staple) prices no longer provide simple and politically efficient foci around which to mobilise urban populations.

This 'core model' may be elaborated to take account of other structural factors, such as the degree of comparative advantage that rich countries have in agricultural production (see below). But, even in its basic form, the model clearly has very considerable plausibility. As a piece of comparative statics, it has a great advantage over Lipton's explanation of urban bias in poor countries in that it appears to simultaneously explain the prevalence of rural bias in rich countries. The real analytic appeal of the rational choice lies however in its claim to go beyond comparative statics, and to satisfactorily account for changes in sectoral policy bias observed to take place as countries become wealthier. This claim is founded on observations about Taiwan and Korea. These are the only two countries that have, since the Second World War, made the transformation from agrarian to industrial societies, and therefore undergone major structural economic changes of the kind that underpin the rational choice analysis of changes in the politics of sectoral bias. And national economic policies have also shifted from urban to rural bias over this period. Can rational choice analysis provide a satisfactory explanation of this policy shift?

After exploring this question in detail (sections VI to VIII), I retain considerable sympathy for the rational choice approach, but question the standard interpretation of the East Asian case on a number of grounds. One concern is that the observed pattern of political activity in Taiwan and Korea is not fully consistent with the predictions of the rational choice model: it is not clear that farmers began to receive more favourable treatment from government solely or even mainly because they became more politically active and effective. A second concern is that the rational choice model appears to exclude an important category of political actor: industrial interests producing agricultural inputs. A third, more abstract, concern is that the rational choice approach is intellectually satisfactory only in so far as it is society-centric, explaining political outcomes as the product of the interaction of organised socio-economic interests. It tends either to ignore the state as a political actor or to take account of it in a rather arbitrary and unsatisfactory way. Before we deal with the East Asian material in detail, it is useful to clarify these general concerns about rational choice analysis and the state.

V. RATIONAL CHOICE ANALYSIS AND THE STATE

In section III, a specific example was given of what I would term misuse of the rational choice paradigm: the attempt to use the (unsatisfactory) idea of state-as-revenue-maximiser to deal with the problem that the simple rational choice predictions about relative political pressures in food and cash crop markets in Africa do not accord with observed reality. A supplementary element sometimes added to the 'core model' of the causes of transition from urban to rural bias constitutes similar abuse of the notion of the state as a rational actor. This supplementary element is to be found, *inter alia*, in the work of Anderson and Hayami [*1986*].

In explaining the association between economic growth and the shift from urban to rural biased economic policies, Anderson and Hayami [*1986: 3*] cite, besides the elements in the 'core model' set out in Figure 1, the following causal factor:

> Second, the declining relative importance of agricultural production and employment as the economy's industrial and service sectors expand makes it less and less costly politically for the government to succumb to farmers' demands for assistance measures designed to reduce the pressure for structural adjustment . . . .

The corollary of this argument, which Anderson and Hayami imply but do not make explicit, is that, at low income levels, the same logic works in a reverse direction: that urban consumers are few in number relative to rural farmers, and that therefore the government (treasury) will, if obliged to subsidise one group or other, prefer to subsidise the smaller group. This is advanced as a *distinct cause* of changing sectoral preferences. At first sight it appears plausible.[10] Careful inspection however suggests that it is a hollow argument, adding nothing at all to the explanation of changing sectoral preferences. For the argument is that the government treasury, which now enters into the model as an independent political actor, will tend to prefer to subsidise the smaller group: food consumers in low income economies, and farmers in high income economies. Why should that be the case? Leaving aside the question whether the food producer versus food purchaser categorisation constitutes the axis around which political support will be purchased, there is no justification for the implied general principle that a given volume of financial resources are politically most effective if concentrated on a particular minority. Why not spread the same volume of resources more thinly over a larger population? Why not subsidise farmers when they are numerous (in low income situations), and food consumers when they are numerous (in high income situations)?

A further example is provided in section VIII of the 'enrichment' of a rational choice model of sectoral bias by the addition of an element relating to the consequences of the self-interested behaviour of a particular category of government agency. The agencies concerned control the level of beef imports into Japan and Korea. It so happens that, in this case, the argument is plausible. The problem is not that rational choice theorists tend to get it consistently wrong when they incorporate 'the state', or particular state agencies, into their models as political actors. What then is the problem?

It is essentially that the rational choice paradigm leaves itself a great deal of freedom to deal with the general dilemma of institutional action within a framework of utilitarianism and methodological individualism. One branch of rational choice theory assumes that state institutions be treated simply as congeries of individuals seeking to maximise their material rewards as bureaucrats [*Tullock, 1965*]. From this perspective, there is no such thing as an institutional actor; the institution merely provides the context within which individuals seek to optimise. At an intermediate level, other rational choice theorists argue that the individual state agency or bureau can be viewed as the basic self-interested political unit and actor [*Niskanen, 1971*]; (and the example of beef import control bureaux in East Asia cited above). Finally, other theorists posit a relatively coherent state apparatus united by (a) the treasury and revenue considerations [*Anderson and Hayami, 1986; Bates, 1981; Levi, 1988* as above]; or by (b) considerations of political and electoral support (Bates, above, on the use of development projects by governments to nourish political support networks; section VI below). Rational choice theorists can elect to understand the state in any one of these ways according to convenience, and thus pick and choose (a) which among a wide range of state-related political actors they wish to incorporate into their analysis, or ignore; and (b) which proximate or ultimate objectives these state-related actors will be pursuing.

The more general point is that there is no theoretical basis for the choices which rational choice theorists make about the specification of the significant actors in any particular context.[11] Further, the deductive basis of much of the theorising provides considerable scope for the attribution of objectives to particular actors. There are no strong pressures to find empirical evidence to support rational choice models in the political *process* – in what people actually do – rather than in political *outcomes*. The combined effect of these two contingencies is the exposure of rational choice theorists to major moral hazard: the temptation, perhaps entirely subconscious, to explain a particular political process by looking first at the outcomes and then framing a model, with selected actors and motivations, that 'explains' the outcome in rational choice terms. There is a slippery slope from rational choice analysis to *post-hoc* rationalisation.

VI. THE RATIONAL CHOICE ANALYSIS: EAST ASIA

A major shift from urban to rural bias has taken place in East Asia in recent decades, especially since the late 1960s. Whether the rational choice approach provides a good explanation is central to its general validity. For Taiwan and Korea provide a good testing ground: rapid

economic growth, and thus rapid structural economic changes, have
taken place in the context of relative stability in the composition and
character of both the Taiwanese (since 1949) and the Korean (since
1961) political regimes. This stability provides a degree of methodological control. If the regime or government is stable (or, undergoing only
incremental modification), it is somewhat easier to test hypotheses that
relate policy change to underlying influences stemming from structural
economic change.

The rational choice analysis of East Asian agricultural policy on which
this section will focus is the book by Anderson and Hayami [*1986*].
Before looking at their central argument in detail, it is worthwhile
mentioning a few contextual features:

TABLE 1

NOMINAL RATES OF AGRICULTURAL PROTECTION IN EAST ASIA, 1955–82

	1955–59	1960–64	1965–69	1970–74	1975–79	1980–82
Japan						
–rice	50	72	99	160	263	249
–weighted average of main crops	44	68	87	110	147	151
Korea						
–rice	−14	−9	6	55	138	154
–weighted average of main crops	−15	−5	9	55	129	166
Taiwan						
–rice	−31	−8	13	4	58	144
–weighted average of main crops	−21	2	2	17	36	55

Note: The nominal rate of protection is defined as the percentage by which the domestic
price exceeds the border price.

Source: Anderson and Hayami [*1986: Table 2.3*].

(1) Like many practitioners of rational choice theory, Anderson and
    Hayami are not political scientists, but (neo-liberal) economists
    seeking intellectual and empirical support for a particular line in
    economic policy: reductions in the high levels of agricultural protec-
    tion prevalent in East Asia.

(2) They deal with Japan as well as with Korea and Taiwan. As is
    explained below, I find this very appropriate to understanding the
    causes of high levels of agricultural protection, although not
    through the same mechanisms as Anderson and Hayami.

(3) Anderson and Hayami use one simple measure of sectoral bias: the nominal rate of protection for local agricultural producers, that is, a measure of the extent to which domestic market prices exceed the prices at which equivalent commodities could be bought on international markets and landed at the ports of the country concerned. Their analysis of sectoral bias is thus concerned only with state intervention to affect the prices of agricultural products. It relates neither to (a) the prices of agricultural producer and consumer goods; nor to (b) the sectoral allocation of government revenue-raising and expenditure. This limitation is not a major problem for the analysis: the dominant fact about Korea and Taiwan in recent decades that needs explanation is the shift from negative to substantially positive nominal rates of agricultural protection (Table 1).[12] Much of the work by Anderson and Hayami concerns the *economic consequences* of agricultural protection. That which relates to the *political causes* revolves around two main propositions:

(1) The first proposition is that the basic motivating mechanism behind the shift from negative to positive agricultural protection during economic growth is the 'core' rational choice model of the politics of food markets set out in Figure 1 – with a spurious supplementary element added (section V). The case is argued deductively in terms of the linkage between the model and policy outcomes; no attempt is made to link either to observed political events or processes.

(2) The second proposition concerns the very high rates of agricultural protection found in East Asia compared with other industrialised countries. This is not an outcome that could be derived from the 'core' rational choice model, since income levels are much lower in Korea and Taiwan than in other industrial countries. It is explained by inserting an additional element into the rational choice model: the political consequences of different rates of comparative advantage in agricultural production between countries. It is argued that a high income country with little comparative advantage in agricultural production will tend to become a food importer. Protection for the farming population can then be achieved through import controls (tariffs or quantitative limits), which boost producer prices for domestic food producers above market levels, while remaining relatively invisible to food consumers or taxpayers, and thus politically unproblematic. High income countries with a comparative advantage in agricultural production (that is, Australia and New Zealand) cannot do the same because market-determined prices for food tend to be below world levels, and there are thus no food

imports to be used as a price lever. Such countries are obliged to
resort to more direct and visible techniques if they wish to support
agricultural incomes: direct subsidies to farmers or direct action to
maintain consumer food prices above market levels by instituting
monopolistic arrangements. Such visible interventions attract the
attention of consumers-cum-taxpayers, and are therefore difficult to
effect. The logic indicates that differences between rich countries in
the degree of protection afforded agriculture should be proportional
to their degree of comparative advantage in agricultural production.
Anderson and Hayami undertake a statistical test of this proposition, both cross-sectionally and over time, using data from East
Asia, the four developed Anglophone food exporting countries
(Australia, Canada, New Zealand and the United States), and eight
west European countries. Their multiple regression analysis indicates that:

> Nearly 70 per cent of the variation [in rates of agricultural protec-
> tion – MPM] is accounted for by differences in agriculture's com-
> parative advantage, agriculture's share of the total economy, the
> international terms of trade between agricultural and manufac-
> tured commodities, membership of the European Community,
> and considerations of food security associated with non-military
> alliance [*1986: 5*].

The broader implication is that rates of agricultural protection in East
Asia are not inexplicably high, but stem from the region's 'very strong
comparative advantage in manufacturing' [*1986: 49*]. One might question the interpretation of the statistical analyses; that is not something I
attempt here. Anderson and Hayami imply that their rational choice
interpretation takes care of all the big questions and puzzles about the
politics of sectoral bias. There is nothing much left to explain. I find that
unacceptable. Even for the East Asian case, the rational choice model is
substantially inconsistent with the facts.

VII. THE POLITICAL SUBORDINATION OF EAST ASIAN AGRICULTURE[13]

The core of the rational choice model lies in the proposition that the
shift to high agricultural protection in Korea and Taiwan was caused by
the increasing capacity of farm interests to influence government policy.
Yet that shift was already under way in the early 1960s, if not before
(see Table 1). It is impossible to construct an accurate picture of the
political history of Korea and Taiwan that is consistent with the notion
that farmers were a significant interest group in the 1960s or, to a lesser

degree, the 1970s. There is not even any evidence of any kind of politically articulated societal demands for higher agricultural output prices in these early decades. The existence of organised agricultural interests is a recent phenomenon.

This is not to suggest that the rational choice model tells us nothing about changing sectoral preferences. For the fact that there is some consistent statistical fit between the predictions of the model and patterns of sectoral bias on a cross-national basis (see above) is strong evidence that the rational choice theorists are not entirely barking up the wrong tree. How far it is the right tree, and how many other trees they may have neglected, are issues that can be illumined by looking at a few aspects of rural politics in Korea and Taiwan – with comparative reference to Japan where appropriate.

East Asian Polities

The Japanese, Korean and Taiwanese polities belong to a recognisable family. For most of the past 40 years, they have constituted variants of a system of 'soft authoritarianism'. Self-reproducing ruling groups, comprising variable coalitions of (a) relatively autonomous public bureaucracies, (b) large-scale capital (the main source of political finance), and (c) the military have managed to keep themselves relatively securely in power by combining – and, in most cases, efficiently deploying – a (variable) range of political resources: effective state apparatuses; the material resources and legitimating authority generated by economic growth; extensive political intelligence apparatuses; executive control of the rules and procedures of electoral systems; and external political support forthcoming because of the sensitive geo-strategic location of the region.[14]

In domestic politics, the main perceived threat to the ruling coalitions has been the alienation and organisational capacity of urban and industrial labour, both manual and white-collar. Considerable political resources have been deployed to meet this threat through varying combinations of ideological, organisational and material co-option, disablement and repression. The agricultural sectors have presented far fewer political challenges and indeed have been important, but passive, supports to the political system.

Following the post-Second World War land reforms and the Korean (civil) War, East Asia's farm sectors comprised, to an unprecedented degree, agglomerations of family-farming households cultivating small land units[15] and united by the near-universality of rice production. This agrarian structure has not determined the shape of rural politics, but it has helped to provide the conditions for two radically different scenarios in relation to interest organisation. On the one hand, the prevalence of family farming embodies potential for the notorious 'potatoes-in-a-sack' syndrome: the weakness of collective consciousness or capacity for collective action at any level. On the other hand, the very universality of engagement in rice production constitutes a powerful, latent, collective interest. These possibilities have worked out somewhat differently in the three countries.

Japan

In the Japanese case, rural electoral power has very considerable substance. The electoral dominance of the Liberal Democratic Party has depended on a combination of (a) a 'gerrymandered' system of electoral demarcation that grossly privileges rural voters; and (b) generous subsidies and protection for the small farm system. Any kind of macro-level class analysis would tend to indicate that political initiative has come from outside the rural sector, and that agriculturalists remain subordinate participants in the ruling coalition. However, farmers have created a substantial autonomous political organisational capacity, especially through their co-operatives, and have therefore entrenched themselves as a powerful interest group [*George and Saxon, 1986*].

Korea

Korea shares with Japan a system of electoral demarcation that has been gerrymandered to privilege rural voters. The rural dimensions of the political system are otherwise substantially different. 'Exclusivity' is the dominant feature of the Korean political system. Power is heavily concentrated in the hands of the state executive, which represents mainly the upper echelons of the military and the public bureaucracy. The role of the legislature is largely symbolic. The main mechanisms through which the state attempts to legitimate itself at the mass level are ideologies of nationalism and claims to competence in achieving economic transformation. The various political parties, especially those which have represented the regime, have relatively little substance to them, being mainly coteries of middle-class urban professionals. No political group close to power has created any substantial organisation in the rural areas.[16] The state agencies that have been responsible for providing services to the farming population have tended to interact with the latter in a directive and authoritarian manner.[17]

The electoral weight of Korea's rural population has not been totally without value. Since the military coup of 1961, all succeeding governments, while remaining ultimately dependent on military force, have striven for electoral legitimation – and have succeeded to the extent of obtaining electoral majorities, even if their 'legitimacy' has been widely questioned. Among other factors, it was the (surprise) failure of President Park to completely command the rural vote in the 1971 presidential elections that helped produce a substantial shift of governmental attention in the direction of the farming population. Not all the consequent policy changes can be said to be pro-farmer. New rice varieties and agricultural practices were promoted in authoritarian ways. Considerable authoritarianism was also embodied in the operations of the Saemaul Movement for 'community development'. There were however some pro-farmer policy shifts, notably (a) a substantial change in the terms of trade in favour of agriculture, especially rice; and (b) a major rural infrastructure programme that made many villages accessible to motorised vehicles for the first time. Until this time, rural communications had lagged far behind more general economic developments [*Moore, 1985b; Wade, 1982*].

The electoral power of the farming population has however been very limited.[18] Rural isolation, the predominance of small-scale family farming and the absence of foci of political organisation alternative to the state and its political intelligence apparatuses have left rural voters very vulnerable to external pressures in casting their votes. The weakness of the farming interest can be illustrated by reactions to a set of policies at the end of 1970s that turned the terms of trade back against agriculture and widened the rural–urban income gap. These included above all the reduction of budgetary subsidies to agriculture [*Moore, 1985a*]. Despite evident dissatisfaction, farmers did not mobilise against the government.

Over the 1980s, the Korean polity has exhibited more fragility and faced more overt public opposition than in the 1960s and 1970s. But farmers have not been in the forefront of this opposition. There have been a few farmers' demonstrations in favour of more agricultural protection, but students, organised labour and the urban middle classes have posed much more direct threats to successive governments. Farmers still lack autonomous political organisation. It is only very recently that there have been signs that the farmers' 'cooperatives', which have in practice been integral parts of the state apparatus, have begun to develop a degree of autonomy for themselves.[19] For the earlier decades there is no evidence of any significant organised agricultural interest on the Korean political scene. As Chalmers Johnson says, economic support for agriculture was motivated largely by different concerns than the quest for electoral support – notably the desire to reduce rural–urban income differentials and so cut the rate of flight of

people from the land into urban slums, where they really could have
caused trouble for the regime [*Johnson, 1987: 157*].

Taiwan

The Taiwanese case material is more rich and interesting than the
Korean, reflecting as it does a more elaborate and sophisticated political
system: one that has been able to combine (a) the effective exclusion of
the 'subaltern populations' from major political decision-making arenas
with (b) extensive mechanisms of political incorporation, mass political
participation and contested electoral selection of occupants of a very
wide range of public posts. The effective management of this elaborate
political system has produced a polity that is both more stable and less
overtly repressive and authoritarian than in Korea, and at the same time
has made possible a gradual transition, accelerated in the later 1980s,
towards a Japanese-type system of one-party electoral dominance combined with genuine tolerance of political opposition, more genuine
electoral competition and increasing respect for civil liberties and human rights.

In the earlier decades with which we are concerned – the 1950s, 1960s
and 1970s – distinctively rural and agricultural institutions played a more
significant role in the Taiwanese polity than they do today. After the
brief period of rapacious Nationalist rule in the late 1940s, participatory
institutions were established on a very large scale. Elections were
instituted for local (township), county and city level executive positions
and for provincial (that is, Taiwan) level legislative positions. The
earlier the period, the less willing was the ruling Guomindang Party to
permit its candidates to risk losing these elections. It was however
willing to tolerate organised opposition, and indeed itself played a role
in orchestrating electoral competition between different factions from
within its own ranks or tied closely to it [*Jacobs, 1980*]. However, in
these early decades in particular, there were a range of other institutions, related to agriculture, some of them participatory and others
exclusionary, which played an important role in the national polity
because of (a) the salience of the ethnic issue (the overt domination of
the Taiwanese by a small minority of Mainlanders organised around the
Guomindang and the state and military apparatuses); and (b) the very
close statistical association between Taiwanese-ness and agricultural
occupations.[20] The density of rural population, the excellence of rural
transport and communications infrastructure, and the high degree of
dispersion of industry into rural areas would have made it very difficult
to manage the polity by keeping the Taiwanese politically dispersed and
fragmented in 'rural idiocy'. A more activist political strategy was

adopted by the regime, and the public institutions concerned with agriculture played an important role as vehicles for the implementation of that strategy.

Taiwan – Exclusionary Institutions

There are two exclusionary agricultural institutions that require mention. The first, the Provincial Food Bureau, was unusual in that it was formally an agency of the Taiwan Provincial Government, yet, unlike almost all other such agencies, was both run largely by Mainlanders and headquartered in Taipei rather than in the Provincial capital of Chung-Hsing.[21] The reasons are clear. The Provincial Government of Taiwan has been granted very little authority, power being concentrated in the hands of the Government of the Republic of China in Taipei, and thus the Guomindang. Most Provincial Government agencies are weak; but the Provincial Food Bureau controlled the rice trade in almost all dimensions, including the procurement, storage, processing and distribution of all rice collected by the state; the management of the rice-fertiliser barter scheme; and the regulation of the private commerce in rice. Especially in earlier decades, when rice was the key consumer good, often scarce, and to a high degree under state control, the Provincial Food Bureau was a strategic organisation. Besides (a) responsibilities for supplying key consumer groups;[22] and (b) opportunities for personal profiteering by staff, the Provincial Food Bureau played an important role in relation to the Farmers' Associations (see below), for it used them as its procurement and storage agents, and thus had direct insight into some of their major economic activities.[23]

The second important exclusionary agricultural institution, the Sino-American Joint Commission on Rural Reconstruction (JCRR) has received much more publicity than the Provincial Food Bureau, although its actual role has been kept obscure – almost mythic – through techniques that are commonplace in Taiwanese public life: abundant descriptive listing of achievements; generous praise; and the absence of analysis of any kind, especially written.[24] The JCRR (1948–79) has been endowed with a reputation as a highly effective agency for the promotion of agricultural development on Taiwan. There is no reason to suspect that this reputation is substantially misleading. The important feature of the JCRR for present purposes lies however in its relationship to the remainder of the government apparatus on Taiwan:

> Not formally a part of the public service, and until 1978 run jointly by Chinese and American staff – although the latter decreased in numbers over time – it has had privileged access to American aid

funds, considerable *de facto* influence derived from the American connection, the ability to pay high salaries to attract good people, and a degree of freedom from the constraints on action which impinge on public bureaucracies. In the late 1940s, the 1950s and the 1960s, the JCRR controlled the bulk of public (and therefore, total) agricultural investment. As a matter of oft-stated principle, it never undertook field programmes itself, but worked only in collaboration with other public or quasi-public agencies (e.g. Farmers and Irrigation Associations). Its influence over its 'collaborators' was however immense. The Provincial Department of Agriculture and Forestry, for example, was restricted solely to an implementation role, and had no say in policy.

The JCRR has frequently been described as the *de facto* Ministry of Agriculture. This is to a large degree true, but also both underestimates and exaggerates its influence, It is an underestimate in the sense that, for the reasons given above, the JCRR had an even greater capacity than a ministry to initiate and monitor action in the field and within subordinate institutions. It is an exaggeration because in certain respects the JCRR was excluded from influence over key macro-economic policy decisions affecting agriculture. It had no responsibility for foreign trade decisions affecting, for example, the degree of import protection to be given to agriculture. This was and remains the sphere of the Ministry of Economic Affairs [*Moore, 1985a: 154–5*].

The JCRR represented farmers' interests as it conceived them; it did not represent farmers. This remained true after the JCRR was replaced by a purely Chinese agency in 1979. Like the JCRR, neither the Council for Agricultural Planning and Development (1979–84) nor the Council of Agriculture (1984 onwards) found place for any farmers' representatives on their advisory or governing councils. They remained 'technocratic'. At the same time, the absence of a Ministry of Agriculture – which had been abolished when the Guomindang government shifted to Taiwan – was felt to be of material and symbolic significance. The establishment of a Ministry became part of the programme of those who favoured a better deal for agriculture. Far from these interests being dominant, they failed to obtain their way, for example in 1983 when it was decided to merge the Council for Agricultural Planning and Development and the Bureau of Agriculture of the Ministry of Economic Affairs to form the Council of Agriculture. In late 1987 and the first half of 1988, when the gradual political liberalisation led for the first time to a major series of demonstrations by interest groups that felt excluded from the political system, and the first

ever 'farmers' movement' [*Hsiao, 1992: 64–5*], farmers' demands included the establishment of a Ministry of Agriculture.[25] The
Guomindang finally conceded the point. When unprecedentedly-open
elections were held in December 1989 in a political system much libera-
lised under President Lee, the establishment of a Ministry of
Agriculture was part of the Guomindang's electoral platform. It is
significant that, at the same time, the Guomindang promised to establish a Ministry of Labour and to undertake a range of measures to
improve working conditions and employees' rights [*Lasater, 1990: 38*].
Responding to relatively unrestrained electoral competition, the
Guomindang was reaching out to the major socio-economic interests
that had hitherto been excluded from effective participation in politics.
As is explained in section VIII below, previous refusals to establish a
Ministry of Agriculture reflected the self-interest and power of the
bureaucrats who 'represented' agriculture in the policy-making process.
It is very difficult to reconcile this interpretation of Taiwanese agricultural politics with the assertion of the rational choice theorists that, since
by the 1980s real rates of agricultural protection in Taiwan were among
the highest in the world, it follows that farmers exercised major influence over national economic policy.

Taiwan – Participatory Institutions

Among the participatory institutions associated with Taiwanese agriculture, by far the most widely publicised are the Farmers Associations. It
has very often been claimed that these 'democratic', 'self-funded' locally
(township) based organisations have made a major contribution to
agricultural development, and exemplify what can be done from the
grassroots. The autonomy and power of the Farmers Associations were
however severely constrained. For present purposes, one can simply list
the main ways in which the Farmers Association system was manipulated by the regime to perpetuate the political weakness of the farming
population:[26]

(1) Although the Farmers Associations were federated at county and
    national levels, the higher levels were kept very weak, both politi-
    cally and in terms of the economic activities in which they were
    encouraged or permitted to engage. Even the basic, township
    Farmers Associations were discouraged, to an economically 'irratio-
    nal' degree, from engaging in joint economic enterprises with neigh-
    bouring Farmers Associations.[27] Economic and political power was
    kept localised and dispersed.

(2) Farmers Associations, like other 'autonomous' organisations, were

obliged to employ Guomindang and political intelligence *apparat-chiks* in their 'security' departments. The apex organisation, the Provincial Farmers Association, had a high proportion of Mainlanders on its staff. Appointments of senior executive staff were at all levels subject to 'guidance' from above.

(3) Electoral systems were designed to disperse power and facilitate Guomindang control, sometimes by playing different local factions off against each other. At the township level, Representatives were first elected by the members. Representatives then had to meet to elect, from among themselves, a Board of Directors and a Board of Supervisors. Representation to higher levels (that is, from township to county, and from county to provincial/national level), rather than being *ex officio*, was arranged through separate elections. Farmers Associations' territorial boundaries were identical to those of local administration (and of the Guomindang), making it possible for the Guomindang to maintain one faction in power in township adminis-tration, and another in the township Farmers Association. Equally, control over local agricultural resources was kept dispersed by organising Irrigation Associations solely around watersheds (which invariably differed from territorial administration) and keeping them totally separate from Farmers Associations.

(4) Close supervision was maintained over Farmers Associations, and their activities were constrained by detailed procedural regulations and reporting requirements, and by restrictions on their activities, notably (a) a prohibition on financing investment through borrow-ing, and (b) refusal to permit expansion of the one really profitable economic activity, the credit service, into the establishment of a rural bank. These restrictions made it difficult for Farmers Associations to become major providers of commercial services, and thus indirectly important political organisations, like agricul-tural co-operatives in Japan.

The essence of what is said above is expressed with admirable brevity by Edwin Winckler, an expert on Taiwanese politics:

> The Nationalists weakened small-scale Taiwanese rural elites through land reform, then coopted them by placing then in charge of state rural agencies. The Nationalists inaugurated local elec-tions that, confined to the subnational level, served mostly to divide parochial local elites against each other [*Winckler, 1988a: 61*].

As is explained in section VIII below, 1972–74 was a very significant period in the shift from urban to rural bias in Korea and Taiwan. It was in these years in particular that the governments began to award rice producers large annual rice price increases – a practice that continued without interruption for about a decade (Figure 2). The reductionism at the heart of the rational choice paradigm almost obliges us to interpret this as evidence that it was at this time that farmers became especially powerful. There is no independent evidence for this, and alternative explanations of the rice price increases are presented in section VIII. There is however an important piece of evidence that runs directly contrary to the reductionist interpretation. In 1974, the Taiwanese government introduced a range of measures to assert even more direct control over Farmers Associations and Irrigation Associations. In particular, chief executive officers, even at the level of township Farmers Associations, were henceforth to be directly nominated by the state, rather than 'chosen' locally by members' representatives.[28] Such an open (and largely uncontested) attack on the very limited autonomy of farmers' organisations is hardly consistent with the notion that farmers had just become significant players in the power game.

The final point to make about Taiwan concerns the nature of the societal interests that have been inducted into the Guomindang Party and given a greater degree of autonomy as the polity has been permitted to become more pluralistic. While a great deal about Taiwanese politics remains obscure, observers seem clear that the Guomindang has focused its recruitment and promotion activities very much on *businessmen* – as opposed, for example, to professionals, white collar employees, manual labour or farmers [*Winckler, 1988b: 169*]. More generally, *businessmen* have become increasingly prominent in politics and, recently, have exhibited a capacity to organise autonomously of political parties and then bargain with them [*Lasater, 1990: 59*]. It would be a particularly blinkered form of reductionism that insisted that politicians from one societal group (business) were incapable of representing the interests of another (farmers). But it seems certain that the domination of local level politics by businessmen (and by 'money power') both indicates and helps to explain the near-absence of farming issues from the political agenda.

VIII. EXPLAINING THE EAST ASIAN PUZZLE

It seems almost impossible that the core rational choice model of the politics of food markets should not account for some of the shift from urban to rural bias in East Asia. The degree of fit between the predictions of the model and global patterns of sectoral bias is too close for the rational choice approach to be rejected. But, equally certainly, it does not provide the degree of explanation for changing sectoral preferences in Korea and Taiwan that its proponents claim. How else then do we explain that shift? Three other partial explanations are suggested by such evidence as is available.

(1) It seems likely that the rational choice theorists have simply ignored a major category of societal actor that emerges during economic growth and becomes an important part of the coalition in favour of rural bias at high income levels: the manufacturers and suppliers of farm machinery, equipment and agro-chemicals. These manufactured inputs account for a high proportion of the production costs of agriculture in high income economies, and their producers and suppliers are reckoned to be among some of the most effective components of the 'agricultural lobby' in such countries [*Self and Storing, 1962: 208; Body, 1984*]. What is the evidence about their political role in Korea and Taiwan?

It is quite clear that the material size of these interests grew very substantially in Korea and Taiwan in the post-war period, but especially in the 1960s. The structure of the agricultural economy changed very considerably, with these manufactured inputs accounting (a) physically, for continuing growth in agricultural production in a situation where land was very scarce and labour rapidly becoming so; and (b) economically, for a rapidly increasing proportion of production costs [*Moore, 1985a; 1988*]. The indices in Table 2, compiled from such relevant long-run statistical series as I have been able to locate, illustrate the rapid growth in the domestic production and use of manufactured farm inputs in the 1960s, compared with the 1950s.[29] The economic basis for a pro-agriculture lobby in manufacturing and distribution was created. It would be surprising if this lobby had not materialised to play much the same kind of role as in Western Europe and North America: orchestrating and supporting pro-agriculture policies in the name of farming. Indeed, the exclusionary nature of the Korean and Taiwanese political systems and the relatively privileged access of large-scale capital to decision-making would tend to provide political opportunities for at least some powerful producing interests, especially perhaps in the chemical industries. The presence of these interests behind the shift to agricultural protection would certainly help to account for the fact that this shift began before the issue of agricultural prices was on the public political agenda. Unfortunately, direct information on the role of these interests in

TABLE 2

INDICES OF THE PRODUCTION AND USE OF MANUFACTURED AGRICULTURAL
INPUTS IN KOREA AND TAIWAN, 1955–74

	Korea				Taiwan		
	(a)	(b)	(c)	(d)	(e)	(f)	(g)
Year	Production of chemical fertiliser (weight)	Use of chemical fertiliser (value, constant prices	Use of other agro-chemicals (as (b))	Farm inventories of machinery and equipment	Use of chemical fertiliser (weight)	Input of mechanical labour into farm production (horse-power day equivalents)	Production of power tillers (numbers)
1955	neg.	36	3	22	86	neg.	neg.
1956	0	42	5	24	97	neg.	neg.
1957	0	41	6	25	101	neg.	neg.
1958	0	46	6	27	104	1	neg.
1959	0	43	6	35	104	4	neg.
1960	1	55	8	35	103	7	neg.
1961	5	58	5	30	97	12	40
1962	6	57	9	44	107	22	37
1963	8	56	15	47	114	27	42
1964	11	61	30	61	134	34	48
1965	13	68	20	69	122	35	64
1966	14	73	23	74	127	61	68
1967	32	84	40	77	139	55	95
1968	82	84	51	99	147	71	113
1969	95	93	64	104	149	84	118
1970	100	100	100	100	100	100	100
1971	102	105	104	118	126	125	146
1972	107	112	116	147	122	134	119
1973	114	132	127	182	142	161	99
1974	127	141	218	213	174	n.d.	121

Source: Columns (a) – (d) from Ban *et al.* [*1980: 105, 419, 419 and 421*] respectively;column (e) from *Taiwan Statistics Data Book* (various issues); column (f) from Shei [*1980: 792*]; and column (g) from *Industry of Free China* (various issues).

policy-making is wholly lacking. The argument is quite consistent with the rational choice approach. The puzzle is why the rational choice theorists have ignored this important interest group.[30]

(2) There is some evidence that some of the most effective proponents of agricultural protection in East Asia are state agencies that, institutionally or as an aggregate of individuals, benefit from the policy. Consider the agencies which control beef imports into Japan and Korea. Protection levels for beef producers have tended to be very high, especially in Korea [*Anderson and Hayami*, 1986: Tables

A1.1–A1.3]. Yet the ownership distribution of beef cattle in Korea is very dispersed, much more so than for dairy animals (in Korea) or for hogs in Taiwan, where large-scale producers increasingly dominate.[31] The logistic obstacles to the autonomous political organisation of Korean beef producers are very considerable. Insofar as they are organised, this seems to be a result of the initiative and leadership exercised by small groups entrenched in state agencies who control beef imports in the name of local agriculture, but to their own direct benefit. The organisations which licence beef imports make very handsome profits, and share these with a limited number of wholesalers with whom they have privileged relations. On retirement, the officials of the import licensing agency may take up posts in the wholesaleing firms.[32]

There is, however, a more general point about the effect on intersectoral policies of the pursuit of self-interest by the personnel of state agricultural agencies. It is a point that may be couched in rational choice terms, although it is questionable whether this actually helps us to understand the world. A commonsensical alertness to the motives of interest groups might lead us more directly to the same end point. The argument can be couched as follows:

(a) Public sector employees have limited mobility within the public service, and therefore vested career interests in the expansion (or, non-contraction) of the agencies in which they work.

(b) Rapid relative decline in the size of the agricultural economy in a context of successful industrialisation is likely to generate concern in agricultural agencies and encourage staff to engage in political activities (lobbying, dissemination of economic analyses and other acceptable types of argument) aimed at directing additional resources into the agricultural economy.

(c) In Korea and Taiwan, 'green' (environmental) political demands were few but highly oppositional. It was therefore not feasible for agricultural bureaucracies to redefine their role in terms of environmental policy.

The corollary of this argument is that, in relatively exclusive polities undergoing the types of structural economic change outlined above, the 'agricultural agencies' may emerge as significant advocates of rural bias. Is there evidence? For Taiwan in particular, there is. One revealing if tangential piece of evidence relates to the long debate, referred to in section VI above, about the lack of a formal Ministry of Agriculture. A major source of resistance to this proposal has been the staff of the JCRR and its successor institutions, the Council for Agricultural Planning and Development, later the Council of Agriculture. It is ironic that these same people were the major proponents of additional state support for agriculture generally (see below). Their successful opposition to becoming regular employees of a Ministry was based above all on simple self-interest: the special status of the JCRR as a joint Sino-American enterprise had justified staff salaries significantly above those of ordinary government employees; these privileged salaries had not been withdrawn when the Americans left, but would not survive conversion of the agency to ministerial status![33]

This particular point about the muscle wielded by the JCRR and its successors in bureaucratic politics is consistent with broader evidence about their influence over the shift to rural bias.[34] For not only had the JCRR recruited high quality (and well paid) staff, but it had also, during its life, gradually shifted emphasis from a technical to a planning and policy-making role. The educational background of the staff had therefore changed, with economists in particular replacing agricultural technicians [*Yager, 1988: 269–71*]. Senior economists, many of them with postgraduate qualifications from prestigious American universities, were extremely well placed to argue agriculture's corner, both within bureaucratic domains and in published media. And they did argue very widely: there is a large literature (in English as well as Chinese), aimed at both policymaking and academic circles, supporting agriculture.[35] Equally, the same people proved very adept at formulating new public intervention measures to cope with the changing economic conditions of the agricultural economy, thus justifying the continued employment of large numbers of agricultural officials.[36]

Without direct information about the policy-making process in East Asia, it is not possible to test satisfactorily this proposition about the power of agricultural agencies. Indirect indications of the influence of this category of actor are certainly more numerous than indications of the power of farmers themselves.

(3) A different but congruent insight into the importance of 'state' factors in the shift to agricultural protection can be obtained by looking into the details of the timing of this process. In so far as there was a single turning point, this was the acceleration in the early 1970s in the rate of increase of (nominal) producer rice prices in all three East Asian countries: 1972–74 in Japan; 1974 in particular in Korea; and 1973–74 in Taiwan (Figure 2). The effect of these increased producer prices on rates of protection was temporarily nullified by

very high prices in world grain markets in 1973–75 (Table 3), but thereafter (a) both producer rice prices and rates of protection tended to increase relatively steadily; and (b) producer rice prices – which are effectively established by levels of government procurement prices – tended to change in rather similar ways in each of the three countries, with Japan taking the lead and Korea and Taiwan following on a year or two later (Figure 2). How do we account for these patterns? The rational choice model deals with incremental changes in balances of political forces arising from changes in economic structure. It would seem to offer no explanation for such a marked turning point in rice pricing policy as came in the early 1970s.[37]

As it happens, contingent political events in Korea and Taiwan at around this time provide some possible explanation. In Korea, following President Park's unexpectedly poor command of the rural vote in the 1971 Presidential elections, a series of pro-agricultural policies was introduced, including more remunerative rice prices [*Moore, 1985b*]. In Taiwan, Chiang Ching-Kuo, the relatively populist and Taiwanese (as opposed to Mainlander) oriented son of President Chiang Kai-Shek, assumed control of economic policy as Vice Prime Minister in 1969, and became Prime Minister in 1972. He was personally responsible for a pro-rural shift in economic policy [*Durdin, 1975*].

However, a wider understanding of East Asian politics and economic policy-making processes suggests that these contingent changes fit into a more structured pattern, and one of which Japan is an important component. It has become widely appreciated that, in economic policymaking, Korea and Taiwan keep a close eye on each other to see what they can learn. What is more important, each of them not only keeps an even closer eye on Japan but consciously shapes its economic structure and strategy to follow paths analogous to those pursued by Japan [*Wade, 1990: 189 and 334*]. Such learning is greatly facilitated by physical proximity, the common background in the Japanese colonial empire, and the frequency of cultural and business contact. Korea and Taiwan have been copying Japan in respect of a range of 'second land reform' policies designed to increase farm operating sizes, encourage cooperation and collective production, and generally ameliorate the economic inefficiencies caused by the combination of high protection and small-scale farming (see note 36). What more plausible explanation of the patterns in Figure 2 than that they have also been copying Japan over the question of agricultural protection?

States do not copy one another; state agencies and their personnel do

FIGURE 2
PRODUCER RICE PRICES, EAST ASIA, 1955–82

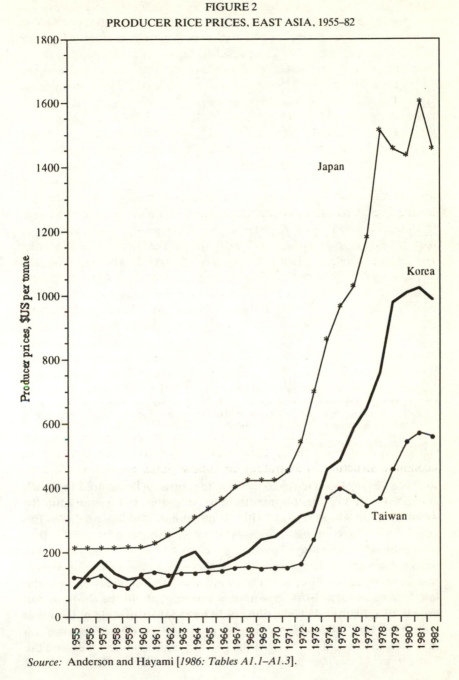

Source: Anderson and Hayami [1986: Tables A1.1–A1.3].

TABLE 3

NOMINAL RATES OF PROTECTION FOR RICE PRODUCERS IN EAST ASIA, 1955–82

Year	Japan	Korea	Taiwan
1955	46	−44	−20
1956	49	−14	−36
1957	53	18	−28
1958	48	−10	−34
1959	56	−22	−39
1960	58	−16	−3
1961	53	−42	−4
1962	72	−34	−11
1963	82	33	−11
1964	96	27	−13
1965	107	−5	−14
1966	107	−6	−15
1967	72	1	−13
1968	98	14	−17
1969	113	24	−5
1970	173	30	−4
1971	220	84	14
1972	233	126	41
1973	123	27	−19
1974	53	7	−14
1975	151	19	−2
1976	274	121	41
1977	300	193	69
1978	285	129	64
1979	304	230	116
1980	210	156	135
1981	211	134	126
1982	326	172	170

Note: The nominal rate of protection is defined in Table 1, and measured here as the ratio of the domestic producer price to the border price.

Source: Anderson and Hayami [*1986: Tables A1.1–A1.3*].

so. Those best placed to make the case for copying Japan are those with (a) access to the relevant information to make the comparisons and (b) recognised positions of authority in the policy-making process. The general acceptance of the legitimacy of the 'copying Japan' process thus has probably permitted those agencies within the Korean and Taiwanese state apparatuses with a self-interest in agricultural protection to be especially effective. They were certainly relatively vocal in the late 1960s and early 1970s in sounding warnings about the threat to the growth of agricultural production posed by rapid absorption of labour in industry,[38] and the wider strategic implications of dependence on imported food supplies.[39] Given the geo-strategic situation then and the evident problems faced by the American forces in Vietnam, these 'national security' arguments presumably fell on very responsive ears. I presume – and it is no more than a presumption – that the same interests were able to take advantage of early indications of the rapid increase in world market cereal prices in 1973 and 1974 to argue the necessity of boosting internal cereal procurement prices on grounds of national security.

IX. THE LIMITS OF THE RATIONAL CHOICE PARADIGM

The East Asian material gives rise to two major concerns about the extent to which the rational choice paradigm can explain sectoral bias. The first concern relates to the extent to which notions of rationally self-interested action may be used to *explain* (rather than 'explain away') the political behaviour of governments or state agencies in an intellectually consistent fashion. For reasons given in section V, I remain a sceptic on this point, and find the rational choice paradigm most convincing when restricted to the analysis of political pressures on governments that have societal origins. In so far as the notion of rational state action is intellectually acceptable, this is likely to be when (a) distinct agencies are identified (as opposed to 'the state' in general) and (b) there is a clear and direct link between the collective self-interest of the staff of those agencies and the policies which they support.

The second concern is more specific to the issue of sectoral bias, more positive in implication, and more original. It is that, insofar as the rational choice paradigm can explain patterns of sectoral bias on a global scale, this involves incorporating into the model a wider range of potential political actors (or, stakeholders in the agricultural economy) than those which appear in existing general models of this process. Reference has been made to aspects of this argument at various points above. I suggest that a minimum list of potentially important stake-holders would be as follows:[40]

(1) *Poor farmers*: (see section IV on the main factors affecting their political role)[41]

(2) *Rich farmers*: (as above)

(3) *Consumers*: (as above)

(4) *Employers*: One would expect them to share the same political predispositions as consumers. At low income levels, (staple) food costs account for a high proportion of employees' expenditure; it is

therefore likely that wage demands and expectations are sensitive to variations in food prices. Employers tend to support policies to keep food prices low. This interest would dissolve at higher income levels as employees and consumers become less concerned with food prices in general, and with the prices of staples in particular [*Bates and Rogerson, 1980: 525–6*].

(5) *Agro-processing industry*: In developing countries in particular, owners of agro-processing facilities are frequently also owners of crop production facilities. In so far as this is not the case, and processors and producers constitute separate interests, one would expect the political stance of (generally large scale, potentially powerful) processing interests to have a significant influence on the nature and intent of state intervention in commodity markets. This set of relationships is under-explored. There is a widespread view that agro-processors take a relatively short term perspective, give priority to acquisition of commodities for processing at low prices, and tend to constitute a significant element in urban-biased coalitions. Such an assumption is not fully convincing on a deductive basis. Agro-processing facilities are generally relatively capital-intensive, dedicated to that particular task, immobile, and, given the typically high costs of transporting bulk raw commodities from field to processing facility, dependent for raw material supplies on a limited geographical area and farming population. Under these conditions, agro-processors, especially if they take a long term view, might be expected to support policies that would provide producers with price incentives to expand production of commodities for processing.

Both at the local and the national (polity) level, there is scope for a wide range of different bargains between agro-processors and (organised) producers about the economic terms of their relationship.[42] One would expect that the same degree of indeterminacy would be found concerning the agro-processors' political stance. It is likely that agro-technical factors will be among the range of variables that will affect the way in which agro-processors use their power to influence public policies affecting producer commodity prices. Processors will be more inclined to exploit producers of permanent tree crops where the latter are 'locked in' to producing a particular commodity for some years. By contrast, the effect of depressing the producer price of annual crops (or those whose production can be terminated at little cost to the producer) will be a more immediate and visible decrease in the supply of products for processing. These are however issues that require empirical research.

(6) *Manufacturers and suppliers of agricultural inputs*: As is explained in section VIII, these interests tend to both emerge in relatively high income economies and, because of the major role of their products in increasing agricultural production, to become significant supporters of policies of rural bias.

(7) *Non-agricultural production in general*: The conventional argument [*Bates, 1981: Ch.4*] is that, in poor economies, non-agricultural producers tend to be (a) individually large but relatively few; (b) concentrated in urban areas; (c) established for import-substitution purposes in protected markets; and (d) heavily dependent on imported current and capital inputs. These four factors combine to make non-agricultural producers a major component of the urban-biased coalition, and one with a particular interest in over-valued exchange rates, which benefit them *qua* importers of inputs, while penalising (mainly agricultural) exporters. This image of the political economy of a stereotypical developing country has no special association with the rational choice paradigm. Indeed, with marginal variations, one could say that it is the common property of the development studies fraternity.[43]

How can the rational choice approach help us to understand the political consequences of changes in this particular scenario? There is no simple answer to this, for the model includes an assumption about economic policy (import-substituting industrialisation) as well as three assumptions about economic structure (few firms, urban location, import dependence). Changing these assumptions, in different combinations, provides scope for a very wide range of alternative scenarios; the issues become too complex to deal with in a model that can be empirically tested. It is for this reason that the core rational choice model of the shift from urban to rural bias (Figure 1) deals solely with the political coalitions that arise in food markets, ignoring non-agricultural production entirely. It would be surprising if such drastic simplification of reality did not entail some loss of explanatory power. This appears to be another fruitful research area.[44]

The implication of the length of this list of stakeholders in the agricultural economy and of the discussion of the way in which the interests of each may be affected by economic structure is that the relationship between economic growth and sectoral bias is less determinant than is suggested by mechanically minded adherents of the core rational choice model.

X. THE STATE AND AGRICULTURE

The academic debate about issues of sectoral bias started from a concern that Third World governments – especially, in the 1960s, the governments of the newly independent African countries – were both exploiting and making a mess of their agricultural economies. The first prominent scholarly publicist of this concern was Rene Dumont, above all in his famous *L'Afrique Noire Est Mal Partie* – published in English as *False Start in Africa [1966]*. The concerns of Dumont and other scholars arguing a similar case [e.g. *Schickele, 1968; Chs.5 and 6; Balogh, 1966: 238–44*] were very empirical: they were trying to draw the attention of policy-makers and practitioners to the fact that governments were setting about 'agricultural development' in ways that ranged between ineffective and disastrous. It was some years later that Mamalakis [*1969, 1971*], Lipton [*1977*], Mitra [*1977*] and Bates [*1981*] published political explanations of this phenomenon of sectoral bias. It is their work, particularly that of Lipton and Bates, to which later research and debate has been oriented. And, as has been explained in this study, the dominant theme in that debate, from the perspective of political explanation, has been the notion that sectoral bias reflects, at least in the short term, the fact that some privileged *societal* interests benefit while other lose. Some of these theorists have implicated 'the state' in the urban bias coalition, but not generally in ways that stand up well to rigorous scholarly scrutiny. In so far as we have acceptable political explanations for sectoral bias, they are essentially 'sociological' explanations.[45]

Reflecting on this debate, I wonder whether we have not missed some of the point of the work of Rene Dumont and the early 'alarmists' by not taking seriously their concern that much of the incipient mess that they detected was traceable in large degree to simple exploitation of the rural population by the personnel of the state apparatus. The introduction into the picture of concepts of class and of competition for resources between different societal groups, while helpful in some respects, may have drawn our attention away from the relationship between the peasant and the state. I suspect that there are issues about the construction and sustenance of state apparatuses, especially at low income levels, which may throw light on what we have learned to call the 'urban bias' problem, and which remain unexplored. The remainder of this study is devoted to a few speculative observations intended to stimulate thinking about this issue.

Every state system requires a personnel network in the countryside to ensure that certain functions are performed. Historically, the personnel

TABLE 4

INCOME LEVELS AND THE EXTENT OF PUBLIC SECTOR PROVISION OF
PURCHASED AGRICULTURAL INPUTS IN SUB–SAHARAN AFRICA

	(a)	(b)	(c)	(d)	(e)	(f)
Country classes (grouped by per capita income level)	Average (unweighted, 1979) % contribution of agriculture to:		No. of countries in which the input was provided at least 80% through the public sector			
	Labour force	GDP	Fertiliser	Seeds	Chemicals	Farm equipment
12 poorest countries	80%	48%	10	10	9	7
12 intermediate countries	82%	38%	7	5	5	5
12 richest coutries	62%	26%	6	7	3	3

Note: Included are all countries for which data were available in relation to columns (c)–(f). No reference time is given for these data; they were implicitly current at the time the report was written.

Source: World Bank [*1981: Tables 3, 32 and 35*].

of most rural state apparatuses have been materially sustained in one of two ways: (a) by permitting them to use their positions in the formal administrative apparatus for self-reward; or (b) by incorporating local societal structures of hierarchy and authority into the state apparatus, exploiting pre-existing systems for the redistribution of economic surplus to 'nourish' the state.[46] However, in the contemporary era, those who control state systems in poor countries face more exacting societal demands than did, say, European states in earlier centuries. Firstly, the legitimacy of governments is increasingly dependent on their capacity to pass some kind of test relating to popular acceptance. If not formal electoral democracy, this implies some plausible claim to represent 'the people', variously defined. That imperative in turn requires a state apparatus that is, in historical perspective, highly activist in relation to popular sentiment: one of its major tasks is to produce and sustain 'legitimacy' for the regime, both by generating positive support and by undermining opposition. Secondly, the idea of 'development' has become increasingly central to popular understandings of the purpose of government, and success in producing 'development' has become a major source of legitimacy. Put more simply, all states are obliged to present themselves as

TABLE 5

INCOME LEVELS AND RELATIVE PREFERENCES FOR AGRICULURAL
EXTENSION AND AGRICULTURAL RESEARCH

Region	(a) GDP per capita, 1982 (to nearest $100)	(b) No. of extension staff per research scientist, 1980	(c) Public sector extension expenditure as a ratio of research expenditure. 1980	(d) Combined research and extension expenditure as a % of the value of agricultural product. 1980
East Africa	200	15	1.4	1.2%
South Asia	300	14	0.4	0.2%
Southeast Asia	700	8	0.6	0.4%
West Africa	900	12	1.0	1.3%
North Africa	900	10	2.8	1.7%
Caribbean/Central America	2,000	3	0.5	0.3%
Temperate South America	2,000	1	0.6	0.4%
Tropical South America	2,100	3	1.1	1.2%
Southern Africa	2,100	2	0.4	0.5%
West Asia	2,200	7	1.0	0.5%
Eastern Europe	2,600	1	0.5	0.4%
Soviet Union	3,700	1	0.5	0.4%
Southern Europe	5,600	3	0.4	0.3%
East Asia	6,800	1	0.3	0.9%
Northern Europe	9,400	1	0.5	0.8%
Central Europe	10,400	2	0.3	0.5%
Oceania	11,100	1	0.3	1.0%
North America	13,300	1	0.5	0.6%

Note: The figures are presented here in very rounded form because the source makes clear that there are many doubts about their accuracy.

Source: Column (a) is from *World Bank Tables*, and columns (b)–(d) from Judd *et al.* [*1983: Tables 1, 2 and 4*].

developmental states. These legitimacy/mobilisation/development imperatives imply state activism. Yet activism implies personnel and thus resources. Governments of poor countries find it difficult to raise resources to openly pay their political cadres from the state budget. They can however use the wide range of state interventions in society and economy justified by 'developmentalism' to create public sector posts to which their cadres can be appointed.

All this seems fairly uncontentious. Where does agriculture fit in? Agriculture is important because these processes outlined above are likely to be especially intense in rural areas and thus within state institutions nominally dedicated to agricultural development. The poorer a society, the fewer alternative means there are of sustaining political cadres outside the state apparatus: there are fewer wealthy people willing to devote their own time to political activities; there are fewer private businessmen who can be persuaded to make donations to finance 'regular' political party activities; and there are fewer non-agricultural state institutions (departments of adult education, social services or electricity; parastatal industries, etc.) with which the burden of sustaining political cadres can be shared.

One would therefore expect that, the poorer the society, the more likely it is that the state will exploit opportunities to establish 'agricultural' agencies in rural areas to 'house' its political cadres. The figures presented in Tables 4 and 5 are at least consistent with that hypothesis. Table 4 indicates a strong connection, on a cross-sectional basis for sub-Saharan African countries, between (a) low levels of income and (b) the depth of the involvement of state agencies in the supply of (marketed) agricultural inputs. The poorer countries are, the more likely are their governments to establish their own (monopoly) organisations for the supply of fertilisers, seeds, agro-chemicals and farm equipment. The implications of Table 5 are slightly less direct. What it provides is evidence of an association between (a) low levels of income and (b) governments' preferences for allocating the joint agricultural research and extension budget more to extension than to research.[47] What is the significance of this pattern? It lies in the fact that agricultural extension is much more 'political' than agricultural research in two senses.

Firstly, and especially at low income levels, where extension personnel are cheap to employ relative to research personnel, a bias in favour of extension provides more opportunities for political patronage, that is, more government jobs to be given away. Secondly, agricultural extension personnel in poor countries are frequently used on a routine basis for political purposes in a way that is not possible in the case of research staff rooted in research stations. For mobility and widespread personal contacts in rural areas lie at the heart of the extensionists' job. They are thus in a position to fulfil the role of cadres working for the regime or ruling party: political intelligence, mobilisation of support, organisation of local political activities and events, etc.

These two sets of figures are congruent with the proposition that contemporary poor states batten on to agriculture to sustain their political cadres, and gradually release their grip as incomes increase and alternative means emerge to support political apparatuses. This hypothesis is not inconsistent with the 'urban bias' literature discussed above, but differs in two respects:

(1) The explanation is fully state-centric, focusing on the implications of differing economic environments for the ways in which states (and regimes) perform their most imperative function – mobilising and deploying the resources (material, organisational, ideological) they need to perpetuate themselves.

(2) The consequences for economic performance do not lie in the realm of inter-sectoral transfers of resources, but in the effect on the economic performance of agriculture of its being subject to the attentions, nominal or real, of so many agencies and officials dedicated in principle to agricultural development. This is not an issue that can be debated here. That there are often considerable costs to the agricultural economy is probably evident to most contemporary observers.

The connection between (a) the extent to which the state latches on to agriculture to support its cadres; and (b) the nature of the sectoral bias that arises from the state's economic and fiscal policies is indirect and non-binding. For example, a state could in principle both subsidise agriculture and use staff positions in its agricultural agencies to sustain its political cadres. My guess however is that the relationship is more likely to be the reverse at low income levels: that the exploitation of agricultural 'service' agencies to provide positions for political cadres is likely to make those agencies unresponsive to farmers' needs, alert mainly to the interests of their own staff, and thus ineffective as political representatives of agricultural interests within the state apparatus. This then may be an additional cause of the low income/urban bias v. high income/rural bias pattern found on the world scale: at low income levels, politically weak farmers receive no political support from agencies of the state responsible for agriculture, whereas at high income levels the same agencies pile in to support farmers in the agencies' own interests.

NOTES

1. There are several other reasons why such straightforward emulation is unlikely, including changing technology and the likelihood that agricultural subsidies will be curtailed through increasing tension between (competing) surplus agricultural producers. The point I am making here is that, even on *ceteris paribus* assumptions about these other factors, the political mechanism linking relative wealth and rural bias is not highly determinant.
2. I have in mind in particular the work of Barrington Moore [*1967*], Ashok Mitra [*1977*] and James Scott [*1976*].
3. A similar attempt to combine conventional class categorisations with categorisations based on membership of economic sectors was made at around the same time by Mamalakis [*1969; 1971*], with the intention of providing a general framework for the study of Latin American politics. Both Lipton and Mamalakis may be seen as responding to a common dilemma: the belief – in those neo-Marxist days – that some kind of class categorisation was essential to any political analysis; and a realisation that conventional categorisations did not take one very far in understanding the politics of Third World countries, and therefore needed some adaptation. Their mistake perhaps lay in their unwillingness to break more cleanly with the notion of classes as political actors.
4. For an explanation and illustration of how empirical research reveals the limitations of the simple society-centric deductive model, see especially Varshney in this volume.
5. For example, if the urban consumer spends 50 per cent of his/her income on maize flour, then a 20 per cent increase in the price of flour cuts the real value of that income by almost nine per cent. If the farmer realises only 40 per cent of his/her income (as producer) from produce sales, and only half of that from maize, a 20 per cent maize price increase would increase real income by only four per cent.
6. One can enrich the underlying model, without altering its basic structure, by assuming that employers, whether in public or private sectors, constitute part of the coalition for low food prices because this helps depress labour costs (see section X).
7. The factors which are likely to affect the degree to which this 'obscurity' obtains are largely self-evident. One of the most important may be whether or not producers can easily make price comparisons through access to a neighbouring country where the same cash export crops are produced, but subjected to a lesser price bias.
8. The weak proposition – that is, that revenue gathering tends to be a major motivation of state action, either as an ultimate goal (enriching those in power) or as an intermediate goal (permitting state managers to command the resources they need to stay in power) – is unexceptionable but rather trite. It does not lead to any unique or original insights into the nature of states or the objectives of state action. And it is to focus on one dimension of the determinants of state action – the 'needs' or 'goals' dimension – without examining how this interacts with the other dimension – the actual possibilities available to achieve objectives. These problems are evident in the book by Margaret Levi [*1988*] which set out to assert the primacy of the revenue imperative. It does not generate the analytical insight which it promises.
9. The empirical validity of this proposition is open to some question. And, to the extent that it is valid, the divergence of interest between different categories of farmers specialising in different products gives rise to the possibility of alternative, competing farmer interest groups. Such a possibility seems more likely to be realised when specialisation by product coincides with (a) location and (b) administrative and political boundaries. The former has long been a factor in, for example, British agricultural politics, with the more powerful (large farm) Eastern cereal growers generally prevailing over the (small farm) Western livestock-rearing industry interested in cheap cereals for animal feed.
10. I have myself elsewhere cited it approvingly [*Moore, 1990: 232–3*].
11. This discretion remains open as long as two basic questions about the concept of the

state as rational political actor remain unresolved: (a) In what sense can the state be considered a unitary actor? (b) What is the state's utility function (that is, its objectives, and preferences among them)? Answers which are consistent with reality are likely to vary according to specific contexts. No general resolution appears likely. Class-theoretic approaches are more constrained in this respect, and their analytic deficiencies are thus more immediately visible.

12. There have been corresponding shifts from urban to rural bias in other areas of government activity, notably, in the early 1970s, (a) abolition of the Taiwanese rice-fertiliser barter scheme, whereby monopsony supply of rice fertiliser at unfavourable rates of exchange (for rice) was used to transfer economic resources from agriculture; (b) the abolition or reduction of various other taxes or charges on Taiwanese agriculture; and (c) the introduction of major programmes of rural infrastructural spending in both Korea and Taiwan. For an overview see Moore [*1985a*] and [*1988*]. The classic quantitative analysis of the dimensions of 'urban bias' in Taiwan in the 1950s and 1960s is by Lee [*1971*].

13. For more details and sources of evidence on most of the points made in this section, see Moore [*1988*].

14. For an economical insight into the characteristics of this 'soft authoritarianism' (his term), see Johnson [*1987*].

15. Since the land reforms of the late 1940s and early 1950s, average farm size in Japan, Korea, and Taiwan has not diverged significantly from one hectare.

16. The Saemaul Movement of the early 1970s appears to have been intended to be a quasi-party, serving to mobilise support for the Park regime among the rural population on a permanent basis. However, the endeavour collapsed [*Moore, 1985b*]. One might however note that the radical Catholic Farmers and Christian Farmers movements, while lacking a mass base, have helped keep governments' attentions on the issue of rural living conditions.

17. For a detailed case study, see Wade [*1982*].

18. Cole and Lyman [*1971: 37–9 and 95*] explain how the formal commitments of the post-1961 military regime to do something for the rural population were honoured only to the extent that there was no conflict with more pressing economic and political imperatives.

19. It was reported in the *Far Eastern Economic Review* (7 Dec. 1990: 53) that the National Livestock Cooperatives Federation, the organisation which serves beef producers, will begin to elect its own local officials rather than having them appointed from above – and thus ultimately by the state.

20. Since Taiwanese owned almost all private property, they also dominated the (non-state) manufacturing and tertiary sectors. However, except for some Mainlanders employed by the state-owned Taiwan Sugar Corporation, Taiwanese accounted for virtually the entire agricultural population. Agriculture accounted for more than half total employment until the mid-1960s.

21. Only two other Provincial government agencies were headquartered in Taipei: the Police Department and the Department of Civil Supplies.

22. The military, public officials and teachers – the key constituents of the regime's support base and of the Mainlander population – were supplied through a ration scheme.

23. It also appears to have consistently underpaid the Farmers' Associations for the provision of these services.

24. The most recent history of the JCRR [*Yager, 1988*] is mainly descriptive and adds little to the earlier and more overtly propagandistic account by Shen [*1970*]. The interpretation presented here is based on the piecing together of various pieces of evidence from the literature and from field research in Taiwan in 1983. Some of the most useful sources are the JCRR's own *Annual Reports* for the first few years of its life. These were written, evidently by Americans, before Guomindang rule on Taiwan was institutionalised. Institutionalisation of rule led to blandness in reporting. A very useful brief analytical account of the political context in which the JCRR operated in

the 1950s and the early 1960s is found in Montgomery *et al.* [*1966*].

25. These demonstrations began in December 1987, and peaked with a large demonstration in Taipei on 20 June 1988. The demands advanced on 20 June were: (1) bans on imports of American agricultural products; (2) extension of social insurance to the farming population; (3) a Ministry of Agriculture; (4) increased procurement prices for rice, and (5) reform of the Farmers Associations to make them more efficient and eradicate Guomindang influence. The first two demands were given special prominence (Guo Jiann-Jong, private communication).

26. More details can be found in Moore [*1988*], Stavis [*1974*] and in a publication by de Lasson [*1976*] which is unfortunately difficult to obtain but extremely insightful. It contains the results of what was to my knowledge the only substantial independent study of the Farmers Association system ever conducted. The Farmers Association system was re-structured in 1950, largely along the lines recommended by Professor Anderson of Cornell University. However, 'three crucial points' in Anderson's report which would have given the system considerably more economic power and organisational-cum-political coherence were not implemented [*de Lasson, 1976: 380–1*].

27. Farmers Associations engaged in a very wide range of income earning activities, including: a rural credit business; grain procurement, processing, storage and distribution on behalf of other government agencies; agricultural insurance; supply of agricultural inputs; marketing and processing of a wide range of products; and the collection of land taxes.

28. A summary of the 'reform' measures imposed on the Farmers Associations is given by de Lasson [*1976: 381*]. The degree of state intervention in Irrigation Associations was greater; they were put under state control until 1982, when a more limited degree of autonomy was again granted. For some details, see Moore [*1989*].

29. The partial exception is fertiliser production in Taiwan. Taiwan was ahead of Korea in both the extent of use of fertiliser and in establishing manufacturing facilities. By the 1960s, fertiliser use was no longer growing very fast in Taiwan (machinery and other agro-chemicals had assumed the lead role), and, even more markedly, the country was shifting out of fertiliser production towards more 'strategic' products, and depending increasingly on imports.

30. One possible reason is that, since rational choice theory is predominantly used as a tool by neo-liberals activated in large degree by hostility to state action and a bias in favour of the private sector, recognition of the 'rent-seeking' political activities of large-scale private business is unwelcome and therefore avoided. Another possible reason is more to do with professional than ideological bias. The core rational choice model of 'politics of food markets' is both amenable to mathematical specification [e.g. *Bates and Rogerson, 1980*], and produces non-obvious predictions. The same is true of the supplementary model of 'the politics of comparative advantage in agricultural production' presented by Anderson and Hayami (see main text). By contrast, the political role of producers and suppliers of manufactured agricultural inputs has neither of these delightful properties.

31. Taiwan does not feature in this particular story because it is a major exporter of meat, pork, rather than rice, now being the major agricultural product. The political energies of large scale pork producers appear to have been focused more on expanding export markets (mainly in Japan) than on obtaining protection against imports. Import competition has been limited because of the national preference for pork over beef, and the fact that Australia and New Zealand do not have the same capacity to capture an unprotected market for pork in Taiwan as they do in relation to beef in Japan and Korea. It is on the latter doors that their livestock producing interests have been pounding.

32. Some detail on the arrangements in Korea is given in by Clifford [*1989*]. Anderson and Hayami discuss this issue in relation to Korea and Japan [*1986: 89–90*]. They are clearly more concerned to expose the malign effects of state-intervention than to ponder the fact that this kind of state-centred 'rent-seeking' constitutes a dimension to

the politics of sectoral preference which is not recognised in their societal-centric rational choice model of the process.

33. The evidence is from my field research in Taiwan in 1983.

34. I do not know how far the Provincial Food Bureau (see above in the main text) comprised a component of this intra-bureaucratic agricultural lobby. It seemed less powerful in the early 1980s than in earlier decades, probably because the rice supplies which it controlled was no longer as scarce and politically strategic as it had been in earlier decades.

35. It is not possible to reference this literature in any comprehensive way. A random example may be found in the article by T.H. Shen [1968], then Chairman of the JCRR. Stressing the contribution of agriculture to economic growth, avoiding any openly jarring note, and taking a positive attitude to the future, he manages to make a case for public investment to ease the changes required to adapt agriculture to changing economic circumstances. The ideological power of this 'lobby' appears to have lain in particular in (a) its capacity to provide good quality papers and speakers to an enormous range of meetings, seminars, workshops and publications; and (b) strong links with American universities, above all, Cornell. There is in fact a very striking example: the earliest authoritative scholarly assault on urban bias in Taiwan in the 1950s and early 1960s was a Cornell doctoral thesis, published as a book by Cornell University Press, and authored by the man who was, in 1988, to become the first Taiwanese (that is, non-Mainlander) President of the country [Lee, 1971].

36. I have in mind in particular a wide range of measures, sometimes termed the 'second land reform', aimed at coping with the increasingly uneconomic nature of small farm production in an environment where rising land values and widespread rural industrialisation encouraged owners to hold on to their land even if they had little economic motivation to cultivate it intensively. These measures included, in particular, the creation (and subsidisation) of various kinds of co-operative and collective arrangements for (seedling) production, machinery ownership and operation, and marketing. My own fieldwork in 1983 [Moore, 1988: 142] indicates that these measures were generally extremely ineffective, and often purely nominal, intended (by officials) to create an impression of activity and (by farmers) as a means of justifying subsidies.

37. It is not possible to conduct the same kind of analysis for other significant agricultural products because virtually all of them face very direct competition from imported substitutes whose world market prices are very unstable. This is especially true of livestock products. Unlike in the case of rice, governments cannot have confidence in their own ability to determine domestic producer prices by setting the level of procurement prices.

38. In both countries, the mid-1960s are generally reckoned to be the time when the labour market began to become noticeably 'tight', when real wages began to edge upwards, and when, therefore, agriculture began to feel the impact of competition for labour in a very marked way.

39. The Yearbook published by the Far Eastern Economic Review includes a brief survey of current events in each country which appears to reflect fairly accurately issues current on the political agenda. The volumes for 1968 (p.312), 1969 (pp.301–2) and 1970 (p.271) make mention of concerns about possible food shortages in Korea, while a similar concern was expressed in relation to Taiwan in 1971 (p.320).

40. Aspects of some of the issues featuring in this list appear, for example, in Bates and Rogerson [1980]. The targets of my critique of 'simplistic' rational choice models are not open-minded scholars such as these.

41. One would however add that, at least in the industrial countries, farmer power appears to be becoming increasingly closely associated with the existence of an autonomous and powerful institutional base in the form of dense networks of agricultural marketing cooperatives. Institutions matter.

42. For an interesting exploration of these political and economic relationships, see Attwood [1989].

43. One additional element which some observers might wish to add is the notion of an

'economy of scarcity', or a 'sellers' market', in which command over goods tends to bring power. In such a situation, producers have little difficulty in disposing of products, and have little incentive to invest resources in expanding their markets by building up the economies of their customers. Thus, fertiliser producers have no incentive to use their political resources to make agricultural production more profitable.

44. In so far as one wishes to explore, within the rational choice framework, the implications of economic growth for the political coalitions which arise in non-agriculture (in general), particular attention should perhaps be paid to the character-istic 'deepening' of inter-firm economic transactions. As (a) production processes become more lengthy and complex and (b) markets become more effective and firms more willing to rely on the market for the supply of intermediate inputs, the ratio of intermediate to final market transactions tends to increase; firms become more dependent on other firms for provision of production inputs and purchase of (unfi-nished) outputs. The political implications of this structural change depend in particu-lar on the extent to which inter-firm transactions cross national borders; for it especially at that point that the state is able to intervene in the market through tariffs and trade and payments controls. However, abstracting from this consideration, it seems likely that the general political consequence of this deepening of inter-firm economic relationships would be to weaken the incentives to engage in collective action on behalf of manufacturing-industry-in-general, non-agriculture, or indeed any broadly defined 'industry' (short of 'the national economy'). For the consequence of firm specialisation is increasing potential conflicts of interest over public policy between firms related through economic transactions: every promise by government to intervene to support the producer price of widgets is simultaneously a threat to the profitability of firms which use widgets in their production process. Everything else being equal, the structural change associated with economic growth probably tends to 'disarm' the industrial lobby which, despite its small size, appears so powerful in developing countries.

45. Perhaps the most plausible exception to this statement lies in the work of Nolan and White [1984] on China.

46. This distinction is much clearer at the conceptual than at the empirical level: many systems combine elements of both.

47. The figures in column b of Table 5 indicate that there is a very strong relationship, at the level of country groups, between average incomes and the extension-research split in terms of personnel. The poorest countries employ 14 or 15 extensionists per research scientists, whereas for the richest countries the numbers in the two categories are approximately equal. There are two possible explanations. One is the political explanation that I advance in the main text. The other is the explanation suggested by the economists who collated these figures: that governments make rational choices in what they perceive to be the social interest. The ratio of extensionists salaries to researchers salaries is so much lower at low income levels, and governments perceive the two categories of staff to be partial substitutes for one another. They therefore respond to these variations in salary ratios by employing relatively more extensionists in low income situations [Judd et al., 1983: 28]. This explanation requires a high level of faith in the rationality and collective interest orientation of governments. However, even if valid, it still does not totally nullify my preferred explanation. For, even when one looks simply at relative expenditures on agricultural extension and agricultural research, side-stepping the impact of varying salary ratios, one still finds that poorer countries tend to prefer extension over research (column c of Table 5).

REFERENCES

Anderson, K. and Y. Hayami, 1986, *The Political Economy of Agricultural Protection. East Asia in International Perspective*, Sydney and London: Allen & Unwin.
Attwood, D., 1989, 'Does Competition Help Cooperation?', *Journal of Development Studies*, Vol.26, No.1.
Balogh, T., 1966, *The Economics of Poverty*, London: Weidenfeld & Nicolson.
Ban, S.H., *et al.*, 1980, *Studies in the Modernisation of the Republic of Korea, 1945–1975: Rural Development*, Cambridge, MA: Harvard University Press.
Bates, R.H., 1981, *Markets and States in Tropical Africa. The Political Basis of Agricultural Policies*, Berkeley and Los Angeles, CA: University of California Press.
Bates, R.H. and W. Rogerson, 1980, 'Agriculture in Development: A Coalitional Analysis', *Public Choice*, Vol.35, No.5.
Body, R., 1984, *Farming in the Clouds*, London: Temple Smith.
Clifford, M., 1989, 'Consumers Corralled', *Far Eastern Economic Review*, 7 Dec.
Cole, D.C. and P.N. Lyman, 1971, *Korean Development. The Interplay of Politics and Economics*, Cambridge, MA: Harvard University Press.
Corbridge, S., 1982, 'Urban Bias, Rural Bias and Industrialisation: An Appraisal of the Work of Michael Lipton and Terry Byres', in J. Harriss (ed.) *Rural Development: Theories of Peasant Economy and Agrarian Change*, London: Hutchison.
Dumont, R., 1966, *False Start in Africa*, London: Andre Deutsch.
Durdin, T., 1975, 'Chiang Ching-Kuo's Taiwan', *Pacific Community* (Tokyo), Vol.7, No.1.
Evans, P.B., Rueschmeyer, D. and T. Skocpol (eds.), 1985, *Bringing the Stae Back In*, Cambridge: Cambridge University Press.
George, A. and E. Saxon, 1986. 'The Politics of Agricultural Protection in Japan', in K. Anderson and Y. Hayami, *The Political Economy of Agricultural Protection: East Asia in International Perspective*, Sydney and London: Allen & Unwin.
Hsiao, H.M., 1992, 'The Rise of Social Movements and Civil Protests', in T. Cheng and S. Haggard (eds.), *Political Change in Taiwan*, Boulder, CO and London: Lynne Rienner Publishers.
Jacobs, J.B., 1980, *Local Politics in a Rural Chinese Cultural Setting. A Field Study of Mazo Township, Taiwan*, Canberra: Contemporary China Centre, Research School of Pacific Studies, Australian National University.
Johnson, C., 1987, 'Political Institutions and Economic Performance: The Government–Business Relationship in Japan, South Korea and Taiwan', in F. Deyo (ed.), *The Political Economy of the New Asian Industrialism*, Ithaca, NY and London: Cornell University Press.
Judd, M.A. *et al.*, 1983, *Investing in Agricultural Supply*, Center Discussion Paper No.442, Economic Growth Center, Yale University.
Lasater, M.L., 1990, *A Step Toward Democracy. The December 1989 Elections in Taiwan, Republic of China*, Washington DC: AEI Press.
De Lasson, A., 1976, *The Farmers' Association Approach to Rural Development. The Taiwan Case*, Goettingen: Institute of Rural Development, University of Goettingen, Socio-Economic Studies on Rural Development, No.19.
Lee, T.H., 1971, *Intersectoral Capital Flows in the Economic Development of Taiwan*, Ithaca, NY: Cornell University Press.
Levi, M., 1988, *Of Rule and Revenue*, Berkeley, Los Angeles, CA London: University of California Press.
Lipton, M., 1977, *Why Poor People Stay Poor: Urban Bias in World Development*, London: Temple Smith.
Lipton, M., 1984, 'Urban Bias Revisited', in J. Harriss and M. Moore (eds.), *Development and the Rural–Urban Divide*, London: Frank Cass.
Mamalakis, M.J., 1969, 'The Theory of Sectoral Clashes', *Latin American Research Review*, Vol.4, No.3.
Mamalakis, M.J., 1971, 'The Theory of Sectoral Clashes and Coalitions Revisited', *Latin American Research Review*, Vol.6, No.3.

March, J.G. and J.P. Olsen, 1989, *Rediscovering Institutions. The Organizational Basis of Politics*, New York and London: The Free Press.

Mitra, A., 1977, *Terms of Trade and Class Relations*, London: Frank Cass.

Montgomery, J.D., Hughes, R.B. and R.H. Davis, 1966, *Rural Improvement and Political Development: The JCRR Model*, American Society for Public Administration, Comparative Administration Group, Papers in Comparative Administration, Special Series, No.7.

Moore, Barrington, 1967, *Social Origins of Dictatorship and Democracy. Lord and Peasant in the Making of the Modern World*, London: Allen Lane, The Penguin Press.

Moore, M., 1984a, 'Political Economy and the Rural–Urban Divide, 1767–1981', in J. Harriss and M. Moore (eds.), *Development and the Rural–Urban Divide*, London: Frank Cass.

Moore, M., 1984b, 'Categorising Space: Urban–Rural or Core-Periphery in Sri Lanka', in J. Harriss and M. Moore (eds.), *Development and the Rural–Urban Divide*, London: Frank Cass.

Moore, M., 1985a, 'Economic Growth and the Rise of Civil Society: Agriculture in Taiwan and South Korea', in G. White and R. Wade (eds.), *Developmental States in East Asia*, Brighton: IDS Research Report 16.

Moore, M., 1985b, 'Mobilization and Disillusion in Rural Korea: The Saemaul Movement in Retrospect', *Pacific Affairs*, Vol.57, No.4.

Moore, M., 1988, 'Economic Growth and the Rise of Civil Society: Agriculture in Taiwan and South Korea', in G. White (ed.), *Developmental States in East Asia*, London: Macmillan.

Moore, M., 1989, 'The Fruits and Fallacies of Neo-Liberalism: The Case of Irrigation Policy', *World Development*, Vol.17, No.11.

Moore, M., 1990, 'The Rational Choice Paradigm and the Allocation of Agricultural Development Resources', *Development and Change*, Vol.21, No.2.

Niskanen, W.A., 1971, *Bureaucracy and Representative Government*, Chicago, IL: Aldine.

Nolan, P. and G. White, 1984, 'Urban Bias, Rural Bias or State Bias? Urban–Rural Relations in Post-Revolutionary China,' in J. Harriss and M. Moore (eds.), *Development and the Rural–Urban Divide*, London: Frank Cass.

Schickele, R., 1968, *Agrarian Revolution and Economic Progress – A Primer for Development*, New York: Praeger.

Scott, J., 1976, *The Moral Economy of the Peasant. Rebellion and Subsistence in Southeast Asia*, New Haven, CT and London: Yale University Press.

Self, P. and H.J. Storing, 1962, *The State and the Farmer*, London: George, Allen & Unwin.

Shei, S.H., 1980, 'Impacts of General Economic Policy on Agricultural Development in Taiwan', in Institute of Economics, Academia Sinica, *Conference on Agricultural Development in China, Japan and Korea*, Taipei.

Shen, T.H., 1968, 'Future Directions in Agricultural Development', *Industry of Free China* (Taipei) Vol.30, No.3.

Shen, T.H., 1970, *The Sino-American Joint Commission on Rural Reconstruction*, Ithaca, NY: Cornell University Press.

Stavis, B., 1974, *Rural Local Governance and Agricultural Development in Taiwan*, Ithaca, NY: Cornell University, Rural Development Committee, Special Series on Rural Local Government No.15.

Tullock, G., 1965, *The Politics of Bureaucracy*, Washington, DC: Public Affairs Press.

Wade, R.W., 1982, *Irrigation and Agricultural Politics in South Korea*, Boulder, CO: Westview Press.

Wade, R.W., 1990, *Governing the Market. Economic Theory and the Role of Government in East Asian Industrialisation*, Princeton, NI: Princeton University Press.

Winckler, E.A., 1988a, 'Mass Political Incorporation, 1500–2000', in E.A. Winckler and S. Greenhalgh (eds.), *Contending Approaches to the Political Economy of Taiwan*, Armonk, NY and London: M.E. Sharpe.

Winckler, E.A., 1988b, 'Elite Political Struggle, 1945–1985', in E.A. Winckler and S.

Greenhalgh (eds.), *Contending Approaches to the Political Economy of Taiwan*, Armonk, NY and London: M.E. Sharpe.

World Bank, 1981, *Accelerated Development in Sub-Saharan Africa. An Agenda for Action*, Washington, DC.

Yager, J.A., 1988, *Transforming Agriculture in Taiwan: The Experience of the Joint Commission on Rural Reconstruction*, Ithaca, NY and London: Cornell University Press.

Reform and Urban Bias in China

JEAN C. OI

Income inequalities between urban and rural areas remain high in China, but the gap has begun to narrow. Peasant incomes have increased dramatically since the post-Mao reforms. Rural areas have new power, but this is a consequence not a cause of the reforms. The improvement in rural conditions reflects a change in the central state's development strategy and ideology, and the local response to incentives embedded in China's reforms. The impetus for these changes is self-preservation of the state and the Chinese Communist Party. The failure to close decisively the income disparities between the urban and rural areas similarly stems from concerns of regime stability and preservation of the party-state.

INTRODUCTION

China exhibits unmistakable signs of urban bias. One recent national survey shows that China has an 'extraordinarily high degree of urban–rural inequality by the standards of other developing countries in Asia.'[1] Whereas the ratio of average urban to rural income is usually well below 2 for other developing countries in Asia, it is 2.42 for China.[2] But China is a case that differs in a number of ways from Lipton's India or the tropical states in Africa that formed the basis of Bates' work [*Lipton, 1977; Bates, 1981*].

Resources are being drained from the rural areas, but unlike Africa, the most dynamic growth is now occurring in the rural sector of the economy, not the urban sector. In the last decade, those in the rural areas have made rapid headway in improving their economic position. Between 1978 and 1990, per capita net income for peasants increased from 133.57 yuan to 629.79 yuan, an average annual increase of 41.4 yuan, up sharply from the 3.2 yuan annual average in the previous 28 years [*Zhang, 1991: 16–17*]. In the first three years of the reform,

The author is Associate Professor of Government, Harvard University. Part of this study will appear in Oi [*1993; forthcoming*]. For their comments on earlier drafts, the author would like to thank Ashutosh Varshney and Andrew Walder.

between 1978–81, per capita rural spending on consumer goods (adjusted for inflation) increased 57 per cent. Most importantly for the purposes of this analysis, the consumption of commodities increased most rapidly in rural, not urban, areas.[3] Tables 1 and 2 show the longer-term increase from 1978 to 1989 in the consumption of various commodities, including food and expensive big-ticket items such as bicycles, colour televisions, refrigerators, and washing machines.

Moreover, industrialisation, the process that usually serves to create urban bias in developing countries, is currently the source of improvement in China's rural areas. China's new rural-based industrialisation accounts for the most rapid growth in the economy since the mid-1980s. It is the wages from work in rural industry that explain the long-term increase in rural incomes noted above, not remittances from those working in urban areas. The growing rural inequality cannot be defined by membership in any particular ethnic or tribal group, geographical location, or participation in special projects devised by central authorities to appease certain sectors of the rural population.

TABLE 1

AGRICULTURAL HOUSEHOLD YEAR–END POSSESSION OF DURABLE
CONSUMER GOODS PER 100 HOUSEHOLDS

Item	1978	1980	1985	1986	1987	1988	1989
Bicycles	30.73	36.87	80.64	90.31	98.52	107.49	113.43
Sewing Machines	19.8	23.31	43.21	46.99	49.79	52.54	53.76
Clocks	24.33	30.95	37.32	50.74	46.92	47.23	48.13
Wristwatches	27.42	37.58	136.32	145.06	161.22	168.9	171.32
Electronic Watches			0	16.13	22.56	25.06	23.49
Electric Fans			9.66	13.63	19.76	28.09	33.96
Washing Machines			1.9	3.22	4.78	6.79	8.15
Refrigerators			0.06	0.2	0.31	0.63	0.89
Motorcycles			0	0.58	0.56	0.91	0.95
Sofas			13.07	18.12	22.93	28.12	33.22
Closets			53.37	59.15	64.27	68.49	72.99
Desks			38.21	43.3	47.18	51.31	53.75
Radio Sets	17.44	33.54	54.19	54.24	52.98	52.17	48.48
Black and White TV Sets		*0.39	10.94	15.76	22.04	28.64	33.91
Color TV Sets			0.8	1.52	2.34	2.8	3.63
Cassette Recorders			4.33	6.6	9.68	13.04	16.23
Cameras				0.33	0.5	0.63	0.79

* This is the total of black and white and colour TV sets.

Source: *China Statistical Yearbook*, *1990*, Beijing: China Statistical Information and Consultancy Service Center, 1990, p.307.

Finally, the development of the rural economy is due primarily to local, not central, initiative. In this article I will show that the central

TABLE 2

AGRICULTURAL HOUSEHOLD PER CAPITA CONSUMPTION OF MAJOR
CONSUMER GOODS

Item	Unit	1978	1980	1985	1986	1987	1988	1989
Grain (unhusked grain)	kg	248	257	257	259	259	260	262
Wheat and Rice	kg	123	163	209	212	211	211	213
Fresh Vegetables	kg	142	127	131	134	130	130	133
Edible Vegetable Oil	kg	1.96	2.49	4.04	4.19	4.69	4.76	4.81
Meat	kg	5.76	7.75	10.97	11.79	11.65	10.71	11
Poultry	kg	0.25	0.66	1.03	1.14	1.15	1.25	1.28
Eggs	kg	0.8	1.2	2.05	2.08	2.25	2.28	2.41
Fish and Shrimp	kg	0.84	1.1	1.64	1.87	1.96	1.91	2.1
Sugar	kg	0.73	1.06	1.46	1.59	1.7	1.41	1.54
Liquor	kg	1.22	1.89	4.37	4.96	5.48	5.93	5.95
Cotton Cloth	m	5.63	4.3	2.54	1.98	1.57	1.5	1.06
Cotton	kg	0.4	0.38	0.43	0.34	0.52	0.32	0.3
Chemical Fiber Cloth	m	0.41	0.94	2.5	2.53	2.28	2.14	1.9
Woolen Fabric	m	0.02	0.06	0.14	0.13	0.12	0.12	0.08
Silk and Satin Cloth	m	0.02	0.06	0.07	0.06	0.05	0.06	0.04
Knitting Wool and Knitwear	kg	0.02	0.05	0.04	0.05	0.07	0.06	0.06
Rubber Shoes, Gym and Leather Shoes	pair	0.32	0.51	0.55	0.66	0.68	0.69	0.67

Source: *China Statistical Yearbook, 1990*, Beijing: China Statistical Information and
Consultancy Service Center, 1990, p.307.

state set in motion a number of reform measures that positively affected
the economic well-being of China's rural inhabitants. These included
revising urban-biased pricing for the procurement of grain and the
loosening of the structure of the rural economy to allow peasants to
diversify to more lucrative cash crops and to engage in non-agricultural
enterprises. However, I will also show that these changes should not be
seen as permanent shifts to a rural bias. The long-term rise in rural
incomes is only a by-product, not a direct consequence, of state intervention on behalf of rural interests. The improvement in the economic
condition of China's rural sector is the result of the efforts of local
officials who are driven neither by urban nor rural bias but by concerns
similar to what Robert Bates terms the 'revenue imperative' [*Bates,
1981*].

In China, local officials have acted to develop the rural economy in
response to the revenue constraints imposed by a bottom–up revenue-
sharing system instituted in the early 1980s that made localities responsible for their own expenses and revenues. Those who have been able
effectively to develop revenue-generating enterprises enjoy the economic returns on their investments and can provide benefits that are
beginning to narrow the urban–rural gap; those who fail have little to

provide the peasants who must continue to endure a low standard of living [*Oi, 1990: 15–36*]. National policies affect the economic well-being of those in rural areas, but the effect of national policies on the rural areas may be mitigated or made worse by the actions of those most immediately and routinely in contact with the rural population.

To understand what has occurred in China's rural areas, one must make an explicit distinction between the central state and its agents. Each is an independent political actor with its own interests and agendas. Those at the local level are capable of diverse independent actions either because of limits on the power of the central government or because the central state allows localities increased autonomy. This autonomy of local political actors is implicit in Nolan and White's critique of urban bias theory when they correctly point out that: 'Chinese peasants are neither unorganised nor inert; they are not captives of the state nor do they lack resources for asserting their interests' [*Nolan and White, 1984: 69*]. But it is not enough to suggest that loopholes exist in the system for the local pursuit of interests. One must incorporate into the analysis the behaviour of local officials as an independent variable capable of determining peasant economic well-being.

In the sections that follow I will first examine the dramatic increase in agricultural income in the first part of the 1980s and its subsequent decline in the mid-1980s. In a later section, I will analyse how the rise of rural industry has increased peasant incomes and has begun to narrow the urban–rural gap in some areas of rural China, despite decreasing agricultural incomes. In the last section, I will consider why the state has not attempted further to close the urban–rural gap.

THE RISE AND FALL OF AGRICULTURAL INCOMES

Beginning in 1979, the Chinese leadership instituted a series of reforms, including increased procurement prices for agricultural crops, decollectivisation of agricultural production, and a return to individual household farming, diversification of the economy, and the reopening of markets. Peasant incomes rose rapidly. This increase came mainly from the price increases in the procurement price paid to peasants for their grain sales to the state [*Travers, 1985: 111–30*]. Grain production increased 27 per cent between 1978 and 1983, with a bumper harvest in 1982 and 1983. By 1983–84, production and procurements reached an all-time historical high, 88 billion jin. State granaries were so full that grain lay rotting on the roadside for lack of adequate storage facilities [*Oi, 1986a: 272–90*]. This allowed rural per-capita income (adjusted for inflation) to show an average annual increase of 11.4 per

FIGURE 1
GRAIN PRODUCTION 1979–91

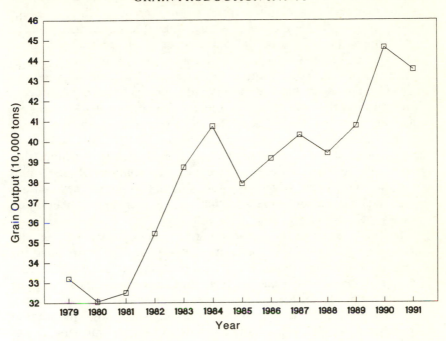

Source: *Zhongguo tongji nainjian 1992*, p.358.

cent between 1978 and 1981, whereas peasant income had increased only 0.5 per cent per year between 1957 and 1977 [*Travers, 1985: 111–30*]. Not surprisingly, rural spending (adjusted for inflation) on consumer goods increased by over 50 per cent from 1978 to 1981. Overall, production of many consumer items increased by at least 100 per cent.[4]

Why were policies favourable to rural interests instituted? This can be seen as an example of rural bias, but in the Chinese case there is no evidence that rural interest groups successfully captured the sympathies of the central leadership or that there was a change in the representation of rural versus urban interests at the seat of power. Those responsible for the major policy changes after 1978 cannot be considered to be a radically new group that clearly represented peasant interests. Likewise, there is little evidence that peasants found new spokesmen for their interests in the upper echelons of power. One can, at most, argue that the experiences of high-ranking cadres during the Cultural Revolution, 1966 to 1976, when many cadres were sent to the farms for hard labour,

perhaps opened their eyes to the plight of the peasant, which in turn
ultimately affected policy. Likewise, there were no dissident political
groups that emerged in either urban or rural areas which successfully
protested against state policies and caused them to be changed. Similar
to the situation described by Bates, the government in China succeeded
in preventing successful overt collective action [*Bates, 1981*].

The political actions by those in the countryside which eventually
persuaded the leadership to undertake the reforms fall into the category
of informal mechanisms by which interests may be pursued. Here, I am
referring to the indirect but none the less effective methods of pursuing
interests through manipulation and circumvention, if not sabotage, of
state policies at the level of implementation. It was such actions that
resulted in the state's failure to extract desired amounts of the surplus
from the countryside. It was the state's failure to increase extractions
when total production increased that forced a change in the state's
policies towards the peasants [*Oi, 1989*].[5]

The combination of the household responsibility system along with
other *material* incentives in the context of the early 1980s provided the
necessary conditions for increased production and sales [*Oi, 1989:
Ch.8*]. Decollectivisation was just beginning, many peasants were 'going
it alone' as producers for the first time. After almost three decades of
collective production when peasants were told when, how, and what to
do each day, not all peasants knew how to be good farmers. It was
certainly not the case that all peasants had the necessary skills to grow
cash crops or engage in animal husbandry. Peasants often remark that
its takes special skills to grow the more lucrative crops, such as watceme-
lon, or to raise chickens or rabbits. It was also a time when there were
few non-agricultural jobs other than those in construction. The growth
of most non-agricultural opportunities, such as work in rural industrial
enterprises, did not appear until about 1984.

Moreover, during the early years of reform, the free markets were
still fairly undeveloped and peasants neither had the information nor the
transport facilities to stray far from their local markets. Markets were
legalised after the Third Plenum (1978) reforms but peasants did not
necessarily first choose the free markets. During the early 1980s when
peasants had few known outlets, selling to the state was a secure and
desirable market opportunity. For example, in 1984 the market price of
grain was lower than the over-quota prices offered by the state. In such
situations, when it was 'difficult to sell grain', peasants vied to sell grain
to the state because of the price as well as for the security.[6]

However, as soon as the context changed and the incentives became
less lucrative than other income alternatives, we see a dramatic change

FIGURE 2
GRAIN ACREAGE 1979–91

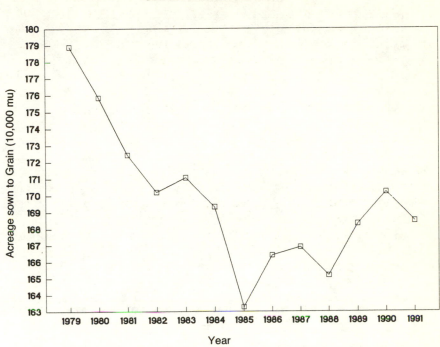

Source: *Zhongguo tongji nainjian 1992*, p.352.

in grain production and the continued impact of the overall urban-biased state policies [*Crook, 1990: 12–15; Crook, 1989a: 9–19*].[7] After steady increases during the first half of the decade, grain production stagnated or declined from the record-breaking harvest of 1984 until 1989.[8] Grain production dropped by 25 million tons in 1985 and failed to surpass the 1984 level until 1989, and even then at lower yields (see Figures 1 and 3). The acreage sown to grain (see Figure 2) has gone down dramatically; and yields per mu of land planted to grain also continued to stagnate (see Figure 3) [*Crook, 1989b*]. The 1989 and 1990 harvests were good, but even at around 412.5 million tons in 1990, grain production did not meet the state-set target of 425 million tons [*Tai, 1990: 54–6*]. A survey of 13,000 peasant households in 155 villages revealed that between 1984 and 1988 the net income from grain production (income from products less production costs) declined 15.6 per cent.

FIGURE 3
GRAIN YIELDS 1979–91

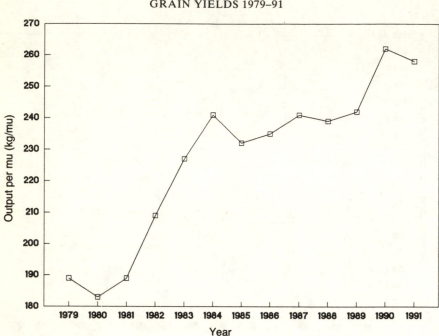

Source: Calculated from *Zhongguo tongji nianjian 1992*, pp. 352, 358.

DECLINING AGRICULTURAL INCOMES: 1985 TO THE PRESENT

With hindsight, it is clear that Deng's agricultural reforms failed to provide a lasting solution to the incentive problem plaguing China's agriculture and to solve the problem of those peasants whose livelihood depended on farming. The problems that I describe below suggest that ultimately the leadership was unwilling to change the economic context and shift its allocation of resources to favour agricultural production and rural interests and was unable to ensure that the protective measures that it did try to institute to protect rural interests were actually implemented.

Pricing Structure

The central state is directly responsible for reducing peasant income to the extent that it abolished the system of unified procurements that had been in effect since the mid-1950s. This policy change, however, is not a case of urban bias. Rather it was to protect the fiscal interests of the central state itself, not to favour the urban sector. In theory this policy also was not intended to harm rural interests. A case can be made that it would, at least in theory, help reduce the burden of having to sell grain to the state.

The unified procurement system, almost from its inception, was a dreaded burden on the peasants. One of the few times that this was not a burden was during the period after 1979 when there was both an abundance of grain and high procurement prices, especially in 1983–84 when there were record harvests. The problem was that the state was obligated to pay the peasants the high over-quota price for all grain above the basic quota amount. At times this over-quota price was higher than the market price. It was during this period when the state had more grain than it knew what to do with that it decided to relieve itself of the financial burden and limit the amount of grain it would buy from the peasants at a set price. Thus in 1985 the central authorities instituted a contract procurement system and restructured the price ratio for quota and over-quota grain sales [Oi, 1986a: 272–90].

The end result for peasants was a mixed blessing. Those who only wished to sell the quota amount to the state benefitted from the restructuring and new price system. The same, however, was not true for those who wanted to sell more than the quota. A study done by a research group under the State Council has shown that many peasants received, on the whole, less income than before for selling their increased output.[9] In 1990 the state further cut the basic quota purchase amount from 75 to 50 million tons. This further hurt peasants because market prices for grain were already low due to the abundant harvests [Tai, 1990: 54–6].

Scissors Effect

As the 1980s progressed, the income of peasants also suffered from the rapidly rising costs of production inputs – a problem common in countries known to have urban bias. The prices for agricultural inputs increased faster than procurement prices. According to one study, the rise in the price ratios between industrial and agricultural goods during 1984–87 deprived the peasants of 37 billion yuan from sales of agricultural goods to the state. The state would need to increase prices between 15 and 20 per cent to bring the price ratios to the 1984 level [Rural Capital Task Force, 1990: 20–25].

Unlike the price for grain, the high costs of inputs was not due to any new legislation by the state. Rather, in this instance, a good part of the problem was the malfunctioning and manipulation of the state distribution system at the local levels. In theory, the input and price problems are compensated for by state provision of scarce and expensive inputs, such as fertiliser and diesel fuel, at low rationed prices, which are given as a bonus for selling to the state. This prospect made state contracts reasonably attractive. The problem was that in many areas the state failed to make good its part of the bargain because of the corruption in the administration of the system at local levels.[10] Peasants sold the grain to the state, but then failed to get the promised inputs from the state [*Oi, 1986b: 230–51*]. This forced peasants either to buy on the open market at much higher prices or not to apply as much fertiliser, which then decreased incomes as the size of harvests declined.[11] To get the recent increase in production, the state had to mandate an increase in the acreage sown to grain.[12]

IOUs

Peasants also suffered when they failed to be paid for the grain they delivered to the state granaries. Instead of getting cash, in a number of areas, particularly during 1988–89, peasants were issued 'white slips' (*baitiao*) – that is, IOUs.[13] Peasants were required to deliver their grain as usual, but they had to wait before they could get cash for their sales.

Was this a case of urban bias? It is difficult to trace the problem to any conscious decision by the central state to favour urban residents; it certainly was not state policy not to pay peasants. The central state, in fact, once realising the anger the IOUs were causing, issued a ban on white slips. This only forced some localities simply to stop buying grain until there were more funds. Peasants were still left in the situation of being stuck with their grain and short of money. Some local authorities continued to buy grain and technically avoided 'white slips' by crediting the savings accounts of the peasants selling the grain at the local savings and loan co-operatives (*xinyong she*). The catch was that peasants had to wait three months to use the money.[14] As with the lack of state-supplied rationed goods, the problem was not with central policies but with implementation at the local levels.

But the cause of this problem can be attributed to the central state's need to ensure increasing supplies of low-priced grain and at the same time its desire to protect its state-owned industrial enterprises,[15] most of which were located in the urban areas. In 1988–89 the central state engaged in a general retrenchment effort. Part of the goal was to free up funds for procurements to resolve the IOU problem. To do this the central state cut loans to other sectors of the rural economy. The chosen target for cut-backs was rural industry, which was seen as the cause of the overheating of the economy, and also happened to be increasingly competitive with the state-owned industrial enterprises for markets and raw materials.

Because credit is given by planned allocations to a locality and because of increasing pressures on localities due to the fiscal reforms that made local spending dependent on locally generated revenues (see below), the cut-backs to rural industry evolved into a major problem that forced local officials to make strategic choices regarding where to use their limited supply of credit. The choices made by many local governments are reflected in statistics which show the shift in investment from agriculture. Despite the fact that local economies were growing, local capital investment in agriculture as a percentage of total investment declined from 39.6 per cent in 1982 to 9.4 per cent in 1988 [*Rural Capital Task Force, 1990: 20–25*]. The decline in the use of rural enterprise funds for either township or village-owned industries has been particularly sharp. If one compares the percentage invested in 1979 to that in 1988, there is a 71.6 per cent decline. Disaggregating that figure, one finds that from 1979 to 1983, when the communes still existed, the amount of subsidies from industry to agriculture averaged about 3.3 billion yuan each year. But from 1984 to 1988, after the communes were disbanded and township enterprises developed rapidly, subsidies averaged only 1.54 billion yuan per year [*Rural Capital Task Force, 1990: 20–25*].

The investment policy of the central state in agriculture clearly has consistently shown an urban bias. Since 1949 agriculture has almost always received a relatively small share of central capital expenditures. The trend, however, has worsened since the beginning of the reforms in the late 1970s. Official statistics show that central-level investment in agriculture has declined significantly from the beginning of the 1980s. For example, in 1980 it constituted over nine per cent, by 1988 it was only three per cent of total investments (see Figure 4) [*Nongye nianjian, 1989: 9*].

The centre tried to counter the effects of this urban-biased development strategy by shifting the burden to the localities. A recent study done by the Ministry of Agriculture points to the great increase of collective funds at the local level and advocates the use of these funds as the solution to the agricultural stagnation [*Rural Capital Task Force, 1990: 20–25*]. Up until the latter half of 1988, localities were encouraged to develop agriculture and use their funds to support agriculture, under various policies such as 'using industry to support agriculture', although the central government took no direct actions that effectively channelled local funds from industry to agriculture. The situation changed dramatically in the later half of 1988 when the central state proclaimed that more funds should be allocated for procurements in particular, and for the agricultural sector in general. The IOU phenomenon was one outcome of the conflict between the centre wanting to reallocate credit and procurements to agriculture and the localities needing to protect their local enterprises. During this period of fiscal austerity, when it was

FIGURE 4
AGRICULTURAL INVESTMENT

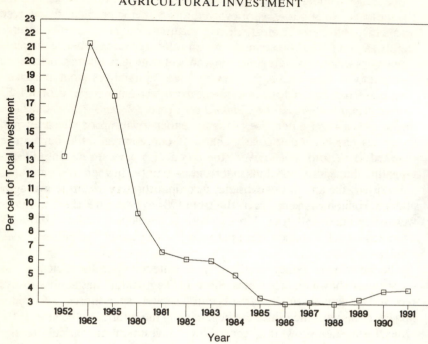

Source: Zhongguo tongji nianjian 1992, p.158; *Zhongguo nongye nianjian 1989*, p.9.

that much more imperative for local government officials to use whatever funds were available for the development of the income-generating
enterprises, local governments diverted funds intended for agriculture
to industry to get higher returns.[16] Agriculture generated almost no
direct income for local governments. Unlike the land which also belongs
to the collective, those factories that are contracted out to individuals to
manage pay rent to the local authorities as well as various fees and
taxes. The term 'cash registers' of local governments sums up nicely the
relationship of local governments to their rural enterprises [*Oi, 1992*].

THE RISE OF RURAL INDUSTRY AND PEASANT INCOMES

Let us now turn to why rural incomes overall increased dramatically
throughout the 1980s despite the declines in returns from agriculture.
Here I will discuss the increasing industrialisation of the Chinese
countryside. In contrast to the disappointing performance in grain pro-

duction, rural industry has been a continuing success story. Why it took off and who was responsible sheds light on the factors that are most important in determining rural income during the reform period.

The green light given by the central authorities for localities to diversify and engage in non-agricultural activity was a crucial first step in the rise of rural industry. The post-Mao leadership made it possible for peasants as well as local authorities who control investment funds to make broader calculations with regard to increasing income and revenues. They no longer were forced to grow grain and rely primarily on returns from grain sales to the state. Investment could be decided based on relative returns compared to other income sources and sales opportunities. Peasants freed from dependence on the commune and grain production increasingly chose to pursue other more lucrative sources of employment, such as growing cash crops, forestry, animal husbandry, fishing and, perhaps, most importantly, work in non-agricultural industry.[17]

Second, once the fiscal reforms were instituted by the reform leadership the problem facing local authorities was how best to generate revenues. Local officials had to become entrepreneurs to ensure their own survival and advance their power [Oi, 1992]. The central authorities wanted to get localities to develop their local economies and generate revenue by making each level of government fiscally self-sufficient – or as the Chinese colloquially phrase it, have each 'eat from separate kitchens'. Each level of government down to the township level was made responsible for its revenues and expenditures, after meeting a tax quota to the next higher level of government. As a result, revenues, income, and returns became as important to local governments as to individuals. The central state encouraged the diversification of the economy and the fiscal reforms forced local governments to find new revenue-generating activities to fund local coffers.

Whether or not to develop rural industry and shift investment to industry was a local-level decision. Consequently, the rapid growth of rural industry and the benefits that it brought cannot easily be categorised as either urban or rural biased. The motives driving this development are suggested by Bates' discussion of the 'revenue imperative' [Bates, 1981]. Rural enterprises yielded the most lucrative returns. Growing in leaps and bounds since the mid-1980s, rural enterprises (xiangzhen qiye)[18] have become the most profitable sector of the rural economy. Increasingly, income from these enterprises has kept many a local government afloat.[19] By 1987 industry had already surpassed agriculture as the dominant source of rural income [State Statistical Bureau, 1988: 214]. In 1987 alone it produced close to 300 billion yuan in income, over 35 per cent of the total rural output, and 16 billion yuan in taxes – twice as much as the agricultural tax. The total gross value of output generated by rural enterprises rose more than ninefold from 49 billion yuan in 1980 to 474 billion yuan in 1987 [*Crook, 1989a*]. In 1988, the total output value rose another 36 per cent and constituted well over 50 per cent of the total rural output and almost a quarter of the total national output. Total revenues (taxes and profits paid to the state) rose over 40 per cent from 1987, taxes alone increased 44 per cent from 1987, with net profits increasing 35.6 per cent.

As an added bonus for rural governments, rural enterprises can absorb the increasing surplus labour created by decollectivisation [*Nongye nianjian, 1989: 19*]. In 1988 alone, the number of workers employed rose almost 8.5 per cent [*Nongye nianjian, 1989: 19*]. The total rural labour force engaged in village and township enterprises rose from 9.5 to 23.83 per cent [*Huang, 1990: 39–46*]. Moreover, the jobs provided by rural industry are lucrative employment opportunities for peasants within the community and for those from nearby areas. During the period from 1984 to 1988 the return in terms of net income per workday increased 45.9 per cent for participation in non-agricultural industries – compared to the 15.1 per cent return for grain [*Sun, 1990: 16–24*]. Many jobs in rural enterprises also have the advantage that peasants need not have any special skills to undertake such work, unlike the skills required to engage in cash cropping.[20]

RURAL INDUSTRY AND NARROWING OF THE URBAN–RURAL GAP

The tremendous growth of rural industry and the economic benefits that it has brought to people in rural areas would be masked, however, if one accepted the finding that there is urban bias in China. The high degree of inequality that I cited in the introduction masks the activity within the rural areas that eventually may alleviate many of the problems that appear as urban bias, that is, the poor economic situation of the rural population. Unlike many developing countries, China seems to have successfully embarked on a course of development that is creating industrial, urban situations and opportunities within the so-called 'rural areas'. Industrialisation, the goal that lies at the root of much urban bias in developing countries, has been occurring most rapidly during the reform period in the rural areas. This type of development offers a number of alternatives that make the situation much more positive than the theory of urban bias would predict.

The theory of urban bias has long been subject to the criticism that it is difficult to draw the line between urban and rural [*Moore, 1984:*

102–22]. The income from rural enterprises and the benefits that it has been able to finance in the rural areas makes it increasingly difficult to draw a clear line between urban and rural in China after the mid-1980s. The term 'rural' has taken on new meaning. In China, since the mid-1980s, about the time of the publication of the Nolan and White article, the character of the Chinese countryside began to change significantly. The structure of the rural economy began shifting from agriculture to industry. Many who live in the countryside are now officially designated 'agricultural' only because of the continued use of the Maoist household registration system, which uses the designation 'agricultural household' (*nongye hukou*) and 'non-agricultural household' to distinguish between those who are entitled to live legally in urban areas (and therefore have access to subsidised grain allocations) and those who are not. In reality, however, an increasing number of 'agricultural households' do not engage in agriculture as their primary source of income. An increasing number of 'agricultural households' now work in rural industry – relegating agriculture to a *sideline enterprise*.

The rapid growth of rural enterprises and the revenues that have accrued to local governments have served to narrow the gap between urban and rural areas and is beginning to counter the overall urban bias that still exists. Wages in some rural factories now come close to rivalling those in urban areas. Moreover, those working in rural enterprises are most likely to receive subsidies that supplement their income and improve their standard of living. Elsewhere I have shown that in areas where rural industry is highly developed, there is a substantial amount of income redistribution and provision of subsidies [*Oi, 1990: 15–36*]. For example, recent survey data reveal that the significant determinant of health insurance is not whether one is an urban or rural resident but whether one works for a state-owned enterprise, that is, organisations known to provide subsidies [*Henderson et al., 1992*]. Many of these state-owned enterprises are in urban areas, but it is not their urban location that predicts benefits. Those in urban areas that do not work in state enterprises are no more likely to have access to health insurance. Next to those who work in state-owned enterprises, it is those in *rural* areas who work in wealthy township or village enterprises who are the most likely to have health insurance.

The problem that remains, however, is that at the same time that the revenues from rural industry are ameliorating urban bias, they are also creating greater inequality *within* rural China. Wages from rural industry have served to promote inequality of rural incomes. According to a 1988 survey, 62 per cent of income from wages is received by the richest ten per cent of individuals. The poorest 20 per cent of the population receives only one per cent of their income from wages. The Gini ratio of inequality *within* rural China is 0.338 [*Khan et al., 1992*].

URBAN BIAS AND THE POWER OF THE COMMUNIST STATE

Despite the progress that some rural areas are making in closing the urban–rural gap, the central state still perpetuates it. Let me conclude this study by considering why the central Chinese state continues the various subsidies that urban residents receive, ranging from low-priced grain to inexpensive housing. Each year the central Chinese state is burdened by the billions of yuan that it spends on grain subsidies for urban residents, who pay less for their grain than the government spends on procurement.[21] In 1992, 14 per cent of China's national budget was spent on food subsidies [*Reuters, 1992*].

Subsidies received by urban residents account for a substantial portion of the urban–rural income inequality [*Oi, 1990: 15–36*]. Researchers have long recognised the economic benefits of the 'unit' (*danwei*) system in urban China, especially in large state-owned factories [*Henderson and Cohen, 1984; Walder, 1986*]. Westerners have often commented on the low cost of urban housing, a dollar or two a month for rent. Khan *et al.* have been able to put a value on the subsidies that urban residents receive. They have found that aggregate subsidies account for 39 per cent of urban income, with the subsidy on public housing being the largest component of urban subsidies (18 per cent) [*Khan et al., 1992*]. The largest single source (44 per cent)[22] of urban income that accounts for the inequality is wages. However, it is when the value of these subsidies to urban residents are calculated with wages that one fully appreciates the magnitude of the advantaged position urban residents have compared to that of those in the countryside.

The obvious solution in the case of grain would be to raise the procurement price – this would certainly undue one of the key indicators of urban bias. But such a solution would require that consumer prices for grain would also be raised to absorb the costs of procurement. This is, of course, where China is stalled and this is where a political decision will have to be made.

Obviously this is a case of urban bias, but the reasons why the central Chinese state is continuing to favour the urban areas lies not in the political activity of any particular interest group in society. Unlike Africa and other developing countries, there is no identifiable group of urban elites that has shaped policy. Likewise, there is no rural elite that has been bought off in order to pass policies detrimental to the mass of the rural population. The group that monopolises policy is the Chinese

Communist Party. In China it is the party's concern for its own *survival* and *legitimacy* that keeps it from making more radical reforms. The urban-biased policies are the insurance policies the regime buys to ensure that those in the urban areas, most importantly the workers, will refrain from political activity that will endanger the stability of the regime. Viewed from another angle, the same bias also reflects the revenue imperative in the shaping of political decisions. It is action by the central state to ensure that workers continue on the job in the large state-owned enterprises that still constitutes the single most important source of revenue for the central budget.

Similar fears have kept rationing and central distribution alive, despite efforts to expand the market.[23] The central government does not want to give up control of the economy. In this case the state is distrustful of relying on market regulation of the economy. The fact that the main benefactors of the rationing system are in the urban areas is a coincidence. This is where most of the large state-owned enterprises are located. It is the profits of the state-owned factories that the central state seems most concerned with protecting, as much as the urban workers who are employed there.

What is ironic is that, despite the centre's attempts to appease the urban sector and maintain urban-biased policies, it is the rural sector that now enjoys new resources to pursue its interests. The fiscal reforms that were instituted to enliven the economy and provide incentives for economic development have also legitimised the retention and autonomy of locally retained revenues. I have shown that the local development effort has resulted in the narrowing of the urban–rural gap. What is perhaps of greater long-term political significance is that this same economic development has inadvertently opened the door to greater political power for the localities to pursue their interests independent of the center's policies [*Oi, 1991*]. Ultimately, this may act as a challenge to the central state's ability to control the economy and society. What must be remembered is that this new power of the rural areas is a *consequence*, not a cause, of the reforms that have begun to narrow the urban–rural gap in China.

NOTES

1. This was a 1988 survey of over 10,000 rural households in 28 provinces and over 9,000 urban households in ten provinces [*Khan et al., 1992: 3*]. A fuller version of [*Khan et al., 1992: 3*] is forthcoming in the *China Quarterly*. On the Maoist era see, for example, Nolan and White [*1984: 52–82*]; Lardy [*1983*]; and Oi [*1989*].
2. This number is higher than that based on the Chinese State Statistical Bureau (SSB)

number, but even if one bases it on the SSB number, it is still 2.19. The difference is due to what Khan *et al.* believe is an underestimation by the SSB of both urban and rural incomes.

3. For further documentation and details see Oi [*1989: Ch.8*].
4. This restructuring of the economy was a key incentive needed to accompany the price increases. For further details and documentation, see Oi [*1989: Ch.8*].
5. It should also be noted that the political climate was ripe for change after the death of Mao Zedong in 1976.
6. The problem of the 'difficulty of selling grain' was not limited to 1983–84. In areas with abundant harvests or those that no longer have funds to continue procurements, peasants still are finding it difficult to sell their grain [*Nongmin ribao, 1990: 2*].
7. Delman [*1989: 42–64*] provides a nicely detailed examination of some of the more technical aspects of the input problems.
8. During this period production costs increased 20.7 per cent, but income increased only eight per cent [*Sun, 1990: 16–24*].
9. The study found that income was reduced by ten per cent [*Oi, 1989*].
10. In areas where the promise of production inputs acts as an effective incentive – where the government has consistently provided the promised inputs – peasants and local officials still turn to grain production as an economically rational use of labour. Grain production remains a prime source of employment [*Rozelle*, nd].
11. While there has been no appreciable decrease in the use of chemical fertiliser, there has been a decrease in the use of manure, which is more burdensome to apply but which has greater benefit to the long-term health of the soil. The use of expensive plastic mulch and pesticides has decreased [*Sun, 1990: 16–24*]. The price of plastic mulch has risen from 2,400 yuan to 6,000 yuan, to as much as 10,000 yuan per ton [*Wu Huien et al., 1990: 3–5, 27–30*].
12. According to the Ministry of Agriculture, 60 per cent of the increased grain production in 1990 was due to the increase in sown acreage [*Tai, 1990: 54–6*].
13. This problem was fairly widespread, although some local officials are reluctant to admit that such problems occurred in their area. Delman [*1989: 42–64*] cites a *Nongmin ribao* article that states that in May 1989 national procurement agencies only had half of the funds needed for procuring the spring harvest.
14. This occurred in one county in Shandong, in 1988 (author's interviews, China, 1990).
15. In China there are three types of enterprises: state-owned, collective-owned, and individual or jointly owned. The state-owned enterprises are generally the largest and those upon which the planned economy is dependent. They enjoy the largest degree of support from the central state.
16. This is not the total explanation for the use of IOUs but it helps explain why some localities ran out of funds when special funds were provided. For details on how money was diverted see Oi [*1991*].
17. The disparity between the relative returns from growing grain and cash crops, forestry, animal husbandry, fishing and non-agricultural industry is substantial. For example, during the period 1984–88 the return in terms of net income per workday increased only 15.1 per cent for grain, but the return from cash crops increased 96.5 per cent [*Sun, 1990: 16–24*].
18. This category includes businesses and industries that belong to township or village governments as well as individual and jointly owned companies. The following statistics include all four categories. However, the collectively owned enterprises are the ones that are the largest and produce the most revenue. In the following discussion I will be focusing on the collectively owned, that is, township and village-owned enterprises unless otherwise noted.
19. For an extended discussion of why local governments have pursued rural industry and the details of revenue extraction see Oi [*1992*].
20. Some peasants have more opportunities than others to pursue these non-agricultural jobs; the growth of rural enterprises varies in different parts of the country. However, despite the differences in rates of development, the number of areas with sizeable

output is increasing. By 1988, 46.6 per cent of all counties in China (1,319 counties) had rural enterprises whose output value had exceeded 100 million yuan, some of which were ten times or more that amount [*Nongye nianjian, 1989: 20*].
21. For a provincial perspective see Wu Yunbo *et al.* [*1990: 20–27*].
22. This number is 51 per cent if the cash income of retired working members is included [*Khan et al., 1992*].
23. The central government has recently eliminated grain rationing in some locations, including in the capital, Beijing. Workers in some enterprises in Beijing will receive a 10 yuan subsidy a month to 'safeguard' their interests, FBIS–CHI–93–088, 10 May 1993, p. 29.

REFERENCES

Bates, Robert, 1981, *Markets and States in Tropical Africa: The Political Basis of Agricultural Policies*, Berkeley, CA: University of California Press.
Chinese Association of Agricultural Students and Scholars, 1989, *First Conference Proceedings*, Ithaca, NY.
Crook, Frederick, 1989a, 'Current Problems and Future Development of China's Agricultural Sector', in Chinese Association of Agricultural Students and Scholars.
Crook, Frederick, 1989b, *China: Agriculture and Trade Report*, Washington, DC: Economic Research Service, Department of Agriculture.
Crook, Frederick, 1990, 'Defusing Peasant Discontent', *The China Business Review* (July–Aug.), pp.12–15.
Davis, Deborah and Ezra Vogel (eds.), 1990, *Chinese Society on the Eve of Tiananmen: The Impact of Reform*, Cambridge, MA: Council on East Asian Studies, Harvard University.
Delman, Jorgen, 1989, 'Current Peasant Discontent in China: Backgrounds and Political Implications', *China Information*, Vol.4, No.2 (Autumn), pp.42–64.
Henderson, Gail and Myron S. Cohen, 1984, *The Chinese Hospital: A Socialist Work Unit*, New Haven, CT: Yale University Press.
Henderson, Gail, Akin, John, Li Zhiming, Jin Shuigao, Wang Jianmin and Ge Keyou, 1992, 'Gender and Welfare Benefits in China: The Distribution of Health Insurance Coverage', paper presented to conference on 'Engendering China: Women, Culture, and the State' held at Harvard University, 7–9 Feb.
Huang Shouhong, 1990, 'Town and Township Enterprises as a Motive Force in the Development of the National Economy', *Jingji yanjiu*, No.5 (20 May), pp.39–46 (translated in JPRS–CAR–90–066, 29 Aug. 1990, pp.34–42).
Khan, Azizur Rahman *et al.*, 1992, 'Sources of Income Inequality in Post-Reform China', paper presented to the Annual Meeting of the Association of Asian Studies.
Lardy, Nicholas, 1983, *Agriculture in China's Modern Economic Development*, Cambridge: Cambridge University Press.
Lipton, Michael, 1977, *Why the Poor Stay Poor: A Study of Urban Bias in World Development*, London: Temple Smith.
Moore, Mick, 1984, 'Categorising Space: Urban–Rural or Core–Periphery in Sri Lanka', *Journal of Development Studies*, Vol.25, No.3, pp.102–22.
Nolan, Peter and Gordon White, 1984, 'Urban Bias, Rural Bias or State Bias? Urban–Rural Relations in Post-Revolutionary China', *Journal of Development Studies*, Vol.20, No.3, pp.55–82.
Nongmin ribao, 1990, 'Why Peasant Households Have So Much Grain' (30 May), p.2 (translated in JPRS–CAR–90–055, 26 July 1990, p.79).
Oi, Jean, 1986a, 'Peasant Grain Marketing and State Procurement: China's Contracting System', *China Quarterly*, No.106 (June), pp.272–90.
Oi, Jean, 1986b, 'Peasant Households Between Plan and Market: Cadre Control Over Agricultural Inputs', *Modern China*, Vol.12, No.2 (April), pp.230–51.
Oi, Jean, 1989, *State and Peasant in Contemporary China: The Political Economy of*

Village Government, Berkeley, CA: University of California Press.
Oi, Jean, 1990, 'The Fate of the Collective After the Commune', in Davis and Vogel, pp.15–36.
Oi, Jean, 1991, 'Fiscal Reform, Central Directives, and Local Autonomy in Rural China', paper presented to the Annual Meeting of the American Political Science Association.
Oi, Jean, 1992, 'Fiscal Reform and the Economic Foundations of Local State Corporatism in China', *World Politics*, Vol.45, No.1 (Oct.), pp.99–126.
Oi, Jean, 1993 (forthcoming), 'Chinese Agriculture: Modernization, But at What Costs', in Robinson and Lin.
Perry, Elizabeth and Christine Wong (eds.), 1985, *The Political Economy of Reform in Post-Mao China*, Cambridge, MA: Council on East Asian Studies, Harvard University.
Reuters, 1992, 'China to Keep Grain Rationing to Protect Poor', *China News Daily* (15 April).
Robinson, Thomas and Lin Zhiling (eds.), 1993, *The Chinese and Their Future: Beijing, Taipei, and Hong Kong*, Lanham, MD: AEI Press.
Rozelle, Scott, nd., 'Principals and Agents in China's Rural Economy: A Decision Making Framework of Township Officials, Village Leaders and Farm Households', Stanford, CA: Food Research Institute, Stanford University.
Rural Capital Task Force, Cooperative Economy Administration and Management Home Office, Ministry of Agriculture, 1990, 'Yindao nongcun zijin zengjia nongye touru', *Nongye jingji wenti*, No.4 (23 April), pp.20–25.
State Statistical Bureau, 1988, *Zhongguo tongji nianjian, 1988*, Beijing: Zhongguo tongji chubanshe.
Sun Zhonghua, 1990, '1984–1988 nian liangshi shengchande weiguan tanshi', *Zhongguo nongcun jingji*, No.3 (20 March), pp.16–24.
Tai Ming Cheung, 1990, 'China's Grain Yields Fall Short of Targets: Harvest of Woes', *Far Eastern Economic Review* (30 Aug.), pp.54–6.
Travers, Lee, 1985, 'Getting Rich Through Diligence: Peasant Income After the Reforms', in Perry and Wong, pp. 111–30.
Walder, Andrew, 1986, *Communist Neo-Traditionalism: Work and Authority in Chinese Industry*, Berkeley, CA: University of California Press.
Wu Huien *et al.* (eds.), 1990, 'Study of Law of Motion of Productivity for the Purpose of Spurring Reform and Development of Agriculture: Theoretical Ideas and Policy Conceptions for the Development of Agricultural Productivity', *Kexuexue yu kexue jishu guanli*, No.2, pp.3–5 and No.3, pp.27–30 (translated in JPRS–CAR-90–048, 5 July 1990, pp.72–80).
Wu Yunbo *et al.*, 1990, 'Study of Remedies to Reduce Grain Business Losses in Heilongjiang Province', *Zhongguo nongcun jingji*, No.5 (20 May), pp.20–27 (translated in JPRS–CAR-90–064, 17 Aug. 1990, pp.46–53).
Zhang Hongyu, 1991, 'China's Land System Transformation and Adjustment of Agricultural Structure: Reviewing China's Rural Reform and Development Since 1978', *Liaowang* (overseas ed.), No.47 (Nov.), pp.16–17 (translated in FBIS–CHI-91–241, 16 Dec. 1991, pp.52–54).
Zhongguo nongye nianjian 1989, 1989, Beijing: Nongye chubanshe.

Rural Bias in the East and South-east Asian Rice Economy: Indonesia in Comparative Perspective

C. PETER TIMMER

This study analyses the rise in protection of rice farmers in East and South-east Asia since 1960. A statistical model of price formation is tested for Japan, South Korea, Malaysia, the Philippines and Indonesia. On average, about 90 per cent of variation in rice prices in these five countries – relative to the world price – can be an attributed to efforts at price stabilisation rather than farmer protection (or discrimination in earlier periods). The shift from urban bias to rural bias is more a result of price stabilisation and declining real rice prices in world markets than basic shifts in political economy.

All Asian countries that have made the transition from poor agricultural society to rich industrial exporter have found the transformation to be very painful for their farmers, especially their rice farmers who make up the bulk of the rural population and who produce the society's staple food. To compensate these farmers for their loss in economic competitiveness and relatively sudden fall in status as the traditional core of cultural and economic values, the most successful Asian countries have systematically protected rice cultivation from cheap foreign competition. This protection has uniformly taken the form of higher domestic prices for rice than the prevailing price in the world market. In some cases the resulting distortions have been quite severe.

During much of the 1980s, the price of rice in Japan was more than eight times higher than the border price, and land prices, labour allo-

C. Peter Timmer is Thomas D. Cabot Professor of Development Studies, At-Large Harvard University. An early version of this study was presented as a paper at the International Conference on the Economic Policy Making Process in Indonesia, Bali, 6–9 September 1990, sponsored by the Asia Foundation. The author, who is responsible for the content of the study, including any errors and omissions, would like to thank Walter P. Falcon, Peter Lindert, and Bill Liddle for very helpful criticism of an early draft and Carol Timmer for her usual insistence that every sentence contribute clearly and effectively to the argument.

cations, rural investments, and foreign trade have been significantly affected. The closed Japanese border for rice has especially exacerbated tensions with the United States, which has surplus rice to sell at the same time that it has a large trade deficit with Japan. Price policy for rice has also been an item of dispute with South Korea, Taiwan, Malaysia, and the Philippines, all of which have protected their rice farmers from foreign competition since at least the mid-1980s.

Indonesia seems to be embarked on a similar path of export-oriented industrialisation. One consequence of such a growth strategy is declining competitiveness of the very small-scale rice farmers who make up the single largest component of the labour force. Through much of the 1980s, rice prices in Indonesia were above the relevant border price. Asian countries, who earlier embarked on a path of growth led by industrial exports, encountered substantial economic and political costs along this transition path, costs which always involved significant protection of rice farmers. This is an appropriate time to ask how Indonesia might manage its own transition away from a rice-based economy toward a broader economy based on services and industrial production, especially one with a high degree of outward orientation.

Indonesia has four potential choices with regard to a policy for the price of rice. The government could tax its rice farmers, the country's single largest block of producers, to finance its industrialisation effort and reap the political benefits of keeping food prices low for consumers. Alternatively, it could protect farmers from foreign competition in order to stimulate increases in crop productivity, rural incomes, and provide a stronger domestic base for food security; as a result of such a policy, consumers would pay higher prices for rice on average. If neither bias is desirable, price stabilisation around the trend in world prices would provide food security at the national level without distorting either producer or consumer decisions in the long run. A last possibility is no policy at all. Rice prices in domestic markets would fluctuate freely with those in world markets, thus garnering all the supposed benefits of free trade without either the costs to the government of market interventions or to the economy of misallocated resources.

Because of the importance of rice to government policy-makers interested in economic growth and political stability and to producers and consumers, these alternatives raise fundamental issues at the core of Indonesia's long-term development strategy. As the country nears the end of its fifth Five-Year Development Plan in 1994, these issues take on even greater importance because of the rapid structural transformation of the economy brought about since the late 1960s. This transformation has occurred in the context of one of the most stable visions of a development strategy – and continuity of policy-makers to carry it out – among all developing countries. Rapid economic change accompanying a stable policy approach is an apparent paradox that needs explaining. The policy debate around the setting of domestic rice prices is an ideal vehicle for the attempt.

The approach is straightforward. This study briefly reviews the basic approaches to commodity price formation and examines the institutional context in which Indonesian rice prices (and fertiliser prices) are set. The key actors are BULOG (the food logistics agency), BAPPENAS (the national planning agency), EKUIN (the Coordinating Ministry for Economics, Finance, and Industry), the Ministry of Finance, and the Ministry of Agriculture. President Suharto personally is the final arbiter of an annual debate over the floor price for rice, which is defended by BULOG procurement.[1]

An analytical approach that is now routine for the government organises this debate. Rice prices and fertiliser prices are analysed for their joint impact on the balance between rice production and consumption. This balance is a major factor determining BULOG's stocks and its ability to stabilise rice prices without resort to large-scale imports. The budgetary impact of the price recommendations is also scrutinised, especially to find ways to reduce the large fertiliser subsidy. In addition, the costs of rice rations for civil service and military personnel and funding for BULOG are important issues for the budget. The decision each year by the President factors all these issues into account, although there seems to be growing emphasis on increasing farm income and ensuring that production is large enough for self-sufficiency in rice to be maintained.[2]

The core of the study is an analysis of how East and South-east Asian countries set their domestic rice prices in relation to international (or border) prices. The argument in the current academic paradigm of neo-classical political economy is that farmers tend to receive more protection as consumer incomes rise and the share of rice in household budgets falls to insignificant levels. The rise in farmer protection, often after prolonged urban bias that favours consumers with low food prices, is thought to reflect changes in the balance of political economy in the country. These changes reflect the greater ease of building political coalitions with the farm population shrinking, reduction in free rider problems, and the lower political costs to elected officials of supplying such protection [Anderson and Hayami, 1986; Lindert, 1991].

The analysis conducted here takes a different approach. Even a casual observer of the Asian rice scene comes away impressed by the extreme instability of prices in the world rice market and by efforts of all governments to prevent that instability from penetrating their borders. How much does the desire for price stability for rice explain the observed behaviour of domestic rice prices, in relation to the world market price? The model developed here specifies that question in statistical terms and tests it for Japan, South Korea, Malaysia, the Philippines, and Indonesia. The results are surely startling: on average, about 90 per cent of the variation in rice prices in these five countries, in relation to the world price, can be attributed to efforts at stabilisation rather than protection (or discrimination in earlier periods) of farmers.

Differences in levels of national income help explain the degree of price stability a country can afford and help explain the switch in policy to parity of real income for rice farmers relative to those of urban workers.[3] After this switch, price stabilisation on behalf of the entire economy is no longer the primary force influencing rice prices. But in the early stages of development, per capita income, and the closely related share of rice in household expenditures, do not explain a large proportion of changes in the domestic price of rice. For this task, the stabilisation model is much more robust.[4]

These results provide the backdrop for considering Indonesia's experience with stabilising rice prices. The country fits well into the overall Asian pattern in view of its low income level compared with incomes in the Philippines, Malaysia, South Korea, and Japan. Does this fit into a regional and historical pattern of economic policy mean the country has no 'freedom' to set its own price policy? Are Indonesian policy-makers merely captive to broader forces? Not entirely, although the question of historical determinism has been raised before in attempting to understand the formation of Indonesia's rice policy [*Timmer, 1975*]. The study closes with a consideration of the opportunities for Indonesian policy-makers to strike an independent path in pursuit of specifically stated objectives and the dangers that lurk on that path.

MODELS OF PRICE FORMATION

Central to any discussion of price policy is the border price, the price for the commodity in international markets, with suitable adjustments made for transportation costs and quality to make the delivered commodity competitive with the domestic commodity under discussion.[5] For the purposes here, the price of rice in the Bangkok market provides the standard against which the domestic rice price is measured.[6] By assumption, if no policies are introduced to alter domestic prices, competition from the international market will force equality between the border price and the domestic price for rice. With no price interventions, the nominal protection coefficient (NPC) should be approximately equal to one (allowing for small differences in quality and transportation costs).

The border price paradigm used by economists to analyse the efficiency of pricing policies argues that NPC = 1 is the optimum. Any deviation from this unitary value, whether NPC < 1 to favour consumers or NPC > 1 to protect farmers, incurs efficiency losses because decisions about rice consumption and production do not reflect the opportunity cost of the commodity to society, that is, its value at the border as an export or an import.[7] Although this paradigm has a very clear logic and is used widely by major donor agencies as the basis of their policy advice (and loan conditionality), there are also significant problems with the paradigm when applied to basic food commodities in the highly unstable world in which actual policy must be implemented. The conclusion about efficiency is valid only in the perfectly competitive, static, partial-equilibrium world in which the underlying assumptions hold. Experience in developing countries since the 1950s suggests that border prices are also important for enforcing dynamic efficiency and speeding economic growth, but this is an empirical lesson and does not come directly from the analytical logic of the border price paradigm itself. More important, the paradigm ignores the macroeconomic consequences of changes in prices. When the commodity in question is important to the macro economy, as rice is to nearly all countries in Asia, the paradigm requires, even on efficiency grounds, significant further analysis before policy conclusions can be accepted.

One further macroeconomic proviso is important. Even if the domestic rice price equalled the border price when using the existing exchange rate, actual incentives faced by farmers and consumers are not necessarily unbiased. In the face of substantial industrial protection and an overvalued domestic currency, tradeable commodities such as rice are severely discriminated against relative to industrial products and nontraded goods and services. A large-scale study by the World Bank conducted during the 1980s found that agriculture typically faced discrimination of 30 per cent or more from such indirect macro pricing and trade policies [*Krueger, Schiff, and Valdés, 1988*]. Such indirect discrimination often outweighed policy efforts to provide positive incentives to the agricultural sector, as measured by the simple nominal protection coefficient for a specific commodity. The statistical analysis conducted in this study does *not* incorporate these indirect effects into the analysis of government efforts to tax or protect rice farmers. Fortunately, all five countries had reasonably neutral macro pricing policies during the period of the analysis, although industrial protection was biased against agriculture in all five countries. The significance of the relatively open exchange rate policy for the general health of the agricultural sector should be stressed. It is highly unlikely that any of the five countries in this study could have maintained a high rate of growth, even with strong incentives through rice prices directly, if the domestic currency had been substantially overvalued for most of the period.[8]

If not border prices and free trade, what? Most poor countries have tried to keep the price of the staple food cheap enough to maintain low wage rates and allow the poor increased access to food at market prices [*Lipton, 1977*]. The World Bank study cited above found that this 'cheap food' bias is stronger at earlier stages of economic development, and it weakens noticeably when the staple is imported. None the less, the underlying macroeconomic bias keeps the statement true on average even when direct policy no longer reflects an urban bias.

There are obvious reasons for trying to keep the price of a staple food as low as possible in a poor country. Especially when a single commodity such as rice provides 50 to 60 per cent of calories on average, and 80 to 90 per cent of the calories of the poor, the food price directly determines the real standard of living in the short run. Raising this price to international parity is the same as making most of the population much poorer. It might be necessary for short-run budgetary reasons; it might be desirable for longer-run economic growth. But it will never be popular as a political decision, and it can cause severe, even irreversible, hardship for the most vulnerable groups. A price policy that keeps food cheap is an understandable, perhaps desirable, response to widespread poverty. Unfortunately, because of its impact on agricultural productivity and rural incomes, a cheap food strategy is also a major factor causing that poverty [*Timmer, Falcon and Pearson, 1983*].

Stimulating growth in agricultural productivity is necessary to start the process of overall economic growth. While this statement would have been highly controversial in the 1960s, it is widely accepted at the start of the 1990s. 'Getting Agriculture Moving', to quote the title of Arthur Mosher's influential book published in 1966, is a complex task involving institutional change, new technology, rural infrastructure, and improved markets. But price incentives are a key stimulus to farmers to experiment, take risks, and invest in the components of higher crop yields. Most countries have found it impossible to increase agricultural productivity very rapidly without price incentives for farmers that matched (or often exceeded) those available in international markets.[9] As the macroeconomic significance of agricultural growth became apparent after the world food crisis of the 1970s, more and more countries ended their cheap food policies in favour of stimulating their rural economies. Border prices were incentive prices, and agriculture thrived.

In the mid-1980s, however, world commodity prices collapsed. A combination of large debts in many importing countries, long-term supply response to the high prices in the 1970s, and the world recession combined to push commodity prices, including rice prices, to historic lows in real terms. If these border prices were passed through to farmers, incentives would be slashed and recent productivity gains threatened. No rice-importing country in Asia permitted such a direct transmittal. Thailand, as a rice exporter, had little alternative to presenting its farmers with the low world prices once the 'rice premium', an export tax that kept the domestic rice price below the world price for many years, was eliminated.[10] Rice farmers in the four importing or self-sufficient countries in this study received substantial protection from world competition during the mid-1980s, even when earlier history reflected a pattern of discrimination.

A pattern of discrimination against farmers when world prices are high (mid-1970s) and of protection when world prices are low (mid-1980s) suggests an obvious policy approach is at work: stabilisation. In principle, a policy of price stabilisation can avoid discrimination or protection in the long run, and the domestic price follows some trend in the world price. When the trend is measured over a long period, such as ten years, the domestic price fluctuates only a little. Year-to-year deviations from the border price can be substantial and might require equally substantial budgetary resources to implement. If the trend is measured over a short period only, such as two or three years, the domestic price can never get too far away from the actual international price, and the budgetary commitments are accordingly smaller.[11]

When price stabilisation becomes an overriding objective of policy, however, and a country becomes rich enough to afford it – rich enough in budgetary resources and ability of consumers to pay – the domestic price can diverge steadily from the border price. When this divergence is in one direction only, protecting farmers from a progressively lower real price in the world market, the empirical record looks as though policy makers have switched from protecting consumers to protecting farmers. Economists who search for explanations of this switch fail to find them in static models of economic efficiency and look instead to explanations in political economy. As noted above, answers have been forthcoming. Unfortunately, they are answers to the wrong questions. The right questions are: why is stabilisation of rice prices so important, and what institutional mechanisms for stabilising prices propel countries down the path that ends up protecting rice farmers? The first question, for a general Asian context, has already been addressed [*Timmer; 1989a, 1991*]. An answer to the second question is attempted here. The Indonesian context is presented in the next section, which is followed by a formal statistical analysis of the process of price formation.

THE INSTITUTIONAL CONTEXT FOR SETTING RICE PRICES

Institutions evolve to solve problems that are important to some set of objectives held by policy-makers. But institutions also have their own momentum, created by prior history and the nature of staff and leadership. Indonesia is a particularly rich example of these principles with respect to setting rice prices and implementing the policies designed to stabilise prices for both producers and consumers. BULOG, the Indonesian Food Logistics Agency, was established almost simultaneously with the New Order government in the mid-1960s as the vehicle to stabilise the commodity economy, especially the rice economy, and to provide rice as partial salaries to the civil service and military (the 'Budget Group'). The success achieved by BULOG in these twin (and sometimes competing) activities has made it one of the most prominent institutions in modern Indonesia.[12]

The basic framework in which prices for rice in Indonesia are debated and policies implemented was formulated in 1967 by Mears and Afiff.[13] Their 'operational rice price policy' called for a floor price for paddy and a ceiling price for milled rice, and an adequate margin between the two prices to allow the private sector to carry out most of the physical marketing of rice. The role of BULOG, the new logistics agency, was to procure enough paddy and rice in rural areas to keep prices to farmers above the floor price and to sell enough rice to wholesalers in urban areas to keep retail rice prices below the ceiling. Floor and ceiling prices were initially pan-territorial to simplify operational instructions to local BULOG staff. If domestic procurement in defence of the floor price was inadequate to meet the needs of defending the urban ceiling price and distribution to the Budget Group, imports from the world market would fill the gap. BULOG held a monopoly on international trade in rice but not in the domestic market, where it was expected to control less than one-quarter of rice traded.

The original Mears and Afiff model was not explicit about the fact that two separate stabilisation functions were being carried out via the floor and ceiling price policy. The clear intent of the model was to stabilise seasonal rice prices, protecting farmers from a collapse at the harvest and consumers from high prices at *paceklik*, the season of scarce rice supplies before the beginning of the main harvest. But the operational capacity to defend floor and ceiling prices on a seasonal basis carried over directly to a capacity to keep prices stable from one year to the next. Indeed, because domestic prices were not linked to world prices in any explicit manner, there was no reason inherent in the Mears and Afiff model why prices needed to be changed at all.

Inflation, the dynamic nature of rice cultivation, and the budgetary costs of importing rice from a changing world market made it necessary to review periodically the price levels to be defended by BULOG in the Mears and Afiff framework. Interestingly, the framework itself has gone virtually unchallenged. Only in the late 1980s, as deregulation in other economic spheres gained momentum, did donors and economic analysts begin to question whether BULOG interventions to defend floor and ceiling prices for rice were economically justified. Until then, the policy debate had been over the price level for rice in relation to four key standards: to the world price measured at the market exchange rate, because of the budgetary implications of any imports needed; to the fertiliser price, as a measure of farmer incentives to use modern technology; to the costs of marketing, as a measure of the extent to which private traders were squeezed by the official margin between the floor price and the ceiling price; and to the *existing* price (after accounting for inflation), as a measure of stability.

Starting in August of each year, evidence about these four standards was gathered to compare them with existing rice prices and to gauge the impact of a range of plausible changes in price. Different agencies have substantially different attitudes about how the rice price should compare to each of the four standards. The Ministry of Finance had the clearest stake in all four standards, and the minister became the key organiser of the analytical process that led up to the annual announcement in October or November of the floor price for rice and prices for fertiliser, in time for decisions about planting the main rice crop. Although the Ministry of Finance had a clear budgetary interest in the decisions about prices of rice and fertiliser and thus had a near veto over pricing changes that require budgetary resources, the National Planning Agency (BAPPENAS) was charged to consider the broader impact of the changes on the whole economy. Accordingly, the integration of all four standards – world prices, fertiliser prices, marketing margins, and price stability – fell largely in the domain of the planning agency (and EKUIN, the Coordinating Ministry for Economics, Finance and Industry, which always worked very closely with both BAPPENAS and the Ministry of Finance). Other agencies and non-governmental organisations such as farmers' groups, students, and business associations were also involved in the process.

The actual mechanism for integrating the four standards into a single price policy involved surprisingly sophisticated analysis of sectoral and economy-wide effects of rice and fertiliser prices. Although no operational computable general-equilibrium model was used to analyse and debate these issues, the complexity of effects of price changes forced analysts to cope with improving methodologies as well as providing basic data and routine analyses to policy-makers. Analysis carried out under the general rubric of determining appropriate rice and fertiliser prices in Indonesia led to new models of marketing margins, determination of the social profitability of the fertiliser subsidy, evidence that consumer responsiveness to price changes for basic foods is substantially greater for the poor, and the hypothesis that price stability has important macroeconomic benefits not reflected in existing micro-based models of risk and instability. None of this work would have been conducted unless policy-makers, especially in the economic ministries, were asking questions about the impact of price policy and appropriate directions for the future.[14]

Two operational agencies also made important inputs into the process of setting rice (and fertiliser) prices. The Ministry of Agriculture had as its natural constituency the millions of rice farmers whose incomes are directly affected by the decisions. Historically, however, the ministry took a heavily paternalistic attitude toward Indonesian farmers, arguing that ministry officials, especially the planning officers in headquarters and the extension agents in the field, knew better than farmers what should be grown and how to grow it. Prices were largely irrelevant in this model of farm decision-making, and the Ministry of Agriculture was outside the core circle of analysts and policy-makers in which the basic debate over price policy took place. This 'top–down', paternalistic attitude in the ministry began to change in the late 1980s, and the new attitudes reflected by senior officials (and their economics skills) assured them a more important role in the future.

BULOG also played a key role in the debate over price policy. As the central institution involved in implementing policy for rice prices, BULOG had a large stake in the choice of a policy that was feasible to implement and did not place financial burdens on the agency without also identifying the resources to meet the obligations.[15] Indeed, for BULOG the price debate was largely a debate over funding mechanisms for the agency. Because it had no direct support from the government budget, all BULOG activities had to be financed by the margins earned on transactions or by indirect subsidies on its operations. The margins and the subsidies were directly affected by domestic commodity prices, as well as by the foreign exchange rate and world commodity prices.

This study is not the place to attempt to explain the complexity of funding mechanisms for BULOG.[16] But the interplay between rice prices determined by policy and the health of BULOG as an institution, both financially and logistically, led the agency to invest heavily in the analytical capacity to understand the issues and influence the policy-making itself.

A major paradox has emerged from BULOG's investments in its analytical and logistical capacity. There can be no doubt that Indonesia's rice markets were substantially more competitive in the early 1990s than when BULOG first faced its stabilisation tasks in the late 1960s. The stability provided by BULOG has induced substantial investment by the private sector in rice marketing. BULOG was able to operate increasingly at the margin of local markets and still maintain a satisfactory degree of price stability. In addition, what was 'satisfactory' was changing as consumers, with higher incomes, were better able to absorb larger price changes, both seasonally and from year to year, and as farmers began to diversify cropping patterns to meet demands from these more affluent consumers. In short, BULOG's role as a price stabilising agency was no longer as important as it once was.[17]

Furthermore, by the late 1980s the analytical skills existed within the agency and elsewhere in the government to manage stabilisation primarily through trade policy rather than direct logistical operations. The large field staff and extensive physical facilities could be privatised, leaving BULOG as a regulatory and trade office, with a far smaller staff, budget, and influence. Such a prospect was obviously threatening to the agency, despite the fact that success itself created it. What alternatives did the government have?

Experience with rice price interventions in the rest of Asia presents a range of possibilities.[18] Several countries, especially those that have industrialised quickly, moved from carrying out simple price stabilisation to providing price supports to farmers at the expense of consumers (and often the budget as well). This path may not have been the only one open to Indonesia, but in the early 1990s, the path of stabilisation and protection was tempting.

To understand the logic and historical precedents for such a path and the policy design behind it, an examination of how price policies evolved over the course of development is essential. The five countries in this exercise, Japan, South Korea, Malaysia, the Philippines, and Indonesia, represent a range of development levels but exhibit several basic similarities with respect to their rice economies. In particular, in the absence of substantial interventions into domestic prices and other forms of subsidies for rice production, all five countries would be rice importers

in normal years.[19] Consistent importer status focuses attention on the
c.i.f. border price and relieves the analysis of the complexity of a
country's switch to export status when the f.o.b. border price becomes
relevant. A single border price thus simplifies the analysis, which uses
actual prices relative to those at the border – the non-intervention level
– as the organising framework for the statistical model in the following
section.

A STATISTICAL ANALYSIS OF VARIANCE IN DOMESTIC PRICES FOR RICE
RELATIVE TO WORLD PRICES

Stabilisation of the domestic rice price can lead to substantial departures
from the world rice price. The simplest way to measure this departure is
to calculate the nominal protection coefficient (NPC), which is the ratio
of the domestic rice price in domestic currency (PD) to the world rice
price (PW), converted from US dollars to domestic currency at the
existing exchange rate (XR). That is:

$$NPC = PD/(XR * PW)$$

The right side of this identity can be decomposed into three independent
factors, each of which can contribute to a change in the nominal
protection coefficient over time: a change in the real price of rice in the
domestic economy (rPD); a change in the real price of rice in the world
market (rPW); and a change in the real exchange rate (rXR).
Converting from nominal prices to real prices requires data on the rate
of inflation in the country concerned (infD) and in the world market
(infW), which is proxied by the inflation rate in the United States
because the world price of rice is quoted in US dollars.[20]

The logic of the decomposition can be followed in three steps:

(1) Multiply the numerator of the NPC definition by infD/infD and the
denominator by infW/infW. Then

$$NPC = \frac{PD * infD/infD}{XR * PW * infW/infW}$$

(2) Let rPD = PD/infD = the real price of rice to the domestic economy;
   rPW = PW/infW = the real price of rice in the world economy; and
   rXR = XR * (infW/infD) = the real exchange rate for the domestic
   economy.
   Then, by rearranging terms:

$$NPC = \frac{rPD}{rPW * rXR}$$

(3) By taking logarithms of both sides of the above identity, the nominal protection coefficient can be decomposed into three additive factors:

$$\log NPC = \log rPD - \log rPW - \log rXR$$

This equation shows that the nominal protection coefficient for rice, the most common measure of protection for rice farmers or subsidies for rice consumers, can vary for three independent reasons – variation in the real price of rice domestically, in the real price of rice in world markets, and in the country's real exchange rate. The debate over urban bias and rural power, to the extent that it is quantitative at all, is primarily concerned with changes in rPD, the real price of rice in the domestic economy. When rice prices fall behind the cost of living, the declining rural–urban terms of trade put pressure on farm incomes. When the rice price rises faster than the rate of inflation, poor consumers complain that their living standard is declining (and the poorest may suffer from hunger and malnutrition).

But even if rPD is constant over time, with no change in this measure of the degree of urban bias, a change in the real price of rice in the world market or in the real exchange rate can cause the nominal protection coefficient to change. A change in either of these variables does not contribute one way or the other to the domestic debate over the degree of urban bias. Indeed, a policy objective of stabilising domestic rice prices in real terms would seek to isolate domestic price formation from changes in rPW and rXR. It is entirely possible to observe a significant change in our common measure of protection for farmers or subsidies for consumers, that is, in the NPC, when the actual policy intent is simply to stabilise the domestic rice price. For the purposes of the analysis here, a change in the NPC caused by a change in rPD will be interpreted as a reflection of policy intentions with respect to farmer protection or consumer subsidies, whereas contributions from changes in rPW and rXR are interpreted as efforts to stabilise the domestic rice price from 'external' fluctuations. Only the empirical record can sort out which variables are most important.

Figure 1 shows the real price of rice in the world market and the trend from 1950 to 1987. The figure plots the price of Thai rice, five-per cent brokens, f.o.b. Bangkok, as deflated by the United States Consumer Price Index (1980 = 1.00). The simple time trend for this 38-year period shows a significant downward slope of $4.83 per metric ton per year. Any country seeking to stabilise its domestic rice price around a long-run trend in the world price must gradually reduce its price over time. At the price level of 1981, when the actual price was exactly on trend, the decline was roughly one per cent per year.

FIGURE 1

DEFLATED PRICE OF THAI RICE AND PRICE TREND

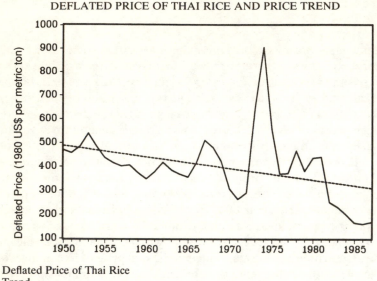

— Deflated Price of Thai Rice
··· Trend

The statistical analysis of variance attempts to explain the difference each year between the rice price a country sets domestically and the actual border price (for Thai rice) for the same year. That is, variance in the nominal protection coefficient, the NPC, is decomposed into relative contributions from each of the three variables designed to indicate the impact of stabilisation and protection policies. The NPC coefficient used here as a dependent variable measures the *ex post* outcome of policy effects. These *ex post* outcomes do not necessarily reflect the *prior* intentions of policy makers to achieve a certain price difference from the world price. The world price itself might not have been a factor at all in the decision-making, or it might have changed substantially after a decision on domestic prices was made and announced. There is no obvious way to sort out these, and other, various reasons for price divergences, except to examine the historical record for consistent patterns. Such patterns are likely to indicate intent, not random movements in the world price.

The results of the analysis for Japan, South Korea, Malaysia, the Philippines, and Indonesia are summarised in Table 1, which shows the percentage contribution of individual or paired independent variables to explanation of the variation in the logarithm of the nominal protection coefficient.[21] The top part of the table shows the results for variation in the logarithm directly (L), whereas the bottom part shows the results for variation in the first differences of the logarithm (DL), that is, in the changes in the (logarithm of the) nominal protection coefficient from year to year.

The results for level of protection (L) and for first differences in the level of protection (DL) shown in Table 1 are quite similar. For the level of protection, variations in the real domestic price of rice (rPD) contribute only modestly to variations from year to year in NPC. The greatest contribution is in South Korea, where 32.4 per cent of the variation in the logarithm of NPC is explained by rPD. The least contribution is in Indonesia; none of the variation is due to changes in the real price of rice. The simple average for the five countries is 13.1 per cent.

The inverse way to ask the question is to examine the joint contribution of the two stabilisation variables – rPW and rXR – to variation in NPC (all in logarithms). The results are nearly a mirror image of those for rPD. In Indonesia, 90.3 per cent of the variation in NPC is explained by the combined variation of rPW and rXR. In South Korea just 58.4 per cent is explained by these two variables. The simple average for the five countries is 85.6 per cent. It is no accident that the percentage explanations from the single variable rPD and the combined variables rPW and rXR usually sum to nearly 100 per cent. If there were no covariance among the three variables, the sum would be exactly 100 per cent, whether done as the sum of a single and paired variables or as the sum of the three variables examined individually.

There is, however, covariance among the three variables, and movements of one can offset movements in the other. A simple analysis of variance would show the individual contributions of each variable so that the sum would be exactly 100 per cent. The results in most cases are not significantly different from those shown in Table 1, except where the overall movement in the NPC is small and the individual explanatory variables show relatively large movements. Indonesia and, to some extent, Malaysia fit this pattern, and the technique used in Table 1 gives a more reliable measure of the impact of the three independent variables in these circumstances.

Normally, explaining variations in first differences in time series data is much more difficult than explaining variation in levels. For the problem at hand, however, the results are strikingly similar. Variations in the first differences in the logarithm of NPC, shown in Table 1 under the heading DL, are not explained by changes in the first differences in the logarithm of the real price of rice in domestic markets – only 12.2 per cent on average. As before, South Korea has the largest contribution from pure price protection to its observed increase in nominal protection. Somewhat surprisingly, Japan and Malaysia have the smallest contribution. In no case, however, does pure price protection

TABLE 1

PERCENTAGE CONTRIBUTION OF THREE INDEPENDENT VARIABLES TO
VARIATION IN THE LOGARITHM OF THE NOMINAL PROTECTION
COEFFICIENT FOR RICE

Independent Variables	Explanation of Variations in the Logarithm of NPC (L) (percent)					
	Japan	South Korea	Malaysia	Philippines	Indonesia	Average
rPD	15.8	32.4	12.9	4.3	0.0	13.1
rPW	51.8	54.8	92.2	23.5	74.9	
rXR	76.1	0.4	43.1	25.8	7.9	
rPD, rPW	78.3	71.6	97.7	23.5	23.5	
rPD, rXR	76.2	58.2	59.3	27.8	9.3	
rPW, rXR	95.7	58.4	96.8	86.6	90.3	85.6
	Explanation of Variations in the first Differences in Logarithm of NPC (DL) (percent)					
rPD	2.3	24.4	1.4	20.9	11.8	12.2
rPW	77.9	45.6	93.6	55.1	73.4	
rXR	0.2	35.9	36.9	16.8	0.0	
rPD, rPW	86.5	70.3	97.2	80.9	85.2	
rPD, rXR	2.6	57.8	36.9	28.8	12.4	
rPW, rXR	91.6	77.7	95.8	86.9	80.0	86.6

Note: rPD = Logarithm of the real price of rice in domestic markets;
         rPW = Logarithm of the real price of rice in world markets; and
         rXR = Real exchange rate of domestic currency per US dollar.

explain more than one-quarter of the changes in the nominal protection coefficient.

The contribution of the two stabilisation variables is uniformly large. On average, 86.6 per cent of the variation in changes in the logarithm of the nominal protection coefficient are explained by variation in changes in the logarithms of rPW and rXR. Even price changes in South Korea are largely explained by these two variables. Nearly all of the changes in Malaysia's nominal protection of rice farmers are accounted for by changes in the world rice price and the real exchange rate for the Malaysian ringgit.

A powerful conclusion emerges from the statistical analysis reported in Table 1. A change in the real price of rice for domestic farmers and consumers explains relatively little of the observed increase in the past 30 to 40 years in the nominal protection coefficient for rice, at least for the countries in this sample. Much of the quantitative work on the political economy of agricultural pricing, and the non-quantitative debate over urban bias versus rural empowerment, has focused on these changes in the nominal protection coefficient. What the political economy literature has missed, somewhat surprisingly in view of the political emphasis placed on food security, is the large contribution to a change in the NPC from stabilisation variables and the small contribution from a change in the real price of rice directly.

This relatively modest contribution of real rice prices in domestic markets to explaining a change in nominal protection can be understood better by examining Figures 2 to 6, which plot the rPD variable for each country along with its nominal protection coefficient. Pure protection for Asian rice farmers is a genuine phenomenon, to be sure, but it is not the same phenomenon that is shown by the time series of nominal protection coefficients. In Japan, for example, pure protection reached its peak in 1968 – and then with a relative price increase of only 50 per cent (see Figure 2). The NPC of more than eight in 1987 is almost entirely a result of fluctuations in world prices and appreciation of both the nominal and the real exchange rate. In fact, the rPD variable had almost exactly the same value in 1987 as it had in 1954 when Japan passed from an NPC < 1 to NPC > 1!

FIGURE 2

NOMINAL PROTECTION COEFFICIENT AND REAL RICE PRICE

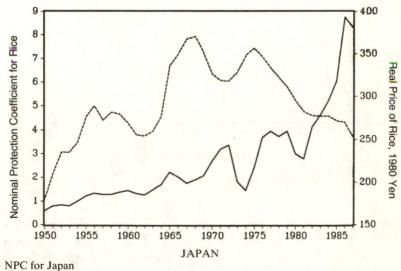

JAPAN

— NPC for Japan
··· Real Rice Price

A more substantial case of pure protection can be seen in the South Korean data (see Figure 3). The peak in rPD occurred in the early 1980s and it has declined only slightly since then. From the mid-1950s to the early 1970s, the rising pattern of pure protection is similar to Japan's. But South Korea then continued to provide more pure protection to rice farmers, whereas Japan's stabilisation policy, in the context of the appreciating yen, seemed sufficient to keep its farmers happy. The real price of rice in South Korea, in relation to prices in the early 1960s when the country was at parity with the world, is actually higher in relative terms than that in Japan. Complaints from agricultural exporting countries that South Korea has imitated the protectionist policies of Japan in its agricultural as well as industrial policies can see clear evidence in Figure 3 that for rice, the imitation has taken the form of leadership!

FIGURE 3

NOMINAL PROTECTION COEFFICIENT AND REAL RICE PRICE

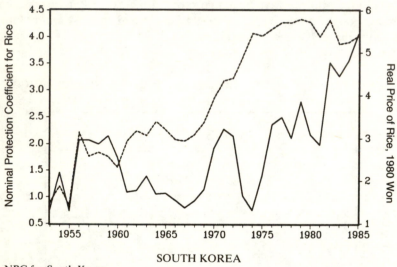

SOUTH KOREA

— NPC for South Korea
··· Real Rice Price in South Korea

Malaysia is often cast as the next follower of Japan, after South Korea. The prime minister has urged his countrymen to 'look East' for lessons on how to develop the country. The path of the nominal protection coefficient from 1974 to 1984 supports the hypothesis, as it rose from about 0.5 to slightly over 2.0 (see Figure 4). The NPC once again conceals as much as it reveals about protection for rice farmers. Real rice prices in domestic currency, as traced by rPD after 1963, when Malaysian rice prices were at parity with world prices, fluctuate in a

fairly narrow range – between 0.95 and 1.25 compared to the 1963 base.
Pure protection as measured in this sense did increase in the late 1970s,
but it has declined since then. It was only 12 per cent higher in 1987 than
in 1963. Malaysia has protected its rice farmers from low world prices in
the 1980s, but most of this protection is an outgrowth of its stabilisation
policy. Little needs to be attributed to more specific efforts at protection. In light of the political rationale for protecting Malay rice farmers
from foreign rice that is nearly always provided by Chinese traders, this
result is all the more surprising.

FIGURE 4

NOMINAL PROTECTION COEFFICIENT AND REAL RICE PRICE

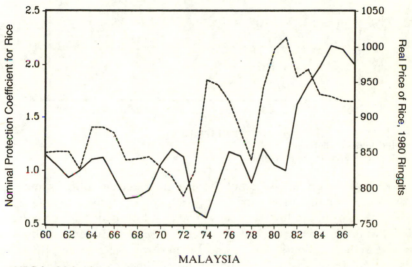

MALAYSIA

— NPC for Malaysia
··· Real Rice Price in Malaysia

The patterns in the Philippines are much more perplexing. The
nominal protection coefficient fluctuates from 0.5 to 1.6, but there is no
apparent trend (see Figure 5). The real price of rice also shows large
fluctuations, again without trend. The statistical analysis reported in
Table 1 demonstrates that the Philippines fits the general East and
South-east Asian pattern in the sense that pure price protection plays
relatively little role in explaining variations in the nominal protection
coefficient. The Philippines is unusual, however, in its lack of any
apparent rationale for change in the real price of rice itself. This
inconsistency in price policy for rice might be a partial explanation for

the failure of the Philippine economy to grow as rapidly as the other countries in this sample.[22]

FIGURE 5

NOMINAL PROTECTION COEFFICIENT AND REAL RICE PRICE

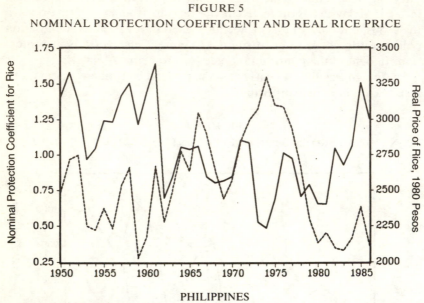

PHILIPPINES

— NPC in the Philippines
··· Real Rice Price in the Philippines

Indonesia is at the low end of the income spectrum in this sample of countries. Nominal protection coefficients for rice hover around unity for most years in the 1970s but show a modest but significant jump in the 1980s to levels between 1.3 and 1.5 (see Figure 6). Is Indonesia about to follow Malaysia, South Korea, and Japan down the path of protecting its rice farmers? Rice is a less important commodity at the start of the 1990s than it was in the mid-1960s, when the New Order government came to power. A policy choice to raise rice prices to benefit the country's millions of rice farmers would be much less damaging to consumer interests and economic efficiency now than 25 years ago.

The pure protection variable, once again, suggests only the barest hint of such a tendency. The rPD variable, plotted in Figure 6, rises significantly above unity in 1968 and 1973, when BULOG lost control of domestic rice prices because of inadequate supplies. Since 1974 real prices of rice in domestic currency have been remarkably stable around their 1971 level. Only in 1986 and 1987 is there a noticeable tendency for the real price to rise above this stable level, but by less than 20 per cent. Significant increases in pure protection for Indonesia's rice farmers

FIGURE 6

NOMINAL PROTECTION COEFFICIENT AND REAL RICE PRICE

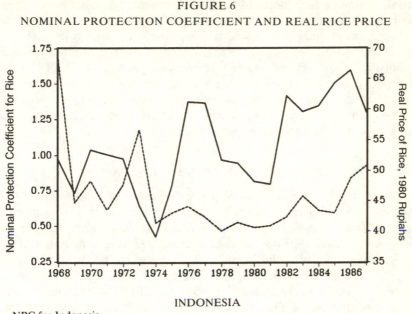

INDONESIA

— NPC for Indonesia
··· Real Rice Price in Indonesia

might be about to begin, but the historical record shows primarily a concern for stabilisation.

Much more of comparative interest can be drawn from Table 1 and Figures 2 to 6. The contributions of changes in rPW, the deflated price of Thai rice, reflect to some extent the financial and institutional capacity of individual countries to isolate themselves from fluctuations in the border price. All five countries manage some isolation, but Malaysia, with a contribution of nearly 94 per cent (in the DL results), is most successful at ignoring the world market, Japan is next with a contribution of 78 per cent, and Indonesia has a contribution of about 73 per cent. Considering the low per capita income in Indonesia, its success in stabilising the domestic rice price relative to the world price must be considered a major bureaucratic success for BULOG.

The results presented here to explain the formation of domestic rice prices relative to world prices, or the nominal protection coefficient, are plausible for all countries tested. As hypothesised, stabilisation objectives play a larger role in explaining variations in the nominal protection coefficient for rice than does an overt effort on the part of policy-makers to raise the degree of protection for rice farmers. The goal of this study has been to set the Indonesian experience with stabilisation of rice prices in a broader Asian context and to understand the nature of the forces at work in Indonesia's decisions about the rice prices to be set and defended. The country fits nicely into the broader model. The specific contribution of each factor for Indonesia reveals two basic forces. First is Indonesia's stage of development; as seen in the early years of the sample, the country was unable to keep price fluctuations in the world market from penetrating its border. Second are the internal political priorities; policy-makers made resources available to BULOG to implement the stabilisation mandate and to control the timing and extent of changes in the real price of rice for farmers. There is a tension between these two basic forces, a tension that is worked out through a process of political economy and debate.

THE POLITICAL ECONOMY OF RICE PRICES IN INDONESIA

Once BULOG regained control of the domestic rice market in 1974, it successfully stabilised rice prices for a decade. Since 1985, the rice market and rice policy have been in considerable turmoil. Neither the large surpluses in 1985 nor the shortages in 1987 were anticipated. Even more unexpected was the President's response to the management of surpluses and shortages. Surpluses were to be exported, at a loss if necessary, to provide warehouse space for BULOG to continue procurement in defense of the floor price. Shortages were to be managed strictly from domestic supplies because Indonesia, in 1984, had achieved self-sufficiency in rice after years of effort. In 1986 FAO awarded the President a gold medal in recognition of this achievement.[23]

Self-sufficiency as a political mandate shifted the nature of the debate about rice price policy and the instruments available to BULOG to implement it. A brief review of the episodes of surplus and shortage reveals how the debate has changed. The slight upturn in pure protection for Indonesia's rice farmers in 1987 struck many observers, familiar with the East Asian model, as an early signal of much more to come. But severe drought in 1991 seriously threatened price stability and the welfare of the poor. After considerable lobbying by the technocrats who manage Indonesian food policy, President Suharto permitted rice imports to maintain levels of BULOG stocks. A potential factor was the national election scheduled six months after the normal peak in rice prices.

The major threat from the rice surplus in 1985 was to BULOG itself. With high procurement, no market operations, and warehouses full of deteriorating rice, BULOG was threatened with financial insolvency, operational gridlock, and rapidly declining institutional legitimacy. A special task force reviewed the situation and made a series of recommendations to remedy the situation. By January 1986, the President approved a special line item in the national budget in response to concern over BULOG's impending financial bankruptcy. Although the budget allocation was never funded because of the collapse of oil prices later in 1986, it focused the attention of senior economic policy-makers on problems with BULOG financing mechanisms and increased their understanding of the large costs of implementing a price stabilisation policy.

Price policy was reconsidered, and a new pricing model was proposed:

> Floor price and fertilizer price policy should be thought of as a short-run tool to manage production trends, subject to constraints imposed by world price levels for both rice and fertilizer and availability of budget resources to finance wide price divergences. Price incentives have been particularly strong for the past eight years. Several years of reduced incentives will significantly improve BULOG's stock position without seriously jeopardizing rural incomes in the short run. Longer-run price policy needs a significant research effort before permanent changes could be made with confidence [*Falcon Team, 1985*].

This call to use price policy to fine tune BULOG's stock position relative to trends in domestic production and consumption required a major ratcheting upward in the agency's capacities to analyse and implement policies that affected the rice economy. The new pricing model was used to reduce incentives gradually to rice farmers. Rice production slowed its rapid expansion and rested at a plateau from 1986 to 1988 that left procurement sharply below the levels of the previous five years. BULOG's surplus stocks were exported and used for distributions to the Budget Groups; by late 1987, after a drought during the dry season, the agency was unable to inject enough rice into retail markets to maintain price stability.

The attention of most policy-makers and analysts was still focused on surpluses and government initiatives to stimulate diversification out of rice. But an Asia-wide drought, plus reduced stocks in the United States because of export subsidies, flipped the thin international market back to shortage. Indonesian rice prices followed world prices up, ending 1988 at rough parity. Because Indonesia had maintained its domestic rice prices well above those in world markets during the worst of the surplus in 1985 and 1986, its price increases were smaller than those in the world market. It seemed as though there was, once again, a longer-run vision behind the stabilisation programme, although the abruptness of the increase in the domestic price was quite unsettling to many consumers and policy makers.

BULOG activities were badly disrupted during the episode. The policy of self-sufficiency meant that imports were not available to replenish the stocks that had been used, with only limited success, to control price increases in late 1987 and early 1988. The government's floor price had been announced before prices rose above normal seasonal levels, and by the procurement season in February, 1988, BULOG's buying price based on this announcement was well below the structure of rural rice prices. Even with the assistance of special task forces, the offer of price premiums by the co-operatives (KUDs), and direct appeals to rice traders, BULOG was unable to replenish its stocks from domestic sources. Prices rose sharply from May to July and stabilised at levels that have been maintained in real terms through early 1992.

Somewhat surprisingly to Indonesia's policy-makers, the rapid succession of rice surpluses and deficits in the late 1980s and early 1990s did not destabilise the rest of the economy to nearly the extent they would have expected, considering the large role rice had played in the economy in the past. Rice is no longer the 'barometer of the economy' that it was even at the beginning of the 1980s.

Consequently, Indonesia appears to be at a crossroad. One path has already been traveled by Japan, South Korea, and Malaysia. It leads to an increasingly protected agricultural sector, the protection made necessary by the stabilisation of rice prices in absolute terms in defense of parity for farm incomes. Despite the distortions such protection must have caused in microeconomic terms, high rice prices do not seem to have exacted a large cost in macroeconomic performance for any of these countries. The political stability provided by the agricultural pricing policies may well have contributed to domestic investment and economic growth, especially during the most painful part of the adjustment process.

Consumers have undoubtedly paid most of the price, but with rice a declining share of their expenditures, complaints and hardship have been minimal. Budgetary costs have often been more burdensome, especially, as in Japan and South Korea, when lower prices were being charged to consumers than were being paid to farmers. Increasingly, the real price may be political in terms of international relations, as the United States in particular attempts to pry open all agricultural markets to which it might export its own farm products.

On this path of rising protection for rice farmers, the price stabilisation agency continues to play a key role. The support programmes used to protect rice farmers require nearly complete isolation from forces in the world rice market. The difficulties of establishing irregular access to world supplies and markets, after self-sufficiency has been reached, have led all countries to use their rice logistics agencies to manage the process. From this comparative perspective, BULOG's institutional future might depend on the new-found support for farmers' interests in the Ministry of Agriculture. A policy of protecting Indonesian rice farmers from world competition by implementing a more vigorous policy of stabilising the real price of rice would provide continued justification for BULOG's extensive field staff and logistical capacity.

A second path would follow the historical route of stabilisation that isolates the country's producers and consumers from year-to-year fluctuations in world rice prices, while staying on a longer-run trend. This policy has served Indonesia and other Asian countries well in the past. When implemented by using international trade as a mechanism for keeping costs low, the positive impact on efficient allocation of resources and economic growth of price stabilisation around a trend in the world price is a powerful argument for following this path. The historical record and results of the statistical analysis presented here, however, suggest that a policy favouring trend stabilisation would face difficulties as an option for the future.[24]

Several factors in Indonesia threaten the political coalition that defends this type of policy and the economic efficiency that is enforced by it. First, there are increasing pressures on farm incomes (at least relatively) as the country's export drive gains momentum, and rural-oriented members of Parliament called for improvements in the terms of trade for farmers as part of the campaign in 1992. Second, the real price of rice in world markets seems to be continuing its long-term decline, and any attempt to follow the trend in world rice prices requires lower rice prices domestically (unless the real exchange rate continues to depreciate). Third, bureaucratic opposition to the gradual loss of an operational role for BULOG as rice shrinks in importance in the economy could significantly impede efforts to deregulate the rice economy and make it more open to world markets. If government policy were to rely more on private traders, in conjunction with variable levies, to stabilise domestic prices, few operational tasks would remain for this powerful agency. Rural politics, bureaucratic politics, and pressures from the world market all seem to conspire against continuation of the efficient policy that stabilises rice prices on trend.

The Asian comparative experience provides little ammunition to counter these pressures once the transition to an industrial economy is well under way. Late in the structural transformation, the static losses in allocative efficiency do not seem to slow economic growth, and policy for rice prices becomes almost entirely a political rather than an economic issue. The problem for Indonesia is its tenuous footing on the ladder of industrialisation. The pressures to raise rice prices are genuine, to be sure, but Indonesia's per capita income is less than one-quarter of Malaysia's and one-eighth of South Korea's. Many poor consumers would face a lower standard of living and the prospect of malnutrition if Indonesia's rice prices continued to rise significantly in real terms. Stabilising rice prices remains important to the economy, to producers, and to consumers, but the 'path to protection' seems unlikely to be the turnpike to riches in the 1990s.

NOTES

1. The fertiliser price is also decided and announced as part of this process because the price of fertiliser determines the cost of the most productive purchased input in the rice-growing process. The two prices have traditionally been linked in the minds of both farmers and policy-makers.
2. For a much more detailed description of this price-setting process, see Timmer [1989b; 1991].
3. Low income countries usually cannot afford wide departures from the world price for long periods of time and so tend to stabilise around the trend in world prices. Rich countries tend to stabilise the real price of rice when measured in domestic currency. Stabilisation is a goal in both rich and poor countries, however.
4. A paper that also attempts to explain the formation of rice prices in Asia includes the role of investments in technology and changing comparative advantage for rice as explanatory variables, while focusing somewhat less on the contribution of stabilisation. See David [1990].
5. This discussion of models of price formation is a very abbreviated summary of Timmer [1986].
6. To be specific, the price in US dollars of Thai five per cent brokens, f.o.b. Bangkok, as quoted by the Board of Trade of Thailand, is used as the 'border price' for all the analysis done here. No adjustments for transportation or quality are made; so nominal protection coefficients for one country (NPC, equal to the border price in dollars divided by the domestic price in dollars) should not be compared directly with those of another country. Each country's NPC series over time, however, is consistent.
7. Countries that switch from import to export status, or vice versa, make the situation more complicated because the border price switches from a c.i.f. basis for importers to an f.o.b. basis for exporters, and the difference can be substantial. For nearly the entire history of all five countries analysed here, the c.i.f. basis as an importer is the appropriate price for comparison in a world of free trade.
8. A partial exception to the prevalence of neutral macro policy is the Philippines. Macro policy and agricultural pricing policy were inconsistent during the period concerned. This inconsistency of policy might be a significant factor explaining the inconsistent results in economic growth in the Philippines, in contrast to the records of the other four countries under analysis.
9. Several important provisos apply. Productivity of individual crops, including rice, can be enhanced through investments in infrastructure, new technology, and procurement programs that reduce farmer risk, even if domestic prices are below world prices. However, the agricultural sector as a whole is unlikely to remain a major source of growth if the price squeeze is sector-wide. Crops into which farmers might diversify in search of higher incomes require incentive prices. An entire literature exists on the

'role of agriculture' in the development process. For recent reviews, see Timmer [1988; 1992].

10. Subsidising the export of rice is an option for rich countries, such as the United States, Japan, and Italy, but would be very costly for a low-income country, such as Thailand, which is a large exporter of rice year in and year out.

11. This discussion of price stabilisation is summarised from Timmer [1989a].

12. This paper can only touch on the highlights of this historical record; the emphasis here is on prospects for the future, especially the potential for significant deregulation of the rice economy as part of the 'winds of deregulation' that have formed a key element of the development strategy in Indonesia since the start of the 1980s. For a much fuller treatment of the historical record, see Timmer [*1990*].

13. The original policy memorandum was revised and published in 1969.

14. This research is summarised in Timmer [*1990*].

15. BULOG's role in fertiliser distribution is largely indirect, via the village co-operatives which are integrated to some extent with local BULOG facilities.

16. See Timmer [1990] for further discussion.

17. This was confirmed in a major speech on 29 April 1992 at a conference celebrating the 25th anniversary of BULOG's establishment. Professor Dr. Saleh Afiff, the chairman of BAPPENAS (and the co-architect of BULOG's original terms of reference in 1967) called for wider price margins to be implemented by BULOG as a way to lower the agency's costs and increase opportunities for the private sector in rice marketing.

18. A review of Asian experience with rice market interventions, plus four detailed case studies, is contained in Asian Development Bank [1988].

19. It is debatable whether the Philippines might be a regular exporter of rice if it managed its macroeconomic and agricultural development policies better. However, with an improved distribution of income – one of the worst in Asia – Filipinos would consume considerably more rice.

20. I am indebted to Peter Lindert for convincing me that this decomposition of the nominal protection coefficient into three components for analysis of variance is a more appropriate procedure than the multiple regression technique used in an earlier version of this study.

21. Naturally, if all three independent variables are included in the analysis, they 'explain' 100 per cent of the variance in the dependent variable because the resulting equation is a definition.

22. For example, between 1970 and 1989, annual per capita income in real US dollars increased by 10.1 per cent in South Korea, 8.4 per cent in Japan, 4.7 per cent in Indonesia, 4.0 per cent in Malaysia, and only 0.8 per cent in the Philippines.

23. Observers who attended the award ceremony in Rome were astonished by President Suharto's familiarity with even small details of the country's agricultural and pricing policies. One African official lamented that, in his country, no one knew as much about agricultural development as the Indonesian president.

24. If the Uruguay Round of GATT negotiations is completed successfully and agricultural trade is brought under GATT rules, a policy of price stabilisation on trend would be threatened. The negotiations themselves, and Indonesia's response to a successful agreement, are unclear as of mid-1992.

REFERENCES

Anderson, Kym, and Yujiro Hayami, with associates, 1986, *The Political Economy of Agricultural Protection: East Asia in International Perspective*, London: Allen & Unwin.

Asian Development Bank, 1988, *Evaluating Rice Market Intervention Policies: Some Asian Examples*, Manila.

David, Cristina C., 1990, 'Determinants of Rice Price Protection in Asia', typescript, Los Baños, Philippines: International Rice Research Institute.

Falcon Team Report, 1985, 'Rice Policy in Indonesia, 1985–1990: The Problems of Success', typescript, Jakarta: BULOG, Sept.

Krueger, Anne O., Schiff, Maurice and Alberto Valdés, 1988, 'Agricultural Incentives in Developing Countries: Measuring the Effect of Sectoral and Economywide Policies', *World Bank Economic Review*, Vol.2, No.3, pp.255–71.

Lindert, Peter H., 1991. 'Historical Patterns of Agricultural Policy', in C. Peter Timmer (ed.), *Agriculture and the State: Growth, Employment, and Poverty in Developing Countries*, Ithaca, NY: Cornell University Press, pp.29–83.

Lipton, Michael, 1977, *Why Poor People Stay Poor: Urban Bias in World Development*, Cambridge, MA: Harvard University Press.

Mears, Leon A. and Saleh Afiff, 1969, 'An Operational Rice Price Policy for Indonesia', *Ekonomi dan Keuangan Indonesia* [Economics and Finance in Indonesia], Jakarta.

Mosher, Arthur T. 1966, *Getting Agriculture Moving: Essentials for Development and Modernisation*, New York: Frederick A. Praeger for the Agricultural Development Council.

Timmer, C. Peter. 1975. 'The Political Economy of Rice in Asia: Indonesia', *Food Research Institute Studies*, Vol.14, No.3, pp.197–231.

Timmer, C. Peter, 1986. *Getting Prices Right: The Scope and Limits of Agricultural Price Policy*, Ithaca, NY: Cornell University Press.

Timmer, C. Peter, 1988. 'The Agricultural Transformation', in Hollis Chenery and T.N. Srinivasan (eds.), *Handbook of Development Economics*, Vol.1, Amsterdam: North-Holland, pp.275–331.

Timmer, C. Peter, 1989a, 'Food Price Policy: The Rationale for Government Intervention', *Food Policy*, Vol.14, No.1, (Feb.), pp.17–42.

Timmer, C. Peter, 1989b. 'Indonesia: Transition from Food Importer to Exporter', in Terry Sicular (ed.), *Food Price Policy in Asia: A Comparative Study*, Ithaca, NY: Cornell University Press, pp.22–64.

Timmer, C. Peter, 1990, 'Food Price Stabilisation: The Indonesian Experience with Rice', typescript, Cambridge, MA: Harvard Institute for International Development.

Timmer, C. Peter, 1991, 'Food Price Stabilisation: Rationale, Design, and Implementation', in Dwight H. Perkins and Michael Roemer (eds.), *Reforming Economic Systems*, Cambridge, MA: Harvard Institute for International Development, Harvard University (distributed by Harvard University Press), pp.219–48 and 456–59.

Timmer, C. Peter, 1992. 'Agriculture and Economic Development Revisited', in Paul S. Teng and Fritz W. T. Penning de Vries (special editors), *Agricultural Systems*, Vol.38, No.5 (Amsterdam: Elsevier), pp.1–35.

Timmer, C. Peter, Falcon, Walter P. and Scott R. Pearson, 1983, *Food Policy Analysis*, Baltimore, MD: Johns Hopkins University Press for the World Bank.

Self-Limited Empowerment: Democracy, Economic Development and Rural India

ASHUTOSH VARSHNEY

This study deals with two questions: (i) what accounts for the rise of the countryside in India's polity? and (ii) how has rural power in the polity affected economic policy and economic outcomes for the peasantry? The rural sector is typically weak in the early stages of development. A powerful countryside, therefore, is a counter-historical occurrence. Universal franchise and a competitive democracy in a primarily agrarian India have led to the empowerment of the countryside. The power of the rural sector is, however, not unconstrained. The first principal constraint is, ironically, the size of the agricultural sector itself. Beyond a point, subsidising a large rural sector is fiscally difficult. The size of the rural population thus cuts both ways: it makes the countryside powerful in a democratic political system but checks this power economically. The second principal constraint on rural power stems from the cross-cutting nature of rural identities and interests. Farmers are also members of caste, ethnic and religious communities. Politics based on economic interests can potentially unite rural India and push the state even more: politics based on caste, ethnicity and religion cuts across rural and urban India, and divides the countryside. Both kinds of politics are vibrant, neither fully displacing the other. The refusal of farmers themselves to give precedence to their farming interests over their other interests and ascriptive identities means that the power of rural India is ultimately

Ashutosh Varshney is Associate Professor of Government, Harvard University. This study draws heavily on the author's forthcoming book, *Democracy, Development and the Countryside: Urban–Rural Struggles in India*, New York, and Cambridge: Cambridge University Press. Earlier versions have been presented at the 1991 Annual Meetings of the American Political Science Association, and in seminars at Harvard, MIT, UCLA, McGill, University of Washington (Seattle), University of Virginia, and the Institute of Social Studies, the Hague. For comments, the author is grateful to Robert Bates, Suzanne Berger, Jonathan Fox, Peter Hall, Ronald Herring, Robert Keohane, David Laitin, Mick Moore, Kalypso Nicolaidis, Ashwani Saith, Peter Timmer, Lance Taylor, the late D.S. Tyagi, Myron Weiner and the Comparative Politics Group at Harvard. The usual disclaimers apply.

self-limited. The urban bias view ignores that farmers, like most of us, have multiple selves and there is no reason to assume a permanent superiority of the economic over the non-economic. As a result, even when farmers become powerful politically, the possibilities of which were underestimated or ruled out by the urban bias theorists, they may not be able to change the economic outcomes completely. They may certainly be able to prevent the worst-case scenarios, but find it hard to realise the best-case scenarios.

This study presents three arguments. The first concerns what has become conventional wisdom in political economy – namely, that the historical trajectory of rural power is marked by a paradox.[1] It is argued that in the early phases of development when rural dwellers constitute a majority of a country's population, they have historically been the weakest. As the process of industrialisation makes a society overwhelmingly or predominantly urban, the power of the rural sector increases [*Bates, 1981*]. It is also recognised that the power of farm groups in advanced industrial countries is reflected in the high protection granted to agriculture [*Anderson and Hayami, 1986*].

The explanations for why this is so are both political and economic. Mancur Olson's argument [*1965*] about the organisational advantage of small groups is normally used to account for the high level of rural organisation. Compared to the third world, the size of the farming community in the first world is smaller, making it easier for the rural sector to organise for political action. The economic argument, on the other hand, is that, being small relative to other sectors in the economy, the farm sector in industrialised countries can be subsidised by the government with lesser fiscal difficulty than if the farm sector were large. Moroever, a small proportion of the household budget is spent on food, making it possible for governments in the developed world to raise farm prices without hurting consumers much.

India defies this historically derived proposition. It is a poor country with over 60 per cent of the population still in agriculture. Yet the rural sector has acquired considerable power in the polity. By now, about 40 per cent of India's parliament has a rural background as opposed to about 20 per cent in the 1950s. Rural mobilisation on prices, subsidies and loans dominated non-party politics in the 1980s. All political parties support rural demands for more 'remunerative' agricultural prices and for higher investment of public resources in the countryside. And finally, some of the key bureaucratic bodies involved in policy-making in

Delhi are by now substantially rural in social origins (although for rural politicians that may still not be adequate).

What is the explantion for the progressive empowerment of India's rural sector? Is it that the introduction of universal franchise and a competitive party system in an early stage of development has led to such an exceptional outcome? As is well known, universal franchise in the currently advanced countries was introduced much after the industrial revolution; not so in India. Independent India was born agrarian as well as democratic. This conjunction, this study argues, has led to the empowerment of the rural sector in the polity.

If democracy has indeed empowered the peasantry, does not the fact that India remains a poor economy put some constraints on rural power? The demand for higher crop prices, for lower farm input prices, for waiver of agricultural loans, and for higher rural investment is routed through the state, because the state makes the decisions on input and crop prices and on public investment. However, if the state responds to the democratically-induced rural pressures by increasing crop prices, lowering input prices and waiving loan repayments from India's nationalised banking system, it must either raise consumer prices to finance the resource transfer, or bear a burden of subsidy on its budget (for other options including taxation, see section IV). With incomes as low as they are in India, and food being the largest item in the typical household budget, food prices for consumers cannot be increased beyond a point. Higher prices will only lead to lower food intake (by the poor in particular) and to accumulating food surpluses. Indeed, in contrast to the bleak production scenario of the mid-1960s, India today suffers from the embarrassment of food surpluses coexisting with widespread hunger. The state, therefore, goes for the second option: namely, increase producer prices (to appease the farmers), not increase consumer prices (or not by the same margin as producer prices), and subsidise the difference through its budget. Are there limits to such subsidisation? With agriculture being the largest sector in a poor economy, the scale of the subsidy required is potentially very large. Unlike advanced industrial economies, subsidisation of the large agricultural sectors in the Third World is thus inherently problematic for public finance. My second argument thus is that the two tendencies – a political tendency increasing the rural pressure in the polity, and an economic tendency arising out of the aggregate poverty of the country – are increasingly at odds. India's poverty, and the compulsions of economic development, are putting a check on the political, rural tide.

The economic constraint on rural power, however, is not the only constraint. My third argument is that in the ultimate analysis, rural power is *self-limiting*. For rural power to push the state and economic policy more in its favour, it must present itself as a cohesive force united on economic interests (higher producer prices, larger subsidies and greater investmnent). Rural India has chosen not to construct its interests entirely economically. While politics based on economic demands is stronger than before, politics based on other cleavages – caste, ethnicity, religion – continues to be vibrant. Politics based on economic interests potentially unites the villagers against urban India; politics based on identities divides them, for caste, ethnicity and religion cut across the urban and the rural. There are Hindu villagers and Hindu urbanites, just as there are 'backward castes' in both cities and villages. Until an economic construction of interests completely overwhelms identities and non-economic interests, rural power, even though greater than ever before, will remain self-limited. The ultimate constraint on rural power may not be the 'urban bias' of the power structure, as the influential urban bias theorists [*Lipton, 1977; Bates, 1981*] have argued. It may well stem from how human beings perceive themselves – as people having multiple selves. An abiding preponderance of the economic over the non-economic is not how this multiplicity is necessarily resolved. The cross-cutting cleavages as a constraint on rural power will be the third main theme of this study.

Section I documents the rise of rural India in the polity. Section II examines whether the rise in political power has changed economic outcomes in favour of the countryside. Noting a disjunction between political power and economic outcomes, section III starts an investigation of why the gap exists. Proximate reasons are examined first, the underlying reasons probed next (section IV). Section V asks what the implications of the study are for the urban bias theory.

I. THE CHANGING SHAPE OF INDIA'S POLITICAL UNIVERSE

For the purposes of identifying the trajectory of rural power, it will be helpful to divide the polity into three parts: party politics, non-party politics, and bureaucracy. State-level party politics in India has always been dominated by rural politicians. The political leadership at the topmost tiers of the polity, however, was primarily urban to begin with. Over time, the top tiers also changed their character. Consider the occupational background of the lower house (Lok Sabha) of the Indian parliament. Figure 1 captures the time trend with respect to three key groups – agriculturists, lawyers and businessmen. It is generally accepted that the rise in agrarian representation has affected most political parties. The trend, of course, is more pronounced in the case of parties with an overwhelmingly agrarian base, such as the former Lok Dal and today's Janata Dal. The Lok Dal formed an important constituent of the central government between 1977 and 1880, with Charan Singh, the most powerful rural politician of post-independence India, holding key cabinet portifolios. In 1989–90, Janata Dal formed the government in Delhi. Devi Lal, a rural patriarch from state politics, became Deputy Prime Minister and Sharad Joshi, the best known non-party peasant leader, was appointed as agricultural adviser, a Cabinet rank position.

FIGURE 1

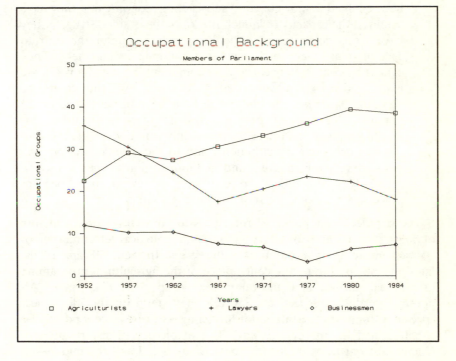

Source: Lok Sabha Secretariat, *Members of Lok Sabha*, various issues.

In non-party politics, led by a score of peasant organisations, agitation for higher agricultural prices and subsidies and for a waiver of agricultural loans emerged in several parts of the country in the 1980s. Non-party peasant leaders – Sharad Joshi, Mahendra Singh Tikait,

Narainswamy Naidu – became household names in various parts of India. They presented urban bias arguments and pressured the elected politicians and government to accept their demands. The basic conflict in India, according to Joshi [*1984*], is between the city and the country-side, between India and *Bharat* (an indigenous term for India). Alarmed by their popularity, this is how *The Times of India* commented on these movements:

> The peasants have started to flex the political muscles that their economic betterment has given them . . . In national terms, (they) cannot claim that (they) have received a raw deal. Witness the manner in which agricultural inputs have been subsidised for the past two decades . . . But it is precisely because the farmers have been enabled to move beyond subsistence economy that they have acquired the capacity to launch the kind of sustained struggle they have. It is going to be difficult to either contain them or to accommodate them in the current economic arrangement. They cannot be contained because they command the vote banks in the countryside to which every party seeks access. And they cannot be accommodated because there is a limit beyond which the urban population cannot be expected to transfer resources to them. For to allow agricultural prices to rise unduly is to undermine the very basis of economic development, add to the woes of the poor in both urban and rural areas and fuel unrest in urban centers which is already proving difficult to control . . . A new spectre of peasant power is likely to haunt India in coming years.[2]

The parallel development of rural pressure in two important sectors of politics – party and non-party – led to an ideological reformulation of politics on the agrarian question in the 1980s. In the 1950s and 1960s, land reforms used to be the centrepiece of the agricultural programme of political parties. Agricultural prices occupy that place now. All political parties, irrespective of where they stand on the ideological spectrum, support the demand for higher agricultural prices and call for a better deal for the countryside. The ideological transformation of Communist parties is by far the most dramatic.[3] Until the mid-1970s, they used to argue that higher agricultural prices, particularly those of food crops, hurt the poor peasants and the landless labourers. These classes were, after all, net buyers of foodgrain. By the early 1980s, the Communist parties began to argue that all sections of the peasantry benefited from higher agricultural prices, not simply the surplus farmers.[4] Before the fiscal and balance of payments crisis of 1991 emerged, several parties supported the demand for a waiver of agricultural loans, too. At the institutional and ideological plane of party politics, there are few dissenting voices left. A *Bharat*–India divide has become an important idiom of Indian politics.

But is it an idiom only? Has the ideological reformulation of party politics had an impact on economic policy? Agricultural policy norms have changed significantly. India's agricultural policy was changed in the mid-1960s after Nehru's death. Abandoning the principles of low agricultural prices and labour-intensive agricultural development, the post-Nehru government made producer price incentives and investments in new technology the governing norms of agricultural policy. It is noteworthy, however, that this change took place much before pressures for higher prices emerged in the polity, indicating that a change in policy principles actually led to a new definition of agrarian interests, not vice versa. However, once the new definition of agrarian interests acquired political momentum, the government reworked the principle of price incentives in a manner more favourable to the countryside. The touchstone of the original definition of incentives was a cost-plus formula, where farm costs were taken to mean input costs, over which a margin of profit was given. By 1980, agriculture-industry terms of trade were added to the cost criterion, thereby including not simply the changes in the costs of farm inputs but also rural consumption goods. This change in norms implies the possibility that even if the terms of trade went against agriculture, due to a reduction of agricultural costs (which would tend to depress agricultural prices), such gains would not be transmitted to the entire economy. The terms of trade would be adjusted in favour of agriculture politically. Finally, after the arrival of the National Front government in power in December 1989, agricultural loans up to Rs 10,000 were waived for farmers on the ground that unfavourable terms of trade had actually mired the peasantry in a debt crisis.[5]

The structure of state institutions responsible for agricultural policy has also been an object of considerable political struggle. Since the mid-1960s, the Commission on Agricultural Costs and Prices (CACP) has been the institutional centrepiece of agricultural policy. Initially envisioned as a purely technical body consisting of economists, statisticians and agricultural administrators, a governmental decision in the mid-1970s gave the CACP a 'farmers' representative' appointed from among the politicians, and another decision in 1984 split the Commission into three technical members and three farmers' representatives. These decisions were made in response to the constant political criticism that decision-makers in the CACP were urban technocrats. They had academic or bureaucratic knowledge of agriculture but, not being agriculturists themselves, had little understanding of the complexities of agriculture. In all three sectors of the polity rural power has thus unambiguously increased.

Why Has Rural Power Risen: The Role of Democracy

There are two aspects to the rise of rural India. Its representation and voice in the politics above (parliamentary politics, state institutions) has significantly gone up, and the politics below (mass political mobilisation) is also marked by increasing rural organisation. A democratic political system is related to both.

The changing configuration of political elites: The existence of a democratic polity in a country with a large rural population explains the changes in India's elite politics. In a poor and largely agrarian country with low literacy rates characterising most of the countryside, the first politicians were predominantly urban. A substantial number were trained in law, the profession that led the national movement. The nation's democratic leadership, however, made a conscious decision to involve the countryside in the mainstream politics. Nehru's economic model was driven by an industrialising zeal; his political model, however, was aimed at politicising the rural periphery in a nation-building effort. The Congress Party consequently moved into the villages to enlist popular support. Moreover, the Congress government became involved in development though various schemes – building roads, schools, better communication systems, irrigation systems, co-operatives, etc. The party and government were thus increasingly visible in the rural areas and were also great sources of patronage and power. As a result, the district and state wings of the party ruralised first. Over time, rural politicians built their careers upwards to reach Delhi, the topmost level of the polity.

Rural pressure on the state institutions was partially a result of the changing social base of political parties. In 1965, Agriculture Minister C. Subramaniam was shocked to discover that the agriculture secretary could see agriculture 'only in the files'. A decade later, the first rural politician was appointed to the Commission for Agricultural Prices and Costs, and by 1985, the Commission was split into two halves – one technocratic, the other rural political. Not only has the Indian politician changed, but so has a good deal of the bureaucracy, though to a lesser degree. Rural politicians may want the upper levels of bureaucracy to follow their wishes more or to be more like them, but that is a statement on what they would ideally prefer, not a judgment of how the present looks compared to the past.

The analysis above may account for changes in elite-level politics, but not in rural mass politics. How does one explain the vibrancy of rural collective action on prices and subsidies (and, of late, loans) in India?

Explaining rural collective action: India's democracy not only leads to a ruralisation of the power structure; it also facilitates rural collective action. The logic of this relationship can be stated as follows. Rural price mobilisation is, after all, a protest against state policies. If the state can repress farmers with impunity, rural mobilisation can be easily stilled at its birth. A democratic system, however, puts serious constraints on the state's repressive capacity *vis-à-vis* the peasantry, particularly as farmers themselves are well represented in the upper tiers of the polity.

This is not to say that the Indian state has not repressed farm mobilisation. Several farmers lost their lives to state police in the initial stages of the mobilisation. But such repression had to cease soon. Every police firing on the agitating farmers in Maharashtra led to an explosion in parliament in the first years of price protest.[6] Subsequently, the state developed a strategy of conciliation. Or, if it found farmers' demands excessive, it simply adopted a posture of protracted inaction, hoping to win the battle of attrition: farmers, after all, must return to their farms at critical junctures in the crop cycle.

Repression was not really the planned strategy of the Indian state even at the early stages. Rather, the sight of rural dwellers blocking roads was enough of a frustrating novelty for *district level administration* to view the rural crowds as dispersable with a show of might. Once such mobilisation acquired legitimacy, thoughts of dispersing agitators through police firings withered away. Legitimacy of these movements has thus made a difference to the behaviour of the coercive institutions *vis-à-vis* agitating farmers. A somewhat dramatic example – with significant symbolism – of the change in state behaviour was the arrival of thousands of farmers in Delhi about the same time as the Indian Prime Minister wished to hold a mammoth rally of his party in the autumn of 1989. Eventually, farmers held their demonstrations in the heart of Delhi and the Prime Minister was forced to move his rally to the outskirts. Farmers' rallies have become a normal feature of political life in Delhi.

To be sure, rural collective action, even in a democracy, is not without cost. Being away from the farm can lead to losses; time and energy must be spent on organisation; weather is not always kind to those blocking roads or those participating in sit-ins; and the *ex-ante* possibility of police repression, despite its improbability, always remains.[7] What is critical, however, is that in democratic systems, the costs of collective action are significantly lower since repression cannot normally be exercised with impunity. Opposition parties have a vested interest in embarrassing the government, as they do in India; a free press puts constraints on the government, as it does in India; and support groups form easily, as they do in India. Mechanisms counter-vailing repression are built into the system.[8] Controlling for the custom-ary obstacles to rural collective action in the Third World (size, dispersion, poor communication), the nature of the political system thus makes a difference. On rural collective action, a democratic polity may well account for the observed differences between India and most of Africa.

II. POLICY OUTCOMES FOR FARM GROUPS

If rural power has gone up in the polity, policy norms have become more favourable to the countryside, and the institutional centrepiece transformed in favour of the villages, have the outcomes also changed for the countryside? Move fundamentally, has the increasing rural power affected incomes in the countryside – and how?

Terms of the Existing Debate

A raging controversy has marked the intellectual debate about whether farm incomes have declined or gone up in India. Four kinds of indicators have been used for supporting these positions: (i) agriculture-industry terms of trade, assuming that a decline in agriculture's terms of trade represents a loss in the rural sector's income (and vice versa); (ii) comparing government prices with free market prices, assuming that if the latter is higher, the government purchases, substantial and rising, can be said to discriminate against the countryside; (iii) comparing price trends with supply trends, assuming that if the relative supply of a given crop goes up, its price must fall (and vice versa), and if it does not, the producers of that crop are the beneficiaries; and (iv) comparing price trends with cost trends, assuming that if the input costs for a crop go up faster than output prices, incomes or returns from that crop must decline. I shall call these the terms of trade argument, the price differential argument, the relative supply argument, and the cost escalation argument respectively.

The terms of trade argument: For ascertaining whether or not a political bias exists, the customary emphasis on inter-sectoral terms of trade can be quite misleading.[9] First of all, empirically, inter-sectoral terms of trade do not show a conclusive trend in either direction, agriculture or industry, but secondly and more importantly, in and of themselves, terms of trade are an inadequate measure for calculating returns to a sector.

Figure 2 plots the latest time-series. No trend in either direction is visible for the entire period: it is a random walk. Upward and downward trajectories are essentially short run. Other exercises carried out for a longer period show similar results – absence of a long-run trend but upward or downward trends for short periods of time [*Thamarajakshi, 1977; 1969*]. At any rate, even if one could find a clear trend, do declining terms of trade mean deteriorating incomes? Returns to farming, or incomes from farming, and agriculture's terms of trade are two very different concepts. Returns to farming (farm incomes) can go up even while farm sector's terms of trade decline. Stated another way, while agriculture's barter terms of trade may deteriorate, its so-called income terms of trade may well improve.

FIGURE 2

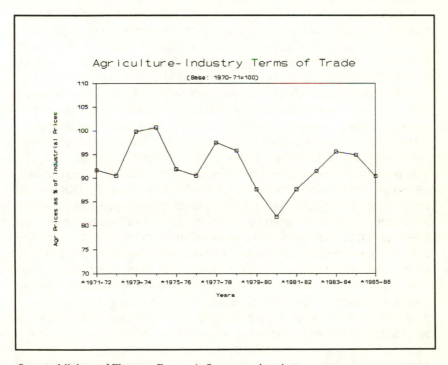

Source: Ministry of Finance, *Economic Survey*, various issues.

Terms of trade may go against agriculture for purely economic reasons, without requiring political manipulation: (i) new technology and skills may reduce the unit costs of agricultural production (costs per acre divided by yield per acre), while industrial costs remain unchanged; (ii) contrariwise, compared to the farm sector, increases in import costs may affect the non-farm sector more; and (iii) rising incomes in the society may lead to a larger expansion in the demand for non-agricultural goods than for agricultural goods. It is in the third case that, given costs, declining terms of trade may also mean declining returns from farming. Case (i), on the other hand, is a classic example of how a decline in agriculture's terms of trade can actually coexist with increases in returns from farming. As new skills and technology reduce unit costs and increase production, a decline in agricultural prices may reduce the rate of return *per unit* of output (that is, per quintal) but higher yields (quintals per acre) may lead to higher returns *per acre*, ensuring a rise in farm incomes[10] – and all of this while prices of industrial goods bought by the farm sector remain unchanged.

Looking at the issue this way, one may add, is not simply a logical exercise. Japanese rice agriculture is the best-researched historical example of agricultural growth despite a stagnation in terms of trade. Between 1880 and 1960, for a period of 80 years, the real price of rice remained stable while rice output increased [*Hayami, 1972*].[11]

A political datum is also worth adding. Unlike several economists and party politicians who continue to use terms of trade to make arguments about declining agricultural incomes, the non-party peasant leaders heading the price agitations have found little use for such abstractions. The most important peasant leader in the country today, Sharad Joshi, wants only returns over costs, not higher returns and better agriculture-industry terms of trade: 'It needs to be clearly understood that we are not discussing . . . intersectoral terms of trade. We are talking about agricultural prices as compared not with non-agricultural prices but as compared with . . . (the) cost of production.'[12]

To sum up, a deterioration in terms of trade necessarily means declining incomes only in a static framework – when agriculture is experiencing no technical change. (That is the context in which the early twentieth century Soviet debate took place.) The obverse is true in a dynamic setting: if new technologies are introduced, agriculture can grow and farm incomes can go up even as agriculture's terms of trade decline.

The price differential argument: This argument was popular in the 1960s and 1970s. To support their 'urban bias' arguments about India, Theodore Schultz and Michael Lipton relied heavily on the gap between the government procurement price and the free market price for food crops. The argument was twofold: (i) procurement prices paid by the government were anywhere between 10 and 25 per cent lower than the free market prices in the 1960s and 1970s for wheat and rice, and (ii) since the government procured roughly 25–30 per cent of the marketed surplus of wheat and rice, government procurement prices depressed farm prices in general and reduced farm incomes.[13]

The first part of the argument was an incontestable fact until the mid-1970s, but the conclusion drawn was questionable. It was perfectly plausible to argue that procurement, by withdrawing a certain quantity from the market, was bound to push up the open market prices; and that therefore the weighted average of the procurement and market prices was the price at issue, not the differential between the procurement and open market price [*Mellor, 1968; Hayami, Subbarao and Otsuka, 1982*].

Starting with the late 1970s, developments in the food economy destroyed this argument as accumulating surpluses made the concept of a *procurement* price, fixed lower than the market price, redundant. Instead, the government price became the *support* price below which prices of wheat and rice would not be allowed to crash. Farmers would simply be supported at this floor. Indeed, there are states now – Punjab, Haryana, Uttar Pradesh, Andhra Pradesh – where the government is the main buyer of grains, since prices in the open market are typically lower than the government price.[14] And in states where open market prices are higher, government buying is a relatively minor operation.[15]

The relative supply argument: Analysts have also focused attention on inter crop pricing, or what may be called *intra*-sectoral terms of trade. Wheat and rice have attracted maximum attention for two reasons. First, their prices affect the incomes and welfare of a large majority of rural (and urban) population. A second reason, however, is avowedly political. In some intellectual and political circles, there have been suspicions, even allegations, that the country's price policy is biased in favour of wheat and against rice. The evidence for the claim is that if the economic laws of supply and demand were any guide, rice prices should have risen faster than those for wheat because wheat output has increased more than rice output. That the eastern and southern part of the country is predominantly rice-growing whereas the north is overwhelmingly wheat-growing is cited to be the source of the regional bias[16]

This argument died a natural death with a change in agrarian practices. The wheat–rice differential could not be sustained in the 1980s. Punjab and Haryana in the north took to rice cultivation in a big way and rice ceased to be a crop confined only to eastern and southern India.

The cost escalation argument: Costs of production have moved much faster than the prices received by farmers, indicating, according to this argument, falling farm incomes.[17] At this point, economists working in the vast network of India's agricultural universities constitute the bulk of the group making this argument. Gunwant Desai, summarising *58* papers presented on 'farm price structure' in the 1986 annual meeting of the Indian Association of Agricultural Economics, notes: 'papers on input–output prices are nearly unanimous in pointing out that despite increases in farm output and its prices, the farmers' net income has not increased because of increases in the prices of inputs' [*Desai, 1986: 433*]. Over the last decade, the cost escalation argument has become the dominant argument of those arguing for an increase in producer prices, supported, among others, by the Commission of Agricultural Prices and Costs (CACP).

FIGURE 3

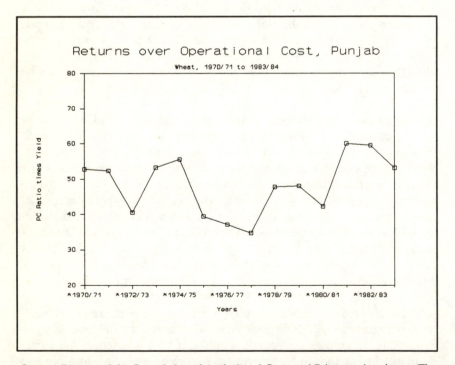

Returns over Operational Cost, Punjab
Wheat, 1970/71 to 1983/84

Source: Reports of the Commission of Agricultural Costs and Prices, various issues. The remaining graphs, unless otherwise stated, are also based on these reports.

Resolving the Debate: Constructing a Return Index and Its Results

Of the four arguments, the implausibility of the first three has already been demonstrated, but what about the cost escalation argument?

The cost argument contains a *non-sequitur*. It draws conclusions about farm incomes from price–cost ratios. Both cost and price data are about unit costs (costs per quintal) and unit prices (prices per quintal). One increasing faster than the other simply indicates the price–cost ratios per quintal, not returns per acre. The latter would also depend upon yields – that is, how many quintals are produced on a given hectare/acre of land. It is perfectly possible for unit costs to increase faster than unit prices but if productivity (yields per acre) goes up by a compensating (or higher) proportion, the returns can still be the same (or higher).

Let us see the logic of the above proposition. Defining returns as a function of price–cost ratios multiplied by yield, we can write the relationship as,

$$R = f(P/C)Y \qquad (1)$$

where R represents farm returns/incomes, P and C represent price per quintal and costs per quintal, and Y yield per acre. Price–cost ratio

FIGURE 4

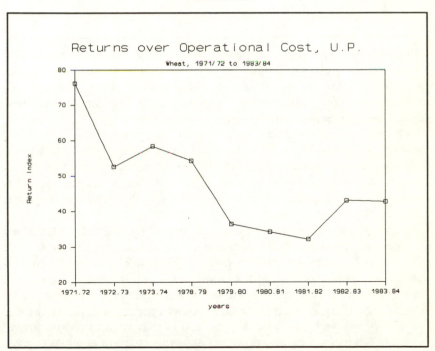

FIGURE 5

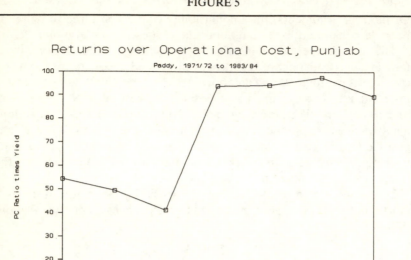

Returns over Operational Cost, Punjab

Paddy, 1971/72 to 1983/84

(P/C) will show us what is happening to the rate of return (per *quintal*). Multiplied by yield Y (quintals per acre), we get a measure for returns per *acre*. We thus get a return index that overcomes the *non-sequitur* of the relative supply argument by including costs and that of the cost escalation argument by incorporating yields.[18]

Let us see the results of the procedure specified above. Consider wheat returns first. Figures 3 and 4 present results form two major wheat states, Punjab and Uttar Pradesh. Figure 3 shows no trend at all in either direction; it is a random walk. A straight line, if drawn, would do violence to the empirical zig-zag. Figure 4 shows declining returns since the early 1970s.

Take paddy returns now. Figure 5, which plots paddy returns in Punjab since the early 1970s, shows an unmistakable upward trend after the mid-1970s. Figure 6 presents paddy returns from another technologically advanced state, Andhra Pradesh. Once again, roughly since the mid-1970s onwards, there is evidence of a mild upward trend, though, clearly, additions of recent years are required for a firmer judgment.

A crop-wise and state-wise disaggregation thus yields a diverse array of results: returns going up, down, or showing no trend at all. We have

FIGURE 6

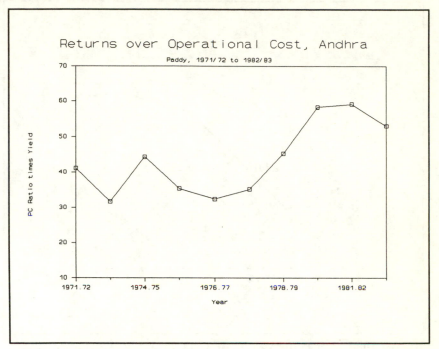

the makings of a paradox here: while the political power of farm groups, as argued before, has been rising over time, incomes from farming have risen or declined, depending on what crop one grows and where. If political power were neatly to translate into economic outcomes, returns from both crops should have increased: first of all, farmers have pressed for price increases for all crops; second, these crops are grown by, and constitute the main source of income for, a large fraction of the farming community; and thirdly, their prices are determined by the government.

Why has a disjunction between the political and the economic emerged? The disjunction would not exist if politics were entirely determinative. Is it that we have conceptualised power incorrectly and that urban bias, operating in an unidentified part of the power structure, limits the impact of the rural power charted above? Or should we go beyond a model driven purely by political determination? Let us first see if there are purely technical, or purely economic reasons for the disjunction.

FIGURE 7

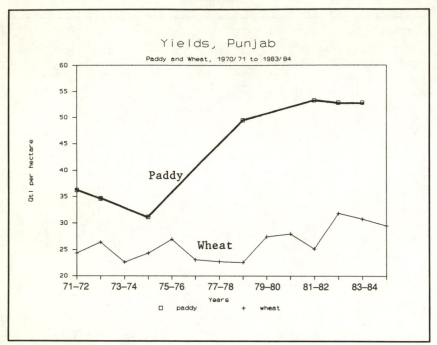

III. THE DISJUNCTION BETWEEN THE POLITICAL AND THE ECONOMIC:
    PROXIMATE CAUSES

(i) The Role of Technology

The first resolution of the paradox comes from the role of technical
change. Figure 7 shows how wheat and rice yields have changed over
time in Punjab, indicating faster technical change in rice as compared to
wheat, at least since the mid-1970s. Wheat drove the first flush of green
revolution. By the mid-1970s, however, as the rate of increase in wheat
yields decelerated in technologically advanced states, rice varieties
initiated the second round of green revolution in these states.
Differential rhythms of technical change, thus, constitute a factor countervailing (or augmenting) the political power of farm groups.

    A technology-based resolution of the paradox between politics and
economics, however, does not answer a different kind of question: why
could the government not neutralise the income effect of a deceleration
in technical change? Recall the return measure from equation (1).
Other things remaining the same, technical change, *by increasing yields*
(that is, the value of Y), would lead to higher returns. But the other
things do not have to remain unchanged. Apart from yield (Y), returns

are also determined by the price–cost ratio (P/C). Wheat returns (or, equivalently, returns from any crop experiencing a deceleration in technical change) can be restored if the government increases support prices (thus pushing up the value of P), or decreases the price of major cost items (thus lowering C), or does both. We know that the central government sets P and significantly affects C by setting the price of fertiliser which typically accounts for the largest farming expense under new technology.

That the rural political power met with a counteracting force in technical change can thus only be a proximate explanation for the disjunction, necessary but not sufficient. It is still to be explained why the government did not, or could not, increase wheat prices or reduce fertiliser and other input prices to an extent that would offset the slowing down of technical change and restore (or increase) returns, despite mounting political pressures in favour of such an increase both in party and non-party politics as well as within the CACP.

(ii) The Demand Constraint: How the Poor Affect the Income of Surplus Farmers

A lack of purchasing power in the economy provides the first answer to the question raised above. A 'basket case' in the 1960s, perpetually dependent on American wheat, India has of late been running a food surplus. Government foodgrain stocks have been accumulating since the late 1970s. The closing stocks had accumulated to nearly 30 million tons, one-fifth of the total food output in the country, when the severe drought of 1987 brought the stocks down to ten million tons.

India's food surplus, however, is a pseudo-surplus for large masses of people remain half-fed. Those who need food do not have the incomes to buy the accumulating government surpluses at the price at which they are offered. This simple economic logic means that the producer prices for wheat, if the government had not intervened, would have fallen, costs of production notwithstanding.

In the 1980s, stocks have tended to exceed the storage capacity in the country: '. . . (E)xcess food stocks reflect misallocation of our scarce resources and also increase risks of loss through spoilage' [*Ministry of Finance, 1985: 18*]. This was also the nearest the government came to admitting a truly bizarre problem: considerable quantities of grain rotting in a poor country where the spectre of hunger still haunts millions.[19]

Though inhuman in view of the hunger at home, exporting grain is, in principle, a solution to the domestic demand constraint. In reality, this

solution was not practical either. The government 'found it impossible
to export wheat and rice for the international prices were often lower'.[20]
Moreover, 'an adequate level of food stocks provides an important
hedge against both uncertain weather and inflation' [*Ministry of
Finance, 1985: 18*]. Only small quantities could be exported, whenever,
given price fluctuations in the world market and the relative price
stability of Indian markets, border prices went above the domestic
prices.

(iii) The Rising Fiscal Burden

An emphasis on the demand constraint leaves yet another issue unresolved. In principle, the government can lower the consumer price to
draw down the surplus and simultaneously increase the producer price
(or lower the price of inputs) to satisfy farmers. All that is required is
the subsidisation of the difference between producer and consumer
prices. Did the government choose this path?

The government has provided a substantial subsidy to farmers but
even high levels of subsidy have not been adequate from the farmers'
viewpoint. As Figure 8 illustrates, since the early 1970s, subsidies in the
Indian economy have risen threefold, from one per cent of GDP to
three per cent. The rising curve of the central government subsidy, our
main concern here, is due mostly to food and fertiliser subsidies. The oil
price hike led to a sharp increase in fertiliser prices in 1972/73, requiring
a subsidy to maintain fertiliser consumption and agricultural growth
rate. Figure 9 shows that food and fertiliser subsidies have constituted
between 55 to 65 per cent of total central subsidies, with the curve rising
more sharply in recent years.[21]

A larger increase in wheat prices or a substantial decrease in fertiliser
prices would have been simply translated into higher subsidies. In a
way, Indian agriculture is thus becoming a victim of its own success. The
government is clear about the source of the problem:

> In part, the problem reflects the success of our farmers and our
> agricultural strategy in raising food production to record levels.
> The problem has been aggravated by high levels of procurement
> without a corresponding increase in the off-take from the public
> distribution system . . . (T)here has also been a rapid increase in
> the volume of fertiliser consumption in the country. This, along
> with the rise in the cost of fertiliser imports and domestic pro-
> duction, has resulted in the growth of fertiliser subsidy from Rs.

FIGURE 8

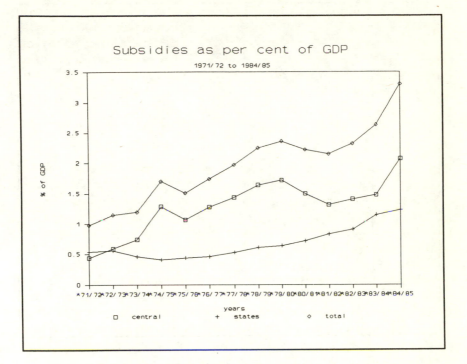

600 crores to over Rs. 2000 crores in the current year [*Ministry of Finance, 1985: 18*].

To sum up, an amalgam of forces, not simply rural power, has determined farm incomes in India. The rising peasant power in the political system has run up against three countervailing factors: differential rhythms of technical change, income distribution in the society, and the mounting fiscal burden of agricultural subsidies. As a result, *the best-case scenarios are not what agricultural groups have been able to achieve. Worst-case scenarios are what they have been able to prevent.* Continual increases in farm returns irrespective of the rhythms of technical change would have been the best case scenario, and a fall in producer prices as a result of accumulating surpluses, the worst case scenario.

FIGURE 9

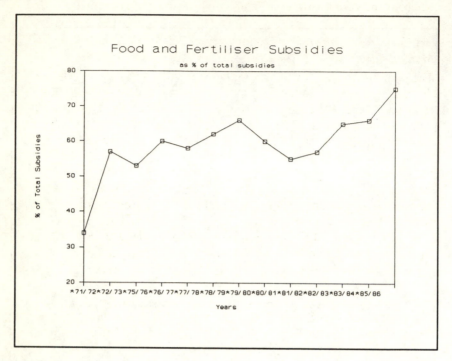

IV. TOWARDS AN UNDERLYING EXPLANATION

The closure of the explanation above is an analytical artifact. Technical change, income distribution and fiscal constraints are assumed to be given in some sense, as indeed they appear to be on first reading. But are these constraints in some sense technically binding or are they politically changeable? For if they are politically manipulable, another set of questions needs to be addressed. Could not something be done about reversing the deceleration of technical change in agriculture? Could not the purchasing power of the poor be increased? Could not a higher fiscal burden be borne?

A related group of questions also follows. How do technical change, income distribution and fiscal constraint make their presence felt in the political process? If all political parties are for higher prices, if farmers are also putting pressure on the government, if the Commission on Agricultural Prices and Costs is getting increasingly ruralised, if its terms of reference have been changed in favour of the countryside, then where is the counter-pressure emanating from?

Are Economic Constraints Technically Binding or Politically Manipulable?

The first constraint, technical change, has two sides: one relating to the technologically advanced areas and the other to the technologically backward areas. Higher outlays of public funds, undertaken in response to political pressures, may help disseminate technology in backward areas but such outlays alone may not be able to deliver the goods in the technologically advanced areas. For a new variety of seeds not only depends on higher fiscal allocations but also on the state of the biochemical sciences. A new seed suitable for India's agronomic conditions cannot be fiscally willed into existence by the political bosses.

In other words, for the technologically advanced areas, technical change may be a serious constraint, not politically manipulable, whereas for backward areas the constraint can be overcome via a greater provision of irrigation, fertilisers and seeds.

Income distribution, the second proximate constraint, is also not easily manipulable. Since blocked demand for food will emerge from the underfed poor, an income re-distribution aimed at the lowest deciles of the population is required. A redistribution of incomes towards the poor typically requires land reforms, transfer programmes or food-for-work schemes. Three decades of research have shown that land reforms are easy to legislate but monumentally hard to implement. And sizeable food-for-work programmes that run down the surplus in the short and medium run, or rural development schemes that create sustained increases in the incomes of the poor, can be run only if the state is prepared to bear the consequent fiscal burden.

All roads, therefore, lead to the third, fiscal constraint. Whether the issue is dissemination of the existing technology or creation of a new one, whether the solution is running large-scale food-for-work programs or designing other transfer programmes, whether the way out is increasing producer prices and/or lowering input prices – in all cases, the fiscal burden on the state will increase.

Can the State Pay More? The Fiscal Possibilities in Theory

In principle, higher farm subsidies can be provided if the government does one or more of the following: (i) increase consumer prices to reduce the burden on the exchequer; (ii) increase government revenue to finance higher subsidies; (iii) increase budget deficits, if raising more revenues is difficult; and (iv) cut government expenditure elsewhere if increasing deficits is ruled out for some reason. The impracticability of the first option in the light of a demand constraint has already been demonstrated.

What about the other three options? Why have these logical possibilities not become empirical realities? The question leads us into the political economy of public finance, an under-researched and complex subject.[22] Some of its salient outlines are sketched below. It will be first demonstrated that the state can pay more to the farmers, and then an attempt will be made to answer why it does not.

Taxes have been the main source of government revenue in India. Since the mid-1970s, tax receipts have ranged between 15 and 17 per cent of GDP. Because the proportion of indirect taxes has risen from 63 per cent of the total tax intake in 1950–51 to nearly 85 per cent by now, it is generally agreed that increasing tax revenue essentially involves raising the proportion of direct taxes in the total receipts [*Acharya, 1988*]. Further, since increasing the tax rate for existing tax-payers, beyond the salaried class, has only led to widespread tax evasion,[23] a generally proposed solution is an agricultural income tax, without which a sizeable increase in tax revenues is not easily achievable in India.[24]

Agricultural incomes have remained virtually untaxed since independence. But if they were taxed to finance higher agricultural subsidies, it would only be a pseudo-solution for the farmers: what was given from one hand would be taken away from the other. Moreover, an agricultural income tax entails some formidable administrative and political difficulties. It has often been recommended by economists but always rejected by politicians:[25] 'It is often been stated that exclusion of agricultural income . . . constitutes an important explanation for the weak revenue-raising capacity of the personal income tax. Taxing agricultural income presents many conceptual and administrative problems . . . The Centre has no intention of seeking any change . . .' [*Ministry of Finance, 1985: 35*].

What of the other two options – increasing budget deficits to finance agricultural subsidies, and, if that is not possible, cutting government expenses elsewhere? The government stated its view in the following manner: 'if subsidies continue to grow at the present rate, they will either be at the expense of developmental expenditures or they will lead to higher budget deficits which, in turn, will affect cost and prices, thereby increasing demand for further subsidies' [*Ministry of Finance, 1985: 19*].

How valid is the claim that if farm subsidies increase, it will either lead to higher budget deficits, or if budget deficits stay at the same level, higher subsidies will be at the cost of development expenditure?

Let us look at the other major expenses in the government budget. Figure 10 presents the results. The main triad of government's budgetary expenses – defence, interest payments and farm subsidies – comes more fully to light.[26] The argument that budget deficits must increase as farm subsidies go up can hold, *if and only if* other budgetary heads that have also contributed to higher deficits cannot be cut.

FIGURE 10

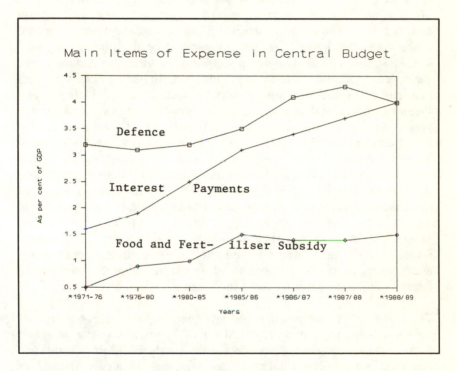

In sum, whether or not farm subsidies can increase is thus an issue that can be reduced to the following choices. Can defence outlays, the current expenses of the government and the deficits of the public sector be reduced? The answer to each question is yes, for these are political decisions. There is nothing technically sacrosanct about defence expenditure staying at three per cent of GDP, or increasing to over four per cent; the defence outlay depends on what the state perceives to be desirable for the country's defence. Interest payments can be cut if the

202 BEYOND URBAN BIAS

state *elects* to impose stronger discipline on the public undertakings, instead of financing their deficits. And, finally, the administrative expenses can be reduced. There is a range of choices available to the state. In the end, the government has been more willing, or has found it easier, to bear some increases in the fiscal burden, but not others.

Why the State Does Not Pay More? From Fiscal Possibilities to Political Realities

Why has the government, despite rising rural protest and power, chosen to bear burdens that cut into the resources potentially available to the rural sector? Two disaggregations are required. First, it is necessary to disaggregate the state. The rising rural power in parliament, in the party system and in the non-party street politics gets substantially dissipated inside the state organs. From the viewpoint of decision-making, the state institutions substantially penetrated by rural politicians – for example, the Commission for Agricultural Costs and Prices – are less powerful than the institutions such as the Finance, Defence and Planning Ministries that, for a variety of reasons, do not subscribe to the view of rural politicians. The Finance Ministry in particular stands out in its influence over the conduct of economic policy. Secondly, rural identities also need to be disaggregated. That the peasantry is on the rise for prices and subsidies is what meets the eye. But hidden underneath are the multiple identities that clash with the economic identities of farmers. Governments so far have not risen and fallen on prices and subsidies, nor have peasant-based parties come to power, despite rural India constituting an overwhelming majority in the country. The reason is that rural voting has expressed a variety of concerns that seem as real as economic concerns. The cross-cutting nature of rural identities and interests limits the pressure rural India can exercise on the state.

The towering finance ministry and economic policy: Three ministries are directly involved in agricultural policy – agriculture, planning and finance. These bureaucracies are driven partly by their institutional concerns, not purely by political considerations. However, if conflicts arise between their respective positions, the resolution of the conflict is a political matter, handled typically by the Prime Minister.

What are the characteristic tendencies of these bureaucracies?[27] The Agriculture Ministry is normally driven by an intrasectoral view of agriculture. Its task is to increase agricultural production and if price incentives and input subsidies are deemed necessary to achieve that, as is likely to be true in the short run, a case for higher prices and subsidies will be made.

The first pressure on the Agriculture Ministry may arise from within the Ministry, if the Food Department is placed within the Agriculture Ministry. The functioning of the Food Department/Ministry is directed more at food distribution than at production, and to encourage higher take-off from the public distribution network, it may wish to lower the consumer price. Further pressures against higher food prices typically emanate from the Planning Ministry. Given the large weight they have in the various price indices, food prices affect the general price level in the economy and, by extension, the real value of plan investments. The Planning Ministry would like greater agricultural production, but the economy-wide macro implications of food prices are normally its greater concern.

The most powerful representative of the macro (inter-sectoral) view is, however, the Finance Ministry. The Planning Ministry deals mostly with the design of economic policy; the Finance Ministry is involved with both the design and the actual, day-to-day conduct of economic policy. The power of Finance lies squarely in the fact that it holds the governmental purse, a power superseded only by that of the Prime Minister. The Finance Ministry is intimately concerned with the general price level in the economy and with the macro balances (budget, trade and foreign exchange). Farm subsidies can affect the budget balance, and the fertiliser-intensity of the green revolution inevitably influences the trade and foreign exchange balance.

Normally hidden behind the principle of governmental secrecy, some of the key inter-bureaucratic dimensions of the problem have come out in the open in the 1980s. Agriculture Ministers have been repeatedly pushed to explain why producer prices cannot be raised further. Some have candidly stated the intersectoral nature of food prices:

> I have many responsibilities that are equally important. Agriculture Ministry is my responsibility – my task there is to raise production. Food Ministry is also my responsibility – my task there is to feed people. I have to look at both . . . The ultimate decision lies with the Cabinet . . . One has to see how much cloth there is for the coat . . . The views of the Planning Commission, Finance and Civil Supplies have to be obtained [*Singh, Rao Birendra, 1980a: 251–2*].

The demand constraint and rising surpluses of the last decade have given the inter-bureaucratic struggle a distinct flavour. They have added to the customary power of the Finance Ministry over economic policy by giving its position an ideological legitimacy. In the 1960s, with deficits in food supply, the Finance Ministry was concerned about the impact of higher food prices on inflation. However, Subramaniam, as Agriculture

Minister, could present the forceful argument that without price incentives and input subsidies, food production would not rise either. With surpluses emerging in the 1980s, the production argument is losing its bureaucratic vigour, even as it is acquiring ever increasing political strength in party and non-party politics. The following statement by the Agriculture Minister in the early 1980s could well have been made by the Finance Ministry:

> How can (the) increase in production be possible if there were no remunerative prices? This is a very . . . simple thing to understand . . . (T)he farmers' standard should rise . . . But we cannot compare our conditions with the conditions in other advanced countries . . . Japan and USA being prosperous countries, the contribution of their farm sector to the gross national income is only 6 to 7 per cent . . . (T)hose countries are able to provide huge subsidies to sustain their farm production. Why? This is because only a very small percentage of their population is employed in agriculture. In Japan . . . (t)hey procure.rice for instance by paying several times the international price. But can we afford to do that in India? If we go to the same level of procurement, by raising the procurement price without raising the issue price, according to the estimates of my Ministry, we have to pay subsidy to the extent of 300 crores per year. Can we take upon ourselves that burden? Do you want this country to develop in every field, or do you want this country to spend all its resources on the development of farming and thus all the time remain a poor country? [*Singh, 1980b: 422*].

Two points emerge. First, as farm pressures in the party and non-party politics have increased in the 1980s to the extent that there are virtually no dissenting voices left in party politics arguing against the farmers' demands, the interbureaucratic politics of the state institutions have, ironically, gone in the other direction. In the end, the noisy parliamentary uproars and the agitational politics of non-party organisations have been dispersed by the quiet power of the Finance Ministry. Second, by concentrating on the character of the Commission on Agricultural Costs and rices (CACP), the rural politicians have been attacking the wrong target. The idea that more rural politicians and fewer urban-trained technocrats in the CACP would redress the grievances of farmers is fundamentally flawed. By having politicians as members, the CACP is certainly more visible than before, but it remains a minor player in the state structure. It has a recommendatory status only. The final decision is taken by the cabinet. The CACP can raise clamours for higher prices but if it cannot even carry the Agriculture Minister with it, it will at best make a marginal difference to the decision.[28] For crops experiencing a technical deceleration, and for situations requiring larger resources, the CACP may not be enough. The more powerful institutions of the state must be penetrated, or forced to change.

Diagram 1 schematically represents the refractory process. The analytical space is divided in two parts, political and economic. The political realm, in turn, has two parts. Realm A represents the trends in party and non-party politics, showing an unmistakable rise in rural power. This is the segment most visible to the eye. Realm B depicts the intra-state, or inter-bureaucratic realm, where the power of Finance, or its ideological hegemony, bends the trajectory of Realm A to produce the economic outcomes in Realm C, outcomes that do not correspond to the trajectory in Realm C. Without Segment B, or without technical change being a variable, the trajectories of Realms A and C could have been similar.

The celebrated works on agrarian political economy works have only partially mapped the analytical space. Michael Lipton [1977] concentrated on Realm C, inferring the shape of Realm A therefrom. Ashok Mitra [1977] also focused on Realm C without taking technical change into consideration and the fiscal politics it creates in Realm B. Bates [1981] dealt with Realms A and C, arguing that a downward trend in Realm C is a result of trends in Realm A. The puzzle for Bates was: why, despite the countryside constituting a majority in the population, there was no upward trend in Realm A. That even an upward trend in Realm A may not directly determine results in Realm C was not his concern. Not part of his empirical universe, rising rural power was missing in his analytical space, too. The state remained undisaggregated, the Finance Ministry did not enter the scene, and the possibility of disjunctions did not appear.

What can alter the situation for the farmers? If a peasant-based party captures power in Delhi, politics can be in command. In the final analysis, the issue boils down to whether or not a peasant-based party can come to power – individually, or, as an overwhelmingly dominant partner in a coalition.

The multiple selves of farmers and self-limited rural power: In a parliamentary system, a majority of total *votes* is not required to gain a majority of representative seats; a plurality of votes is enough. Since 70 per cent of the country's population is rural, the support of a majority in the countryside should, in principle, suffice to capture power. A sectional strategy based on an urban–rural divide should therefore be

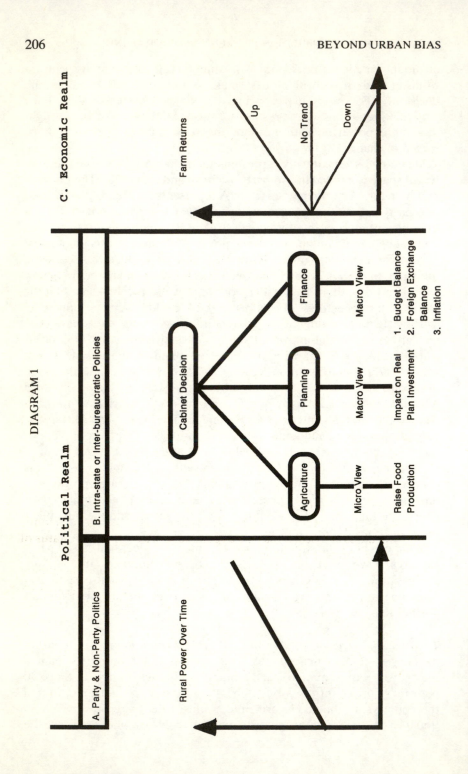

DIAGRAM 1

adequate for gaining a plurality of total votes in a predominantly rural country.[29] Why, then, does a sectional rural strategy fail?

How farmers vote, and how they define their interests at the time of voting, may have little to do with prices and loans. Besides, half a million may show up for agitations between elections, making political news, but an equal number may stay back distrusting the caste of the leaders of the agitation or the social composition of the leaders' main support base. Those who stay back do not form part of the news.

The array of choices at the time of voting may be as follows: should I vote for a party representing my caste, or a party representing my religious community, or one expressing my region's interest, or a national party that advocates the country's unity over everything else, or for a charismatic leader, or for a party that best represents my occupational interests. A farmer may well vote on caste, religious or regional considerations; even worse, those who participated in price agitations between elections may vote on non-economic grounds during elections. In other words, a single issue, or a set of economic issues, may clash with other considerations that determine how farmers define their political interests and vote. The description below of electoral behaviour in Uttar Pradesh during the 1980 parliamentary elections illustrates the problem. The Janata Party comprising, among others, Charan Singh's peasant-based Lok Dal party had broken up, each party of the erstwhile Janata coalition contesting separately, and Mrs Gandhi's party, Congress (I), was bidding for a return to power.

> On the face of it, the election seemed to turn overwhelmingly on the issue of high prices, scarcity of essential commodities, the sugar cane price and the availability of agricultural inputs needed by the *kisans* (peasants) in the previous growing season . . . Whether or not a voter blamed the government for the economic difficulties and scarcities . . . depended more on the caste status of the respondent than on their economic position . . . Brahmin voters favorably disposed to the Congress . . . blamed the Janata government . . . Yadav *kisans*, who were inclined toward the Lok Dal, however, blamed only the Janata government and excused Charan Singh who had been in office only a short time . . . In other words, the (economic) issues in the campaign were as much the excuses for voting behaviour as reasons for it. The really central issue . . . in Uttar Pradesh at least . . . was whether the voters identified with the middle cultivating castes or with the Congress coalition [*Brass, 1985: 198*].

More critically, consider the lament of Sharad Joshi, the most successful peasant mobiliser in the country, on how difficult it was for a movement based on economic demands to go beyond where it stood:

> Men do not like to appear to be fighting for bread or even for butter. They like to feel . . . that there is a principle involved. Castes, language, religion and region provide ready-made principles for which men can be made willingly to die and brutally to kill. It is perhaps related to the primary urge to seek security in community. May be, the fraternity of an economic class has identity of interests but not the means and structures for securing them [*Joshi, 1988: 67*].

Joshi goes on to add how the emergence of religious strife completely overwhelmed a powerful peasant movement, based on economic demands and led by the Bhartiya Kisan Union (BKU), in Punjab in the 1980s.[30]

The further march of rural power may not be possible unless farmers define their identity primarily as farmers, not as members of a caste, linguistic or regional community. The challenge before these movements is to create these necessary conditions, that is, to transform the way farmers define their interests and identities. For at least some time to come, they are unwilling to let their multiple selves be reduced to a narrow economic groove. A rise in religious upsurge in recent years is affecting not only urban India but also the countryside. In an election charged with religious and identity issues, the Janata Dal, which incorporates the Lok Dal of yesteryears, picked up a mere 12 per cent of India's vote, whereas the party representing Hindu nationalism made the most gains in June 1991. There are no indications that the cross-cutting identities and interests would be resolved in favour of economic interests, defined as higher prices and subsidies.

V. CONCLUSIONS

About a decade before Lipton published *Why Poor People Stay Poor: Urban Bias In World Development*, Samuel Huntington presented an argument about 'The Green Uprisings: Party Systems and Rural Mobilisation' [*Huntington, 1968*]. Lipton in 1977 wrote how powerless the countryside was; Huntington in 1968 talked of 'ruralising elections', elections that ruralised a polity dominated by Westernised post-independence elite (Sri Lanka, 1956; Turkey, 1950; Senegal, 1951; Jamaica, 1944; Lesotho, 1965). 'The urban classes have been able to win most of the rounds of struggle with the countryside', wrote Lipton. Huntington argued:

> Electoral competition in postcolonial countries thus seems to direct the attention of political leaders from the urban to the rural voter, to make political appeals less modern and more traditional, to replace highly educated cosmopolitan leaders with less educated local and provincial leaders . . . The effect of democracy is to disperse power among a plurality of more traditional elites. By increasing the power of rural groups democracy also tends to promote policies aimed at rural and agrarian rather than urban and industrial development [*Huntington, 1968: 445*].

Lipton 'first noted urban bias in (his) analysis of India in the 1960s' [*Lipton, 1977: 18*], precisely the time political scientists were reporting that the national leadership of the Congress Party had shifted from Nehru, a man educated at Harrow and Cambridge, to Shastri, a politician who had never been outside his country before becoming Prime Minister. They were also writing that the party leadership in Madras state had moved from Rajgopalachari, an anglicised Brahmin lawyer, to Kamraj, a man from a peasant background with very little formal education.

For some reason, the political economy field did not communicate with political science in the 1960s and 1970s. If it had, an urban bias argument without a distinction between democratic and authoritarian political systems would not have been made. In a primarily rural society, a democratic political system is likely, over time, to ruralise the political system and economic policy. An SLFP would begin to defeat a UNP (Sri Lanka in 1956); a Shastri and a Kamraj would begin to dominate the Congress Party (India after the mid-1960s); a Mahathir Mohamad would replace the generation of Tunku Abdul Rahman (Malaysia in the 1980s); and an Andrew Jackson would defeat a John Quincy Adams (the US in 1829).[31] Authoritarian polities do not have to seek electoral legitimacy in the same way, so they are not under the same rural pressure. An undivided Punjab was split into India and Pakistan in 1947, with the better-endowed west going to Pakistan, and the less developed east coming to India's share. After four decades of development, reports Holly Sims, agriculture in India's Punjab has left Pakistani Punjab considerably behind [*Sims, 1988*].

One should not push this argument too far. Pro-rural policies and economic outcomes can exist in authoritarian polities, too. It depends on the ideological proclivities of the political leadership (Widner, this volume). Indonesia under President Suharto is by far the best known example. His pro-rural inclinations have lifted Indonesia's agriculture out of its 1960s morass (Timmer, this volume). Perhaps other examples can also be cited. The point simply is that *there is no systematic ruralising tendency in authoritarian polities*. Urban bias can flourish, at times with reckless abandon.

Economic counters to the urban bias can also be found. If the source of public revenue is not agriculture, industrialisation or state-building would not necessarily squeeze agriculture. Minerals can be one such source, oil another. Having these resources, of course, does not mean that public revenue would be spent wisely. A profligate state can squander away the asset and catch the Dutch disease: due to various economic fall-outs and indirect effects, agriculture could still lose out. The same can be said about states blessed with the bounty of foreign aid. A few national budgets are known to have been almost entirely funded by acts of strategic friendship – and for long years. In all of these cases, a structural opportunity to leave the countryside unharmed does exist, although some states may not cash in for various reasons.[32]

Other problems arise for the urban bias argument when we realise that even after rural groups acquire a great deal of power and manage to influence economic policy, the policy outcomes may still not be favourable at all times. Reduced to its core, the urban bias view is that the countryside suffers because it has no power in the polity. Influencing economic policy through accretions of political power may not, however, be enough to determine economic well-being in the countryside. Understanding this disjunction requires going inside a state to determine exactly how rural groups and their representatives function in pursuit of their aims and what forces are encountered. More importantly, it also requires determining whether rural groups can actually cohere politically around economic interests. The disjunction between the political and the economic in India is due not to the eccentricities of the Indian case but, rather, the relationship between political power and economic outcomes has to be more comprehensively imagined. The refusal of farmers themselves to give precedence to their economic interests over their non-economic interests or ascriptive identities may seriously constrain their power. Much of the political economy literature, governed by the assumption of rationality, ignores the fact that farmers, like most of us, have multiple selves and there is no reason to assume a permanent superiority of the economic over the non-economic.

Urban bias thus may not be as ubiquitous as we, the students of political economy, have often believed. Nor does its reversal in the political system guarantee continued rural well-being, although it does perhaps produce happier outcomes for the countryside than is generally the case otherwise. From the perspective of the countryside, the real issue, it seems, is procuring appropriate economic policies, the appropriateness depending on the context of the country in question. Unfortunately, there is no good theory of policy change or of conditions under which policies change. Short of that, a democratic political system would be the second best alternative for the countryside.

NOTES

1. The terms 'rural sector', 'peasantry' and 'farmers' are used interchangeably in this study, despite a tradition of controversy on this point. It has often been argued that a distinction needs to be drawn between 'peasants' and 'farmers', the former defined as those producing for home consumption, the latter for the market. While this duality may be perfectly legitimate for historical cases drawn from Europe, advances in agricultural technology are making this distinction increasingly anachronistic. In terms of economic motivations and participation in market exchange, the upper and middle peasantry, and even the lower peasantry, do not any more appear to be fundamentally different from the class of farmers. Social distinctions within the rural sector exist, but they have to be construed differently, not in terms of 'peasants' and 'farmers'. After the scientific advances of the last three decades, the so-called peasantry in many parts of the Third World has used the new technology in a rational manner, thereby aiding the process of modernisation rather than restraining it. One major objection to using the term 'rural sector' remains, however. In the Third World, increases or decreases in rural power and welfare may not affect the class of agricultural labourers; therefore, the term rural sector, whenever used this study, makes no assumptions about the directionality in the welfare or power of agricultural labourers. The awkward position of landless agricultural labourers in the rural sector is discussed in detail in Ashutosh Varshney [*forthcoming: Ch.5*].
2. *The Times of India*, 3 Feb. 1988. This editorial was written after an agitation in Western Uttar Pradesh in the winter of 1987–88.
3. A similar transformation marks the position of the BJP, customarily an urban-based party. For details, see Varshney [*forthcoming: Ch.5*].
4. See Surjeet [*1981: 16*]. Surjeet is a politburo member of the Communist Party Marxist (CPM) and the party's prominent theoretician.
5. The estimated cost of this waiver to the country's credit system ranges from Rs 500–700 billion. Hard statistics are not available, but it should be clear that the magnitude is very large. In January 1991, they would have translated into $25–35 billion (by the exchange rate existing at the time).
6. The Lok Sabha Debates in 1980 and 1981 reverberated with rancorous debates over the police repression of the Joshi-led agitation. The State legislature in Maharashtra also exploded with charges and countercharges between the treasury and opposition benches, but police firing on agitating farmers ceased after that.
7. Moreover, political opponents can always plant criminals among such rallies, provoking the police and administration – the sort of disruption normally achieved through destruction of public property. Such political games are not unknown in movement politics.
8. The repression-resisting capacity of a democracy, as Robert Dahl [*1971: Ch.2 and 3*] explains with great clarity, will not apply to some groups – those whose numbers are so meagre that they are electorally important, and/or if the group is geographically concentrated, and/or the dominant ideology in the system makes discrimination of

certain groups more acceptable than that of others. Dahl explains the position of American blacks before the mid-1960s in that way; the argument can be extended to quite a few groups in India but not to farmers.

9. For arguments for and against see Mitra [*1977*]; Tyagi [*1979*]; Kahlon and Tyagi [*1980*]; and Kumar [*1988*].

10. Raj Krishna [*1982*] provides a simple mathematical proof of this. Symbolically, if Q and F are total output and total input, and Po and Pi are output and input prices, then return-to-cost ratio (r) can be written as PoQ/PiF. Let the terms of trade be defined as $p^* = Po/Pi$, and total factor productivity as $t^* = Q/F$. In growth rates, then, $\hat{r} = p^* + t^*$. Thus, profitability can be raised by improving terms of trade (p^*) without technical innovation ($t^*=0$), or by improving productivity (t^*) at unchanged prices ($P^*=0$), or by improving both.

11. In the Indian debate, too, technology has recently been factored into the terms of trade arguments [*Tyagi, 1987*].

12. See Joshi [*1986*: 'The *Aakrosh* Syndrome']; also author's interviews with Joshi, Pune, India, 3 and 4 Dec. 1984.

13. 'Around 1967–68, about a quarter of Indian cereal marketings were publicly procured, at prices about 25 per cent lower than were obtainable in the market . . . In the 1970s, compulsory procurement of wheat, while not fully enforceable, has been used by the government .to hold farm-gate prices . . . Government procurement, at low prices . . . has been substantial enough to depress farm prices' [*Lipton, 1977: 295*; page citation here and later from the Indian edition, published by Heritage Publishers, Delhi, 1978].

14. Some farmers none the less sell grain to private traders because with the growth of government purchases have come the bureaucratic problems of late payments, long queues and malpractices by the staff of the Food Corporation of India.

15. Since the mid-1970s, Punjab, Haryana and Uttar Pradesh have typically accounted for over 90 per cent of the procured wheat. Over 80 per cent of the government rice stock has also come from these three states and Andhra Pradesh.

16. First made by Mitra [*1977*]. The regional argument acquired a high political pitch during the Janata years in Delhi (1977–79). Heated debates took place in parliament.

17. Price–fertiliser cost ratios formed part of Lipton's argument too but by now, the argument has been generalised to include all costs, not simply fertilisers. Lipton's use of the fertiliser cost data was prompted by the fact that fertiliser costs are typically the largest expense of farmers.

18. It should be emphasised that the formula developed above does not give us exact returns; rather, it yields a return index. Exact returns, using the same symbols, can be written as

$$R = (P-C)Y \qquad (2)$$

The problem with formula (2) is that it gives us *nominal* returns, not *real* returns. For formula (2) to give us real returns, we need a price deflator, which is a monumental difficulty in that no uniquely acceptable deflators for measuring farm incomes exist. Because of the way weights are assigned to different commodities, the applicability of both the wholesale price index and consumer price index has been seriously questioned for calculating real farm incomes from nominal figures. Formula (1) surmounts this difficulty: it divides prices, a nominal measure, by costs, another nominal measure, instead of subtracting one nominal measure from the other, which would in the end still leave us with a nominal magnitude. Formula (1) thus yields a proxy for exact returns, *a second best* measure which overcomes the inherent difficulties of the ideal solution, and suffices for the purposes of judging the directionality of farm incomes (whether they have gone down or up over time).

19. No good estimates of how much grain rots every year are available. Nor, given the political sensitivity of such an issue, can it easily be known. It is widely believed, however, that anywhere between two and four million tons of grain are lost this way.

20. Author's interview with Rao Birendra Singh, Agriculture Minister (1980–86), Delhi, 18 Sept. 1986.

21. In India's case, food subsidies of the last ten years or so cannot be called consumer subsidies. Given the demand constraint, if the market had been allowed to rule, prices would have come down, both for consumers and producers. The food subsidy increased because the floor at which producers were supported was too high for poor consumers. A food subsidy is a consumer subsidy in situations of shortage but a producer subsidy in the context of surpluses. The fertiliser subsidy, however, may not entirely benefit farmers. Domestic costs of fertiliser production in India are high and given the cost-plus pricing principle, even inefficient fertiliser producers get protection. In other words, for a portion of fertiliser supplies (excluding international imports, that are still substantial, and the relatively efficient fertiliser producers at home), the fertiliser subsidy in India is in fact a subsidy to fertiliser producers, not to farmers. What is pertinent for the fiscal burden argument is that, whatever the reason behind subsidies, their rising burden goes against farm interests.

22. One of the few political economy works on public finance is Toye [1981]. Ending with 1970, Toye's work does not deal with the period marked by farm subsidy issues.

23. Although tax evasion has often been pointed as the culprit that has driven a gap between the expected and actual revenue collection, it should be pointed out that despite evasions, a tax–GDP ratio of 17–18 per cent is quite impressive for a country at India's GDP. It can none the less be shown that, even at the given level of income, tax receipts can go up. See below.

24. The most widely known case for an agricultural income tax is Ministry of Finance [1972], also known as the K.N. Raj Committee. The Raj committee was constituted at a time when the left dominated India's economic policy-making under Mrs Gandhi, and the talk of taxing the new agricultural rich was widely prevalent. It should be noted, however, that the left was not the only advocate of taxing the beneficiaries of the green revolution.

25. Even while the left dominated policy circles under Mrs Gandhi in the late 1960s to mid 1970s, Mrs. Gandhi's response to proposals for taxing the agricultural rich was fairly straightforward. She 'told the planners unequivocally that . . . none of the experts in the Planning Commission . . . seemed to have . . . a realistic appreciation of the political' factors . . . Agriculture could not be taxed for political reasons . . . [Economic and Political Weekly, 1974].

26. Of the three, interest payments have increased most sharply over the last decade and a half. The government has borrowed, mainly domestically, to fund public investment, to meet deficits of the public sector and to even finance the current government expenses.

27. For details, see Varshney [1989].

28. Once again, of the politicians, only Sharad Joshi has realised this point: 'What means does (the CAPC) have at its disposal for evaluating the repercussions (of agricultural prices) on the cost of living, wages, industrial costs? What does it know of the overall needs of the economy and balanced price structure? These are matters dealt with . . . in much higher forums – the ministries of Planning, Finance, Agriculture, Commerce, the Planning Commission, the Reserve Bank.' [Joshi, 1984: 33–34].

29. Qualitatively, the problem is the same as that of a strong women's movement finding it difficult to turn itself into a women's party despite women constituting, typically, more than half of a given population.

30. Also author's interview with Sharad Joshi, Delhi, 12 Jan. 1991.

31. One should expect that in other democracies in the Third World, too, a similar tendency – rural empowerment – would obtain. Stable Third World democracies have been few and far between. The link has been briefly noticed though not yet systematically developed. On Costa Rica, see Colburn in this volume. For Zimbabwe during its first ten years of democratic politics (1980–89), see Bratton [1987] and Herbst [1988]. For Sri Lanka, Mick Moore notes that ethnic identities overwhelmed farm identities as a result of which Sri Lanka's rural sector did not acquire the same power as India's

rural sector did [*Moore, 1985*]. Ronald Herring [*1988*] points out that the rural folk in Sri Lanka had no special reason to organise as economic (as opposed to ethnic) political groups since the economic policy of Sri Lankan government was already substantially pro-rural. While arguing a case for Kenya's rural exceptionalism in Africa, Bates notes how the pursuit of power became interlinked with a nurturing of the rural constituency in Kenyan politics and how electoral competition, though more limited than in Asian democracies but keener than in most African polities, produced a tendency towards pro-rural economic policies in Kenya [*Bates, 1989*]. It would be interesting to see whether other democracies in the Third World – Botswana, Trinidad and Tobago, Jamaica, Venezuela since 1959 and Chile between 1932 and 1972 – support the proposed link between democracy, rural empowerment and rural well-being in the Third World.

32. The final chapter of Bates [*1981*] anticipates some of these possibilities. And in Bates [*1989*], he presents Kenya as an exception to the urban bias of Africa.

REFERENCES

Acharya, Shankar, 1988, 'India's Fiscal Policy', in Gustav Papanek and Robert Lucas, *The Indian Economy: Recent Developments and Future Prospects*, Boulder, CO: Westview Press.

Anderson, Kim and Yujiro Hayami, 1986, *The Political Economy of Agricultural Protection*, Sydney: Allen & Unwin.

Bates, Robert, 1981, *Markets and States in Tropical Africa*, Berkeley, CA: University of California Press.

Bates, Robert, 1989, *Beyond the Miracle of the Market: The Political Economy of Agrarian Development in Kenya*, Cambridge: Cambridge University Press.

Brass, Paul, 1985, 'Congress, the Lok Dal and the Middle Peasant Castes: An Analysis of the 1977 and 1980 Parliamentary Election in Uttar Pradesh', in Brass, *Caste, Faction and Party in Indian Politics*, Vol.II, Delhi: Chanakya Publications.

Bratton, Michael, 1987, 'The Comrades and the Countryside: The Politics of Agricultural Policy in Zimbabwe', *World Politics*, Vol.36, No.2, January.

Dahl, Robert, 1971, *Polyarchy*, New Haven, CT: Yale University Press, 1971.

Desai, Gunwant, 1986, 'Rapporteur's Report on Farm Price Structure', *Indian Journal of Agricultural Economics*, Vol.41, No.4, Oct.–Dec.

Economic and Political Weekly, 1974, 25 May.

Hayami, Yujiro, 1972, 'Rice Price Policy in Japan's Economic Development', *American Journal of Agricultural Economics*, Aug.

Hayami, Yujiro, Subbarao, K. and K. Otsuka, 1982, 'Efficiency and Equity in the Producer Levy of India', *American Journal of Agricultural Economics*, Nov.

Herbst, Jeffrey, 1988, 'Societal Demands and Government Choices: Agricultural Producer Price Policy in Zimbabwe', *Comparative Politics*, Vol.20, No.1, April.

Herring, Ronald J., 1988, Review of Mick Moore, *Economic Development and Cultural Change*, Vol.36, No.3, April.

Huntington, Samuel P., 1968, *Political Order in Changing Societies*, New Haven, CT: Yale University Press, 1968

Joshi, Sharad, 1984, *Bharat Speaks Out*, Bombay: Build Documentation Center, 1984.

Joshi, Sharad, 1988, 'The Outlines of the Second Indian Republic', *Bharat Eye-View*, Ambethan, Pune: Shetkari Sanghathan.

Kahlon, A.S. and D.S. Tyagi, 1980, 'Inter-Sectoral Terms of Trade', *Economic and Political Weekly*, Review of Agriculture, 27 Dec.

Krishna, Raj, 1982, 'Some Aspects of Agricultural Growth, Price Policy and Equity in Developing Countries', *Food Research Institute Studies*, Vol.18, No.3, p.238.

Kumar, Gopalakrishna, 1988, 'On Prices and Economic Power: Explaining Recent Changes in Intersectoral Relations in the Indian Economy', *Journal of Development Studies*, Vol.25, No.1, Oct.

Lipton, Michael, 1977, *Why Poor People Stay Poor: Urban Bias in World Development*, Cambridge, MA: Harvard University Press.

Mellor, John, 1968, 'Functions of Agricultural Prices in Economic Development', *Indian Journal of Agricultural Economics*, Vol.23, No.1, Jan.–March.

Ministry of Finance, 1972, *Report of the Committee on Taxation of Agricultural Wealth and Income*, Delhi: Government of India.

Ministry of Finance, 1985, *Long Term Fiscal Policy*, Delhi: Government of India, Dec.

Mitra, Ashok, 1977, *Terms of Trade and Class Relations*, London: Frank Cass.

Moore, Mick, 1985, *The State and Peasant Politics in Sri Lanka*, Cambridge: Cambridge University Press.

Olson, Mancur, 1965, *The Logic of Collective Action*, Cambridge, MA: Harvard University Press.

Sims, Holly, 1988, *Political Regimes, Public Policy and Economic Development: Agricultural Performance and Rural Change in Two Punjabs*, New Delhi and Newbury Park: Sage Publications.

Singh, Rao Birendra, 1980a, *Lok Sabha Debates*, VII Series, Vol.VII, 29 July.

Singh, Rao Birendra, 1980b: *Lok Sabha Debates*, VII Series, Vol.X, 11 Dec.

Surjeet, H.K.S., 1981, 'Upsurge', *Seminar*, No.267, Nov.

Thamarajakshi, R., 1969, 'Intersectoral Terms of Trade and the Marketed Surplus, 1951–52 to 1965–66', *Economic and Political Weekly*, Review of Agriculture, 26 June.

Thamarajakshi, R., 1977, 'Role of Price Incentives in Stimulating Agricultural Production in a Developing Economy', in Douglas Ensminger (ed.), *Food Enough or Starvation for Millions*, Rome: FAO.

Toye, John, 1981, *Public Expenditures and Indian Development Policy, 1960–70*, Cambridge: Cambridge University Press.

Tyagi, D.S., 1979, 'Farm Prices and Class Bias in India', *Economic and Political Weekly*, Review of Agriculture, Sept.

Tyagi, D.S., 1987, 'Domestic Terms of Trade and Their Effect on Supply and Demand of Agricultural Sector', *Economic and Political Weekly*, Review of Agriculture, 28 March.

Varshney, Ashutosh, 1989, 'Ideas, Institutions and Interests in Policy Change', *Policy Sciences*, Fall.

Varshney, Ashutosh, forthcoming, *Democracy, Development and the Countryside: Urban–Rural Struggles in India*, New York: Cambridge University Press.

III. COMMENTARY

'Urban Bias': A Fresh Look

ROBERT H. BATES

Focusing on non-conforming cases, the articles in this special issue abandon the method of stylised facts and highlight instead variation over space and time. In so doing, they detect errors of commission and omission in the earlier literature on urban bias. They call for a focus on the economic role of political institutions, the political role of markets for assets, and the political significance of technical change.

INTRODUCTION

When investigating a pattern of behaviour, scholars can choose between two methods. They can agree upon a set of stylised facts and then seek an explanation of them; or they can note a range of variation and search for a set of variables and a model of the relationship among them that would account for it. The first approach, which tends to be deductive, highlights similarities. The second, which tends to be inductive, highlights differences.

In my own work on 'urban bias' [*Bates, 1981a*], I adopted the first method. The articles in this volume adopt the second. Most focus on non-confirming cases: instances in which developing countries have adopted agricultural policies that favour the interests of farmers. In addition, they highlight variability over space and time. Taking a fresh look at 'urban bias' and employing different methods, what have these authors learned?

ERRORS OF COMMISSION

One of the most important lessons is that early studies of 'urban bias' were plagued with possible measurement error. As Timmer points out in his essay, the basic measure employed was the ratio of local to world prices for farm products, adjusted for the real exchange rate. But, he emphasises, domestic prices for commodities tend to change less, and

Robert H. Bates is Henry R. Luce Professor of Political Science and Economics at Duke University, Durham, North Carolina. He joins Harvard University as Professor of Government later this year.

less frequently, than do international prices, and much of the variation in this ratio therefore results from price movements in international markets. When, as in the 1970s, international prices rise but domestic prices remain steady, then students of agricultural policy would see domestic prices lying below world market prices and infer 'urban bias.' When, as in the 1980s, international prices fall while domestic prices remain relatively unchanged, then students of agricultural policy would infer a shift in favour of farmers.

Timmer plays off of this methodological point in three major ways. The first is to urge a move away from a 'domestic origins' explanation of agricultural policy in favour of one based on international trade. In taking this position, Timmer joins many others who point to shifts in the international terms of trade and market conditions, rather than to domestic policy choices, as fundamental determinants of Third World development. Secondly, he urges that analysts focus on the macro-economy rather than the industry or sector as the basic unit of analysis. In choosing pricing policies, policy-makers pay more attention to aggregate prices and trade balances, he argues, than to the relative fortunes of organised interests. Considerations of the aggregate welfare, rather than of distributional consequences, represent the basic motivation for policy choices, he claims; policy-makers appear to place a primary emphasis on price stability rather than on price discrimination in making policy choices.

Clearly, Timmer poses a fundamental challenge to the existing literature on urban bias. His methodological critique threatens to overturn received wisdoms. And the alternative approaches that he adopts represent sharp alternatives to established explanations of policy making. While accepting Timmer's basic point – that changes in domestic prices are smaller and less frequent than those in international markets – I am none the less reluctant to subscribe to his reinterpretations, and for several reason.

Pace Timmer, the local price for farm products is not the only, or indeed the major, factor under the government's control. So too is the exchange rate. And, as much of the literature has emphasised, the politics of the exchange rate are absolutely fundamental to the politics of urban bias [*Krueger, 1992*]. Even were local prices the primary variables under the government's control, a small change in measurement would be called for, rather than a large change in approach. The relevant measure would be the tendency to adjust, or to fail to adjust, the domestic price to the international price; and the appropriate definition of urban bias would be the tendency of governments to persist in holding domestic prices below world market levels when international prices rise or their eagerness to reduce local prices to world price levels, when international prices fall. Given this revised measure and altered definition of policy bias, I am certain that the same pattern would hold: as was detected in the original works in this genre, governments in poor countries would tend to intervene in markets in ways that impose a tax on agriculture, while governments in richer nations would tend to intervene in ways that confer subsidies on farmers.

The basic question thus remains: why do governments behave that way? Timmer calls for explanations that emphasise macroeconomic policy-making and welfare-enhancing economic management, rather than ones that focus on distributional struggles among industries or sectors. I suspect that our differences arise from differences in our field experiences, his largely centring on Indonesia – a nation where macroeconomic policy-makers have long occupied unusually powerful positions – and mine largely taking place in Africa – a continent wherein, notoriously, they have not. That said, I would none the less insist on a political explanation.

In the first instance, we must try to understand why politicians in Indonesia have yielded control over agricultural pricing policies to macroeconomists, while those elsewhere, and especially in Africa, have not. More generally, we *must* understand the politics of the profoundly paradoxical transformation of agriculture's location in the political economy of nations, as these nations develop: its transformation from an embattled majority that is taxed into a minority powerful enough to be subsidised. This transformation implies political struggles: the displacement of agrarian elites, the capturing of the peasantry, urban riots, peasant rebellions, fights between town and country, taxation, oppression, and violence. Welfare-enhancing motivations, such as the search for price stability, may play a role in the behaviour of some technocrats; but these technocrats can only affect the policies of the state as a result of some anterior political struggle – one in which, as a consequence of some political victory, agricultural policy is at last delegated to the economists.

The articles point to a second possible error of commission: that of assuming a clear separation of interests between town and country. The sectoral theory of Lipton [*Lipton, 1977*] and my own interest group approach rest on the presumption of distinct interests, with policy outcomes being characterised in terms of the supremacy of the interests of urban consumers of farm products. We both interpret the relative immiseration of the countryside in developing countries as the outcome of a redistributive struggle.

But what if there is no clear divide? If asset-holders mix their portfolios, holding entitlements to streams of income from both agriculture and industry, it is impossible to distinguish the economic interests of those who live in town from those who live in the country; and policy choices then cannot be accounted for as the outcome of sectoral conflicts. As the contributions make clear, this threat to urban bias theory is not merely a possibility; it is actual. For, as noted by Widner, urban residents 'abroad' in the Ivory Coast maintain close ties – economic, social, and political – with their rural homes. As noted by Oi, industry has moved to the countryside in China and accounts for much of the recent growth in rural incomes. In Kenya, Taiwan, and India, industrial firms, whether as the processors of agricultural products or as the suppliers of farm inputs, represent active agents in the politics of agricultural policy-making, as documented by Moore and Varshney. These observations thus call into question one of the basic assumptions underlying the literature on urban bias: the clear separation between town and country.

There can be no question about the facts: families and firms do maintain diversified portfolios, straddling the divide between town and country, and holding income-earning assets in both sectors. There is less certainty, however, in the interpretation of these facts. More important, surely, than the existence of urban–rural linkages is their incidence and magnitude, and both vary. With regard to the incidence, as Widner stresses, it was clearly significant for agricultural policy in the Ivory Coast that political elites in that country owned cocoa plantations. Elite ties with agriculture characterise as well three other nations in Africa: Malawi, Botswana and Kenya. That political elites were stake-holders in these nations, to use Moore's phrase, would appear to go far in explaining why they pursued policies more favourable to agriculture than those that were adopted by other nations in Africa. Not only the incidence but also the magnitude of cross-sectoral ties can vary. It can vary over space: In early twentieth century Colombia, for example, rural banks borrowed urban capital to finance coffee exports and on-lent the savings of coffee farmers to finance urban industry. In contrast to, say, Uganda, coffee policy in Colombia was rarely debated in terms of 'industry versus agriculture' – and was far more favourable to coffee farmers. The magnitude can also vary over time. As noted by Moore and Varshney, as technical change took place in agriculture in Asia, farmers purchased a greater percentage of their imports from industry; ties grew between firms and farms, sometimes resulting in vertically integrated agro-industries; and agricultural policy shifted away from that characteristic of urban bias. In nations where the magnitude of the urban-based agricultural investment is greater than in others, then, interests arise within industry that favour higher prices for farmers.

ERRORS OF OMISSION

The contributions in this volume thus point to errors of commission in the literature on urban bias. They also point to errors of omission. In part as a result, they critique the original literature for an over-emphasis on the political significance of groups and their interests, and an under-emphasis on the political significance of ideology and the state.

While agreeing with much of this criticism, I must, at the outset, take exception to the assertion that ideology was overlooked in the early works on urban bias. I would point to the comprehensive overview of political and economic thought contained in Lipton's foundational study [*Lipton, 1977*]. And I would also point to my own effort to measure the impact of ideology on the likelihood of state intervention in agricultural markets in Africa [*Bates, 1981b*]. My study confirmed what others [*Mitrany, 1961*] have averred: that socialist governments tend to violate the interests of food producers in general and the peasantry in particular.

For ideological reasons, socialist governments possess deep ties to urban labour; they therefore align with the consumers of food. Relative to others, socialist governments forge large bureaucracies, if only so as to provide a greater range and quality of public services. Producing an unpriced service, these governments are hit hard by increases in wages resulting from increases in the prices of food, and therefore tend to resist such price rises. Socialist governments are committed to industrialisation; often, they are committed to public ownership. As a result, they tend to own more industries than do other governments; and, all else being equal, when wages rise in response to increased costs of food, industrial profits fall. Driven by ideological imperatives to forge financial and political ties with public and private employees and urban industry, socialist governments therefore end up acting as if they were more committed to industrialisation than to economic equality. Ironically, their ideological commitments lead them to violate their egalitarian ethics, as they adopt policies that violate the interests of their poorest citizens – the peasantry [*Bates, 1981b*; *Mitrany, 1961*].

The impact of ideology has thus been more deeply explored than is claimed by some of the contributors to this volume. The authors also call for a greater recognition of the role of state intervention, and in this they are more persuasive. Moore notes the role of public bureaucrats in defending farm interests in Taiwan; Timmer does the same for

Indonesia. Oi notes that in China local functionaries, in search of revenues, advocate the cause of rural interests. These examples can be easily multiplied: As argued by Hayami, quasi-state agencies mobilise political blocs to defend rice-growing interests in Japan [*Hayami, 1988*]. And bureaucrats in the United States helped to spawn the Farm Bureau, a leading defender of farm interests [*McConnell, 1966*]. Few political scientists would to go as far as Timmer, who places the technocrat at the centre of his analysis of agricultural policy in Indonesia. But many, including myself, would agree that agencies of the state not only implement but also help to create agricultural policy. We would agree that state agencies not only respond to organised interests, as the early literature recognised; they also create and mobilise such interests, as documented in these essays. Their significance clearly was underestimated in the sectoral and interest group theories that dominated the earlier literature.

That admitted, a second admission must follow: that acknowledging the significance of 'state actors' is not the same as advancing a theory of their behaviour. The earlier studies stressed the role of such political agencies as agricultural marketing boards; indeed, in the hands of some [*Findlay, 1991*] marketing boards provided the iconography of the predatory state, so pilloried by the neo-classical development economists. The contributions in this volume stress the role of other public institutions and demonstrate that they can promote rather than prey upon rural interests in the developing nations and, indeed, overcome the pressures from urban interests to impose low price policies upon agriculture. Without going further, however, little progress has been made in attacking the fundamental problem: why some states promote rural interests while others do not.

Within these essays, hints emerge, providing guidelines as how best to proceed in analysing 'the role of the state'. As already mentioned, some authors, such as Widner and Moore, point to the *economic* interests of political elites, such as Houphouet's cocoa farms in the Ivory Coast or Moore's 'stakes-holders' in agriculture. Widner, Moore, and others also highlight the significance of the *political* interests of these elites and, in particular, the way in which they must compete for power. While Widner and Colburn caution against any facile equation of democratic politics with the empowerment of farm interests, all authors affirm that the structure of political competition shapes the way in which governments orient themselves toward rural communities and formulate pricing policies for farmers. To provide two examples: competitive elections and the search for political majorities appear to have shaped agricultural policy in India and Korea. And the ability of rural-based political parties to make and unmake coalition governments featured in Varshney's analysis of policy change in India.

The sectoral and pressure group theories of urban bias largely left political institutions out of the analysis. Their significance lies in the way in which they structure the competition for power. It may be useful to summarise some of the propositions that have been advanced regarding their impact upon agricultural policy.

(1) Single party systems lead to a removal of agricultural pricing policy from the political agenda. Under single party systems, political debate does not focus on the relative fortunes of town versus country [*Bates, 1978, 1979*; Widner, this volume].

(2) In single party systems that allow candidates to compete for votes in local constituencies, political competition focuses attention on the ability of politicians to allocate political 'pork', such as jobs or public investments, rather than on their stands on broad issues of public policy, such as pricing policies [*Bates, 1989*; Widner, this volume].

(3) Single party systems that are socialist adopt agricultural policies that are more adverse to the interests of farmers than do single party systems that endorse other political ideologies [*Bates, 1981b*].

(4) In nations with competitive party systems, political competition for votes leads to a shift in policy in favour of rural interests [*Bates, 1978; 1979*]. This competition is sufficient to shift a nation that otherwise might be expected to be 'urban biased', such as India, into the ranks of the 'rural biased' (Varshney, this volume).

Clearly, more work needs to be done on the impact of political institutions on 'urban bias'. In particular, recall Varshney's analysis: India shifted to pro-farmer policies only up to a point; a strong Finance Ministry resisted policies that inflicted too a high a financial cost, thereby curtailing the rise of producer prices. Elsewhere, clearly, Ministries of Finance have not been so powerful; they did little to reduce the costs of pro-urban policies in the nations of Africa, for example. A key question thus becomes: What determines the political power of financial ministries? What shapes their relative power *vis-à-vis* other spending ministries and powerful private interests in their societies? What enables public financial institutions to become relatively autonomous from private interests? A lesson learned from these articles, then, is the necessity of focusing on the sources of power of public bureaucracies and, in particular, public financial institutions, thereby achieving a deeper understanding of the role of political institutions in shaping development policy.

The failure fully to take into account the significance of public bureaucracies and political institutions thus constituted a major error of omission in the early literature on urban bias. Just beneath the surface lurk, as it were, hints of another: a failure to appreciate the *political* implications of *technical* change. As documented in the essays on East and South Asia, where farmers have shifted to modern technologies, they have become more dependent on the provision of off-farm inputs: improved seeds, fertilisers, and chemicals, for example. One result, as already argued, is the creation of an industrial lobby protective of agrarian incomes. There would appear to be others. Modern technologies often require irrigation. As noted in numerous studies [*Moore, 1989*; *Wade, 1982*] irrigation transforms rural households into rural communities, as individual farm families devise institutions to mediate conflicts over the allocation of water supplies. A second consequence of technical change is, that with the adoption of new technologies peasant farmers can become organised, thereby augmenting their political power. The emergence of an organised farm lobby in India would appear to be based in part upon this transformation. Thirdly, when farmers employ purchased inputs, food supplies become more sensitive to relative prices. The implication is clear: government policies that erode incentives are more rapidly and surely punished by reduced production, and governments, behaving rationally, therefore are less inclined to adopt pricing policies that lower the incomes of farmers. Lastly, the conflict between farmers and the state in developing societies derives from the farmers' desire for profits and the state's desire for low farm prices. With technical change, the states can have lower prices, even while farm profits rise. A fourth consequence of technical change, then, is that it creates political space, ameliorating the clash of interests between the farmers and the state.

De Janvry [*1973*] has studied the political origins of technical change in Third World agriculture. Other works have focused on the dire political consequences of technical innovation [*Williams, 1986*]. Less visible, but surely as important, have been the positive political consequences as suggested in these essays: the organisation of peasant communities, their recruitment of industrial allies, their capacity to deter negative pricing policies, and the movement from constant to positive sum payoffs in their games against the state.

There have, of course, been other errors of omission. Certainly in the context of Africa, failure to appreciate the significance of warfare stands as the most glaring. At times of war, food supplies dwindle; civilians cannot compete with armies in areas where food is 'purchased' at the point of a gun; and civilians therefore starve. Civil warfare, banditry, revolutions, and ethnic conflict: these forms of violence have swept Northern and Southern Africa. Famine in the modern era results more from the non-existence of stable governments than from the tendency of established governments to adopt policies that are urban biased.

A last major error of omission was the failure to appreciate the political significance of black markets. Governments may be urban biased; but farmers can elude the structures put in place to implement pricing policies that are not market clearing. Farmers can sell in official channels at times of low market prices and in black markets at times when market prices are high. One implication is, of course, that official policies of urban bias have been neutralised by the use of markets. Another is the need to re-interpret the role of international organisations. International agencies that urge policy adjustments, calling for getting the prices right, *must* be seeking to strengthen public institutions, not to weaken them – as their market oriented language would imply and as their critics would claim. For farmers, using parallel markets, have already got their prices right. It is the governments that have not, at great cost to their budgets and to their national economies. Recognition of the significance of black markets thus leads to a recognition of the real significance of policy reforms: they are oriented at least as much to the strengthening of public institutions as they are to the strengthening of private markets. The failure to analyse black markets has thus led to an overestimation of the degree of urban bias and to a misinterpretation of the political significance of 'market-oriented' policy reforms.

CONCLUSION

The strategy of the articles in this special issues has been to over-sample non-conforming cases – cases in which agricultural policies fail to conform to the patterns characteristic of urban bias. By pursuing this strategy, the articles highlight errors of commission and omission in the earlier literature. They therefore enable us to make progress. Future work, they suggest, should focus more on institutions that structure political competition. It should develop a theory of public financial institutions: one that explains why they provide effective agencies of constraint [*Collier, 1992*] in some countries but not in others. It should focus on the political significance of technical change and productivity growth in agriculture and of markets in ownership rights and claims to income that link the interests of town and country, thereby altering the structure of interests that drive policy choices in developing areas.

REFERENCES

Bates, R.H., 1978, 'People in Villages', *World Politics*, Vol.21, No.1, pp.129–49.
Bates, R.H., 1979, *Rural Responses to Industrialisation*, New Haven, CT and London: Yale University Press.
Bates, R.H., 1981a, *Markets and States in Tropical Africa*, Berkeley and Los Angeles, CT: University of California Press.
Bates, R.H., 1981b, 'Food Policy in Africa', *Food Policy*, Vol.6, No.3, pp.147–57.
Collier, P., 1992, 'Africa's External Economic Relations, 1960–1990', in D. Rimmer (ed.), *Africa 30 Years On*, London: Royal African Society in Association with James Currey.
De Janvry, A., 1973, 'A Socio-economic Model of Induced Innovations for Argentine Agricultural Development', *Quarterly Journal of Economics*, Vol.87, pp.410–35.
Findlay, R., 1991, 'The New Political Economy', in G. Meier (ed.), *Politics and Policy Making in Developing Countries*, San Francisco, CA: International Center for Economic Growth.
Hayami, Y., 1988, *Japanese Agriculture Under Siege*, London: Macmillan.
Krueger, A., 1992, *The Political Economy of Agricultural Pricing Policy*, Vol.5, Washington, DC and Baltimore, MD: World Bank with the Johns Hopkins University Press.
Lipton, M., 1977, *Why Poor People Stay Poor: Urban Bias in World Development*, Cambridge, MA: Harvard University Press.
McConnell, G., 1966, *Private Power and American Democracy*, New York: Alfred A. Knopf.
Mitrany, D., 1961, *Marx Against the Peasant*, New York: Collier Books.
Moore, M., 1989, ' "The Fruits and Fallacies" of Neo-Liberalism: The Case of Irrigation Policy', *World Development*, Vol.17, No.11, pp.1733–50.
Wade, R., 1982, *Irrigation and Agricultural Policies in South Korea*, Boulder, CO.: Westview Press.
Williams, R., 1986, *Export Agriculture and the Crisis in Central America*, Chapel Hill, NC and London: University of North Carolina Press.

Urban Bias: Of Consequences, Classes and Causality

MICHAEL LIPTON

Choice-theoretic accounts of urban bias (UB) in LDCs are popular, because they also 'explain' rural bias in richer countries. Such misguided elegance notwithstanding, class-theoretic (not simply Marxist/productionist) accounts are preferable. Why? (1) UB alleges persistently inefficient and/or unfair (i) anti-rural outcomes, (ii) intra-rurally, biases towards rural elites who in return deliver surpluses townwards. (2) If UB declines for one outcome, it must increase for others – unless pro-urban classes weaken relative to pro-rural. Thus farm-price UB fell in 1975–90 in many LDCs, but – with urban–rural class/ power balances little changed – public-expenditure UB rose to compensate. (3) Yet long-term development transforms such balances, shifting many outcomes from UB to rural bias. (4) Explaining (2) and (3) involves understanding urban–rural class relations. When, and to obtain which, outcomes, do rural elites seek rural rather than urban alliances? Choice/game/coalition theories help, but only within institutionally dense, localised, historical analyses of why classes cohere or disintegrate.

I

This collection deals mainly with the causes of urban bias (UB). Hence the authors address two main questions. Why have some countries less UB than others, or even (allegedly) rural bias? Why is UB reduced, even (allegedly) reversed, in later development?

Some of the attempts in these studies to explain the *causes* of UB do not work well. This is because they assume away, or neglect, the issues of *definition, measurement and evidence* – 'the economic mechanisms and consequences of urban bias' (Moore, p.83) – on which Lipton [*1977*] concentrated. The most striking illustration of the problem is the flirtation of several contributions in this volume with the view that

---

The author is Professorial Fellow, The Institute of Development Studies at the University of Sussex. He is grateful to Mick Moore for very helpful suggestions on a previous draft.

agricultural prices, or terms of trade, can readily be used to develop satisfactory overall indicators of the degree of UB. Yet, if reduced price bias has gone far to eliminating the damage that rural people perceive from overall UB in China, why does the government still need (albeit less than before 1983) draconian restriction on migration to the cities? If in India, why is the gap between rural and urban infant mortality large and increasing? The equation of price bias and urban bias leads to the neglect of important non-price factors in UB, and can produce mis-specification both of the countries with relatively little UB, and of the change in UB during the development process.

My commentary is structured as follows. In section II I rehearse the definition, rules of measurement, and nature of evidence regarding UB, in order to relate them to the causal concerns of the studies in this collection. The relationship requires us to clarify the crucially distinct issues of *extraction* and *recirculation* of various forms of rural surplus [*Lipton, 1989: 97–8*]. Section III reviews the static issue, of why some countries show less UB than others. Section IV examines the changes in UB during development. Specifically, section V examines Moore's antithesis between class-theoretic and choice-theoretic accounts of the causality of change in UB.

Moore's choice/class juxtaposition provides a useful framework for the discussion, in section VI, of the crucial issue of price vs. non-price manifestations of UB. First, I re-establish that UB cannot be measured with price indicators alone. If not, do rural people's prices, relative to urban people's, tend to improve when their relative non-price circum-stances are improving, or when they are worsening? If the relative power of urban and rural classes remains constant, and if the preference ordering of each class stays the same, then a reduction in price UB is likely to accompany an *increase* in non-price UB. If rural 'power' increases relative to urban 'power', better farm prices are likely to accompany a *decrease* in other aspects of UB – for example, in rural underendowment with schools, roads, etc. If preference orderings change, perhaps leading to changed individual decisions about which coalitions to join, an indeterminate pattern of changes in UB is likely; that is, the various rural prices and other endowment indicators, relative to urban, are likely to move in distinct ways.

Finally, in section VII, I turn to three issues, familiar from the literature, on which the studies in this collection cast fresh light. Is UB meaningful where the urban–rural borderline is unclear, or shifting, or where settlement is almost continuous? Is urban bias possible, if there are many rural rich or many urban poor? And how does UB relate to possible 'industrial bias'? In particular, what is the role, in the creation or reversal of UB, of linkage sub-sectors – such as farm processing and input manufacture; the rural non-farm sector; and urban agriculture?

II

UB is defined upon outcomes, not causes or processes [*Lipton, 1977: 44–56*]. It exists unambiguously whenever an outcome, for example, an endowment of schools or a set of prices, persistently favours urban people *vis-à-vis* rural, and thereby harms both efficiency (static and dynamic) and income distribution (especially in ways that deepen poverty). Today, one would add a further condition for *strong unambiguous* UB: that the persistently pro-urban outcome also increases the risk of non-sustainability – fiscal, administrative or environmental.

Such 'all-round bad UB' does exist. For example, the extreme relative rural deprivation of health and educational services in most LDCs risks accelerating urban drift, and hence congestion (with increasing marginal external costs, ultimately unsustainable fiscally or environmentally); curtails services for the neediest; and reduces overall returns to those services. However, if we categorise outcomes only by presence or absence of strong unambiguous UB, these very strong requirements would often leave us unable to judge whether an outcome is urban-biased or not. Hence we should also define two less demanding senses of UB. *Weak unambiguous UB* exists whenever there is a persistently pro-urban outcome that harms at least one of the four goals – static efficiency; dynamic efficiency; a poverty-sensitive indicator of income distribution; and sustainability – without causing gains in any of the other three goals. *Weak ambiguous UB* exists whenever there is a persistently pro-urban outcome that damages at least one of the policy goals, even if it also benefits one or more of the others, so long as the circumstances are such that the damage is agreed to outweigh the benefit. Of course, if 'agreed' is replaced by 'proved', even weak ambiguous UB of an outcome presents a strong and unambiguous case against it.

I should re-emphasise, in the light of the important contributions made by these papers, three propositions in Lipton [*1977*]. First, UB applies to outcomes. The truth or falsity of the UB hypothesis – that UB is prevalent in post-1945 developing (but not developed, nor on the whole pre-1930 developing) countries – is independent of the causation of UB.

This is not to deny that causation is of central importance for other purposes than defining UB. However, causation is not mechanically separable from ideology or history, especially late colonial history, in the way that some expositions of rational-choice theory appear to suggest. Widner (pp.41–2) emphasises the rural origins of the anti-colonial struggle as a cause of the Ivory Coast's lower UB (in respect of some outcomes) than most African countries. This is the obverse of the normal linkage between anti-colonial movements, urban groups, and anti-rural ideologies [Lipton, 1977: 79–82; 1984: 183].

The second proposition is that UB (whether strong unambiguous, weak unambiguous, or weak ambiguous) can and does apply to some sets of outcomes and circumstances but not to others. It applies to relative farm-price outcomes in Ghana but not in Cuba. In Indonesia UB may well, as Timmer argues, no longer be shown in farm prices; but does it still pervade rural vs. urban access to doctors? Even within price policies, allowing for the effects of foreign-trade and exchange-rate policies, farmers' wheat subsidy has turned positive within India – but rice, sugar, and overall farm output subsidies remain negative.

Third, intra-rural outcomes (not only rural–urban ones) can be greatly affected by UB. One of many examples is the pervasive pattern of output price manipulation against farmers, together with compensatory input price subsidies to the larger farmers who sell food or exportables to the cities. 'Today's governments are great friends of agriculture and support it [with] all sorts of subsidies. All these exercises only raise rent and benefit the urban-resident landlord [or big surplus farmer: ML] and hence the towns' (Kautsky, cited in Lipton [1977: 119]).

It is worth putting these definitional issues together in the context of claims that rural 'empowerment', perhaps via democracy, often overcomes UB. Moore (p.87) implies that food price trends are the main piece of evidence in testing such claims. Varshney (pp.4–5) reviews the scope and limits of the World Bank's concentration on farm/non-farm price ratios as the central components of UB in the early 1980s, and elsewhere concentrates on showing that some price biases against Indian farmers have indeed been corrected, perhaps over-corrected, since the early 1960s. But during the same period the ratio of rural to urban infant mortality has increased [Ruzicka, 1982]; agriculture's share in public investment has fallen much faster than its share in GNP or employment [World Bank 1991: iii]; even on the price front there has been persistent UB against farm products mainly produced for rural use (rice, as against wheat); and farm sales have been exposed to negative, and farm purchases to positive, effective protection [ibid.: 44–5]. Concentration on particular outcomes where UB has been reduced, or even reversed, has led several contributors to this symposium to infer that such outcomes indicate increased rural empowerment, and its capacity to reverse UB in many cases. Such inferences are not borne out by other outcomes, which continue to exhibit persistent UB.

Sometimes, as in the case of medical and educational outcomes, India (like most LDCs, and rhetoric notwithstanding) exhibits strong, unambiguous and probably increasing UB. Sometimes – as in the case of rice vs. wheat prices, millet/sorghum vs. wheat research, and investment and research for Eastern and rainfed areas – UB in India has affected intra-rural rather than rural–urban outcomes, concentrating resources on rural areas that provide cities with most food, exportables, skills or savings. Several of the studies in this collection would benefit, if it were possible to disaggregate their analysis of UB, by looking at a wider range of relevant *outcome* indicators.

III

Why do some countries have less UB, on most or all of the important indicators, than other countries with roughly similar levels of development (this section)? In view of the generally agreed fact that most developed countries feature rural bias, on most of the important indicators – from farm protection, through transport and postal subsidies, to tax breaks; and most centrally in urban/rural and non-farm/farm income ratios – what is it about 'development' that is linked to the shift from UB to RB (section IV)? Choice-theoretic accounts of UB – unlike class-based explanations – of their nature appear to answer these questions in the same framework as that used to explain UB itself. That is why Moore (pp.84–5), and implicitly Varshney (p.4), prefer choice-based to class-based explanations of UB.

However, there are strong logical objections to such reasoning for that preference. First and foremost, the reasoning misapplies the 'principle of parsimony', which states that as an explanation X is preferable to Y if X explains a larger set of events, thereby [*Popper, 1934/59: 140–2*] surviving a greater risk of refutation than Y. This principle applies only if X is not in other respects seriously inferior to Y. In particular, if X claims to explain both urban bias in poor countries and rural bias in rich ones, but Y claims only to explain the former, then the 'principle of parsimony' prefers X over Y only if X is at least as good at explaining urban bias as is Y.

Furthermore, as a matter of procedure, it is not obvious that the right way to generalise an explanation X of urban bias in poor developing countries is to adapt or replace it by Y, which explains not only UB but also subsequent rural bias in rich countries. It may well be preferable to replace X by Z, which explains both UB and other contemporary features of poor countries, especially of power-relations there.

But the main problem is pressure towards elegance at too high a cost in accuracy. Physics may (perhaps) 'owe' us a single overall explanation for rising and falling bodies; but reality does not owe us elegant explanations in social science (or even natural science). If history, class, and ideology are important in ways not readily reducible to choice-theoretic formulations, then the three distinct types of outcome – UB in poor countries, RB in rich countries, and the transition from UB to RB (if it happens) – may well not be explained by just one causal sequence or theoretical framework, rather than one each for UB and RB and for the shift – or even several each.

The second objection to preferring choice-theoretic explanations of 'first UB, then RB' on grounds of the 'principle of parsimony' is that their abstract elegance, their overarchingness, is necessarily at the cost of the historical density and specificity of class-based explanations of 'why urban power dominates in such-and-such *types* of societies (initially, of observed times and places)'. The words 'types of' are of course essential – otherwise we deal in lists, not science – but generalisation may best proceed by raising the coverage (and reducing the number) of 'types of *societies*' bit by bit. Instead, the choice-theoretic enterprise appears – perhaps dubiously – to impose in one swoop a theoretical structure that reduces every sort of community to *persons* who maximise 'utility' as 'individuals'.[1]

Third, it is disputable whether the class-choice antithesis is real. Perhaps [*Roemer (ed.), 1985*] even class-based approaches can be 'reduced' to choice-theoretic 'foundations' (see section V below).

Fourth, individuals or their decisions, *pace* Hayek, have no *logical* precedence – in the (dubious) enterprise of establishing 'fundamental particles' for social science – over classes, relations or even macro-variables.[2] Nevertheless, suppose that we neglect all this reasoning. Suppose we force ourselves to choose between choice-theoretic and class-based accounts of why some countries have more UB than others. Provided we are allowed to depart from stereotyped 'common relations to the means of production' definitions of what causes individuals to be members of the same class, then class-based analyses are more *useful* than choice-theoretic analyses, that is, are likelier to suggest policies that can reduce policy bias, because more concerned to identify (and assess the power of) relevant and durable groups.

A prior requirement, in deciding why some LDCs have relatively low UB on most of the important indicators, is to agree on which countries qualify. This means agreeing both on what are 'important indicators' and on their actual levels – the latter not easy in Africa, where extreme UB has helped to bring extremely deficient rural and agricultural statistics. As for the indicators, Widner's crop-specific evidence that the

Ivory Coast 'displays less UB than other African producers of the same major export crops' (p.29) is, in itself, persuasive. Yet Valdès and Schiff [*1992: 6, 18–19*] show that such evidence may not suffice. Direct taxes on crop outputs (net of input subsidies) accounted for just over half the burden on farm output in the Ivory Coast in 1960–82; the rest was due to exchange-rate overvaluation and to the protection of industrial products against competing, cheaper imports. Altogether, the Ivory Coast, with 'taxation' accounting for 49.0 per cent of agricultural output, ranked above 16 of the 17 other developing countries sampled, including Zambia (46.3 per cent) but excepting Ghana (59.5 per cent). World Bank sources for the Ivory Coast, including Africa's most accurate survey of rural and urban living standards [*World Bank, 1990; Kakwani, 1993; Glewwe and van der Gaag, 1992*], also suggest exceptionally wide rural–urban gaps, not just in income but in infant mortality and adult literacy.

This suggests that, if particular UB outcomes or manifestations are limited by an external constraint, such as an Ivoirien monetary and exchange-rate policy tied to the CFA Franc (Widner, pp.33–6) or an IMF agreement, then a given urban/rural power balance will so act as to increase UB in other outcomes not so constrained. This is not, of course, to question Widner's evidence that this power balance was itself somewhat 'ruralised' in the Ivory Coast by virtue of the unusual origins, ideology, and landed interests of the Ivory Coast's political elite; and that this made itself felt in agricultural extension, roads, and other services, so that rural people may have gained from improving *income* terms of trade even though (except perhaps for farmers in the political élite) their *barter* terms of trade were severely repressed.

Before we try to agree on which countries show low UB, we need to separate UB in respect of *extraction* and of *recirculation* of surpluses [*Lipton, 1991b*]. Moore (p. 88) suggests that cash crops are more exposed to price repression in Africa than food crops partly because surplus is more readily extracted from cash crops; that would also explain why recirculation, via research and irrigation, has been much commoner for cash crops. Yet Widner (pp.37, 40) points out that failure to recirculate, especially via research, has been central in Côte d'Ivoire; indeed it underlies the stagnation of African agriculture overall. Lee's work on Taiwan, and Ishikawa's on Japan – both prior to the Timmer–Schultz concept of net surplus (Varshney, p.11) – illustrated that substantial recirculation into agriculture, probably exceeding extraction, was necessary to raise agricultural productivity *before* the period of significant extraction. Only afterwards could extraction exceed recirculation without encountering Varshney's dilemma: that, if farmers are forced to

236 BEYOND URBAN BIAS

invest in agriculture less than they save, that is, to generate a savings surplus for the cities, this gravely impairs their ability at the same time to produce enough farm growth to generate a growing surplus of farm output (wage-goods, that is, mainly food, plus net exportables) for the cities as well.

On the whole, I now see inter-country UB comparisons as an issue, not so much of 'more' or 'less' UB on each of a vector of outcomes, but of the different degrees to which rural extractions are accompanied by rural recirculation. This has happened very substantially in East Asia, even during the early extractive periods before the price adjustments[3] chronicled by Timmer; to a considerable extent in post-colonial South Asia; and hardly at all in sub-Saharan Africa. However, finer distinctions – both among countries and among types of extraction and recirculation, that is, among outcomes – are needed to establish which sorts of LDCs, and at what conjunctures, are more, or less, exposed to what sorts of UB. The contributions to this collection make a useful start.

The main *proximate* cause of UB outcomes, if there are significant numbers of rural rich and powerful people, is that they seek to combine with urban power-groups, rather than with the rural dispossessed, in parties or pressure-groups to secure their aims. The trouble with lists of factors reducing a country's UB such as Colburn's (pp. 61–2) – national democracy, local organisations, foreign resources, 'socialism', a later stage of development, fragmentation of urban interest-groups – is that any or all of the factors can render it *more* or *less* likely that rural 'big men' will seek mainly urban allies. Whether more national democracy, local organisation, urban fragmentation, etc. has this outcome depends on what *types* of institutions develop, and on the incentives and options they offer to rural élites and their alternative allies (urban or rural).

One might ask: cannot the rural rich work with the rural poor to improve rural schools, but with the urban elites to focus input subsidies on big farmers providing cheap surpluses of food and exportables for the cities? Indeed, especially in complex democracies, such multiplex pressuring is feasible, but the question is too one-way in its causality. The rural rich, if they decide in general to align themselves with the urban élites rather than the rural poor (for example, because they are confronted by institutions, themselves rather inflexible, that render the former alignment more promising of net benefit to themselves), become likelier to reside in cities, to use urban schools and doctors, and generally to avoid behaviour that makes them dependent, for benefit, on a low degree of UB.

Decentralisation offers a good example of the ambiguous effect of institutions on UB. Oi (p.130) points out that the falling disparity between rural and urban incomes in China 'is due primarily to local, not central, initiative'. The growth of options to live well through rural industry – by producing in it or by taxing it – must have ruralised the interests and alliances of emerging rural elites in many areas, causing those interests to cohere with those of (some of) the rural 'masses' rather than with those of urban élites. Yet the rural administrators who taxed China's decentralised and growing rural small industries (pp. 141–2) presumably live in rural towns; then rural extraction, for urban recirculation by expenditures on the Kautsky model, is also 'decentralised'. Meanwhile, rural emigration to the perceived advantages of Beijing and Guangdong remains severely restricted (albeit less so than before 1983). Rural industry, however, must have played a large part in China – as elsewhere in East Asia – in reconciling an urban power elite, dedicated to industrialisation, to a more decentralised, less price-based, and perhaps on balance smaller, degrees of urban bias and extraction.

Agricultural processors, urban as well as rural, may find that, because of their interests in maintaining farmers' (suppliers') incentives, they need to avoid extreme UB for some outcomes. This seems important for the Ivory Coast (Widner, pp. 51–2) as well as Taiwan and Korea (Moore, p.106), but the impact on price extraction is ambiguous. Processors want their inputs, that is, specific farm outputs, made cheaper by price repression, but not so cheap as to reduce or destabilise farm supply in ways that reduce or endanger processing profitability. How that affects the UB of price outcomes will depend, not only on the politics of processors' power, but also on the economics: domestic and international elasticities of supply (and hence relations of production) and of demand.

A recurring issue in these contributions is the role of democracy in reducing UB. It is clearly neither necessary (as Colburn's discussion of Cuba shows) nor sufficient. All the same, the correlation between democracy-indicators and UB-indicators across poor countries is probably negative. Varshney's account of farmers' organisation and politicisation to reduce some aspects of price UB in India is compelling, and there are analogies in other countries; this could not have happened to similar effect in a closed society. However, other forms of political opening, such as 'dialogue' in the Ivory Coast, might substitute for democracy in reducing UB (Widner, pp. 28, 50); there is a striking contrast with Malawi, where a similarly 'agricultural', but autocratic, political leadership has exposed small farmers and the rural poor to unremitting price and quota UB and thus excluded them from almost all the gains of growth – and, more recently, undermined growth itself, because resources were shifted away from the more efficient small-farm sector towards protected surplus (mainly tobacco) farmers and their urban allies.

Despite Varshney's statement that in a democracy such as India, 'politics based on economic interests potentially unites the villagers' against UB (p.180), the contrast between Kenya and the Ivory Coast reveals the *contingency* of this result, and hence of democracy as a cure for UB. In Kenya, 'semi-competitive' politics did little to help rural people. According to Widner (p. 57), this was because parliament was weak. Conversely Lele and others interpret Kenya's unusually (for Africa) low non-price UB, for example in allocation of roads and schools, as indicating the rurality and power of middle farmers. This could hardly have been expressed so effectively in a highly autocratic polity; one would therefore expect it to be less important in Kenya around 1987–91 than before or since. But obviously it could have been otherwise: democracy, to the extent that Kenya enjoyed it, could have *helped* an urban alliance to ignore, or extract from, the unorganised rural poor, if the rural rich had so interpreted their self-interest.

The contingent nature of 'democracy as a cure for UB' is illustrated by the Indian states. In Maharashtra and elsewhere, factions within the dominant caste compete for rural power in the democratic arena, inter alia by rival appeals for support from the very poor (usually in ex-untouchable castes). That process softens the impact of the urban alliance by shaking out benefits to the surplusless rural poor. In states with no clear dominant caste, such as Bihar, the urban alliance works much more blatantly. There, its members are pressed little, if at all, by the democratic process to include or woo the rural poor.

In November 1992, though we are not owed elegant unity of explanation for UB in developing and RB in developed countries, a striking example of the latter gave us further pause in arguing that democracy must weaken sectoral bias. French farmers, comprising six per cent of the workforce and on average far from poor, then used violent protest to induce the Prime Minister to commit himself to vetoing a GATT settlement that, as the *patronat* vociferously claims, is clearly in France's interests, as well as the EC's and the world's. In close analogy, throughout Africa (and probably *more* in its more democratic places), organised urban rioters have frequently thwarted governmental efforts to raise the price of non-poor people's foods – not millet, sorghum and cassava, but maize flour, wheat bread, and sometimes meat and dairy products.

This can be interpreted as follows. Hegelian civil society – not only (and not all of) 'the market', but peaceful conflict, and influence upon 'the State', by many different interest-groups and persons – need not reduce UB in developing countries (it may instead ease co-operation within their urban alliances), but on the whole it is likely to do so, for two reasons. First, the poor and rural majorities are better placed to use the weight of numbers (*pace* Olson) if there is freedom to organise and influence. Second, because UB is inefficient in its neglect of agriculture and the small-scale, there is a variable-sum game: the losers from UB, in reducing it, generate extra GNP, from which the gainers from UB can be compensated for sacrificing some of those such gains. This variable-sum game is likelier to be played with strategies leading to outcomes with less UB – and hence higher (GNP) values of the game – if the powerful have to compete within Hegelian civil society, than if they retain political status coercively and fear to lose it if UB declines. Even if such a decline does mean extra GNP that might in principle compensate them for their losses, they fear that their prospects for compensation depend on retaining coercive political status, which in turn depends partly on their maintaining UB.

So Hegelian civil society is strongly and positively correlated with (though neither necessary nor sufficient for) reduced UB. Its unhampered and effective operation is probably similarly correlated with democratic institutions. Therefore, democracy is probably positively correlated with lower UB in developing countries. Analogous reasoning may apply to RB in rich countries.

But there is a major caveat [*Lipton, 1991a*]. Hobbesian civil society – a society whose members implicitly contract that each will allow the State to enforce non-violence upon him or her, provided the State behaves similarly towards all other persons or institutions – is a necessary condition for effective organisation by the weak within Hegelian civil society. If the Hobbesian condition is violated – if the weakness or self-interest of the State is such that it permits minorities of thugs to enforce the interests of urban minorities in Africa, or rural minorities in Europe – then Hegelian civil society is powerless to reduce biases in favour of non-poor and non-efficient minorities, whether UB in Africa or RB in Europe. Thus the positive impact of democracy on Hegelian civil society, and hence on reduction of UB or RB, counts for little, unless accompanied or preceded by an effective Hobbesian State.

IV

Some plausible moderators of UB, such as those considered in section III – for example, democracy and agro-processing – are only tenuously (though positively) related to the level of economic development. There are other 'plausible moderators' that are more intrinsic to the development process. These indirect, cross-section links between development and reduced UB are considered in this section – alongside the direct time-series indicators of dwindling UB in the development process identified by Oi, Timmer and Varshney.

For both sets of indicators, however, there is a basic conceptual problem. The studies in this collection either assert or imply that the declines in UB outcomes are *caused by* 'development', or by its usual correlates. I believe the sequence is mostly the opposite: reduced UB, by increasing static and dynamic efficiency and by (equitably) incorporating hitherto neglected or exploited people, *causes*, or at least accelerates, development. The studies in this collection raise the problem of identifying the causal chain, but (reasonably enough) do not solve it.

The argument that UB gets *less* (or turns into RB) with development because the urban sector becomes *larger* relative to the rural sector is 'paradoxical but nevertheless false'. There are two versions. Olson [*1965; 1982*] argues that small sectors are more powerful because their very smallness renders it easier for managers of a group's agency for collective action – of its party, trade union, or rural or urban movement – to collect dues from members; easier for members to supervise dues-payment by others; likelier that a few defaults would bankrupt the agency; and therefore less tempting for members (adopting non-co-operative strategies in a contributors' version of prisoners' dilemma) to leave to others the paying of subscriptions, the provision of lobbying or canvassing services on behalf of the group, etc. Varshney gives some weight to this argument, as does Bates's work. The other version is that of Anderson and Hayami [*1986*], for whom the advantage of a group with few members (and correspondingly many non-members) is that it costs little to help all members of the group, and that this little is divided among many non-members.

Moore (p.92) convincingly refutes the Anderson–Hayami version of 'small is powerful' by observing that a state could well gain more support (votes certainly, power possibly) by taxing the few to give a little to each of the many, rather than by taxing the many to give a lot to each of the few. The Olson version appears to succumb to an analogous observation, this time on the group rather than on the state: that, even if small groups do have lower per-member *transactions*-costs of maintaining their representative agencies, large groups have more persons, more resources in total, and a prospect of lower per-person operating costs to scale for those agencies. As the size of a supported (for example, urban) group increases and that of a supporting (for example, rural) group decreases, the Anderson–Hayami prediction of diminishing UB fails, if the extra *political returns to the state*, from supporting more people, would outweigh the extra political cost of raising the revenue; then bias (in this case UB) would increase. Similarly, the Olson prediction of diminishing UB fails if, as a group (for example, the urban sector) gets bigger, the *economic returns to the group and its agency* increase more as a result of scale-economies in group organisation and pressure, than they decrease as a result of extra transactions-costs of avoiding free-riding (that is, of preventing group members from benefiting from the agency without contributing time or cash to it).

Obviously, there is some size of group, perhaps a very small size, below which the Anderson–Hayami and Olson arguments do fail for these reasons. Obviously too, the group's wealth and power – and hence threat potential – help to determine that size. If Ghana's 'urban sector' comprised one bankrupt, living alone in a great city surrounded by millions of wealthy farmers, that would not generate much UB. Nor, if there were only one French farmer (and she a poor one) in a nation of net consumers of farm products, would the French state fight, as it now does, against a GATT agreement that involved liberalisation of farm trade – an agreement clearly in the French national interest. Olson (through his concept of 'encompassing coalitions') and Anderson–Hayami do respond to such arguments by seeking to define, and limit, circumstances in which 'small is powerful'. However, the responses savour of *deus ex machina*. They tend to circumscribe and weaken, not to revive, the 'paradox of smallness' as an explanation of why development tends to turn UB into RB for many outcomes.

The paradox of smallness – and, more generally, coalition theory, culminating in tit-for-tat theories of prisoner's dilemma [*Axelrod, 1984*] – comprises perhaps the most attractive, because the least contingent, attempt to link rational-choice theory to changing social reality, such as the declining role of UB during the middle-to-late periods of economic development. Yet the logical rigour of paradox-of-smallness explanations is not much use if such explanations do not work. As for the fascinating developments of game theory culminating in the strong empirical basis for Axelrod's proposition, this makes it easier to explain the stability of a pair of chosen strategies, and hence why UB or RB, once established, persists – but harder to explain how UB can decline, let alone be transferred into RB. Also, tit-for-tat casts no light on the central puzzle of why, and for how long, rural élites will join coalitions with the urban alliance rather than with other rural persons.

This collection reviews two other sorts of explanation of 'declining UB during development' that are broadly consistent with choice-theoretic accounts of individual action: that both middle-period development and reduced UB are contingent upon a reduced role of the State and of its self-seeking agents; or that they are contingent on changed costs of group action associated with changed demographics, especially rising rural population densities. These explanations offer more promise, but require modification, probably via closer reference to the

changing perceived interests of people as members of classes, as well as
to the changing objective power of such classes.

Rural population density, and with it the quality of communications,
tends to increase during middle-to-late development. This not only
simplifies the organisation of rural common-interest groups and reduces
the density advantages of urban ones; it raises the economic (GNP)
costs of some UB outcomes, and/or reduces the costs of avoiding them.
Price bias against agriculture costs more GNP, if aggregate agricultural
supply elasticity is high (relative to non-agricultural); denser rural populations and communications, leading to readier availability of inputs and
knowledge, help to achieve this. The cost of reducing rural disadvantage
in access to health or electricity – in extreme cases of rural dispersion, a
cost so large that anti-rural outcomes may not meet the 'static ineffici-
ency' condition for UB (p.231) – declines as rural densities grow. Such
examples could be multiplied. It may be hypothesised that (a) given
GNP-per-person, UB (and rural-vs.-urban inequality) tends to be lower
where density is higher – in 'India' than in 'Africa'; in Kerala (and
Rwanda) than in Rajasthan (and Zaïre); (b) that development, denser
rural populations (with smaller proportions reliant on arid-zone or bush-
fallow farming or pastoralism), and reduced UB tend to go together.
Moore (p.100) emphasises these points in the case of Taiwan.

A related issue is that of more continuous rural settlement, leading to
a blurred rural–urban borderline, to part-time farming, and above all to
greater economic prospects for efficient rural industrialisation. The
relatively high degree of all these phenomena in Kerala, in South-
western Sri Lanka, and (Oi, p.142) since the late 1970s in parts of
China, underlines the linkage to reduced UB. If urban élite ideology
remains wedded to 'heavy' industries and techniques, these opportunities will be thwarted – typically by licensing and restrictions, often
overtly designed to favour 'small' industry, but in practice protecting the
largely urban not-so-small against the rural smallest. As fiscal crisis
renders these policies less viable, however, the presence of dense or
continuous rural settlement permits a less urban-biased alternative.

Perhaps the most interesting criticism of class-based theories of UB –
and argument for choice-based theories – is that reduced UB is mainly the
result of the changing, and increasingly developmental, choices that it
pays *state* agents to make. For Oi (p.145), increasingly decentralised
Chinese *state* organs became increasingly favourable to rural industry;
persistently anti-agricultural procurement policy is explained, not via
interest-groups, but by rational-choice party (state?) leaders seeking
urban stability. Colburn (pp. 61–2) stresses state openness, decentralisation, or egalitarianism as correlates of low urban bias in Cuba and Costa

Rica alike. Varshney (pp.181, 209) even sees the ruralisation and (as it were) genuine indigenisation of India's *state* elite in the 1960s as a clear political signpost to reduced UB, neglected by economistic writers such as myself; though Indian MPs' and MLAs' self-interest surely depends on where their real estate, friends, shares, schools and doctors are, rather than on whether they were initially 'farmers' (or wish for electoral reasons to describe themselves as such). Moore (p.87) treats Bates's analysis – of how large farmers are, as potentially disruptive members of the urban alliance, 'bought off' (by projects and subsidies) so that they tolerate price bias – as correctly '"importing" the state into the model as a separate and distinct political actor, with its own motivations and objectives'. Moore (p. 116) also rightly argues that 'much of the incipient mess that [*Dumont, 1962,* and others] detected was [due largely] to simple exploitation of the rural population by the personnel of the state apparatus'.

But can we really explain the rise of UB with early development, and perhaps its decline later on, by saying that 'poor States batten on agriculture to sustain their political cadres, and gradually release their grip as [GNP rises so that] alternative means emerge' (Moore, p.119)? Such an explanation begs the question of how States get like that. The states that oversaw agricultural development in eighteenth- and nineteenth-century England, Prussia, the USA, France, and even Japan showed little or no UB. Prices were twisted, if at all, in favour of farmers – for example, until 1847, with the Corn Laws in England. Well into the twentieth century, age-specific urban death-rates in England far exceeded rural [*Williamson, 1991*]. In all the above countries during early modern development, farm–non-farm income disparities were much lower than in almost any post-colonial developing country [*Lipton, 1977: 435–7*].

Rational-choice theorists – following Weber but rejecting his (in every sense) idealistic view of the bureaucracy – tend to see state institutions, whether monolithic or not, as seeking to maximise their own members' interests, subject (more or less) to legal, and sometimes electoral, constraints. Class theorists normally see state institutions as 'executive committees' of powerful and coherent social groups. Both views have elements of truth; furthermore, ideology [*Lipton, 1977: Ch.4*], and even Fabian goodwill, also motivate state agents. However, the view that 'the state' exogenously chooses to feed off farmers, because that is all the food there is, and grazes more widely when (and if) this ceases to be the case – and the implicit attribution of UB to State action – is surely oversimple. In almost all LDCs, taxable capacity per person is much more in the richer (and more unequal) cities than in the villages. Yet governments seek to run states by 'taxing' (in the broadest sense) mainly the villagers. This has to be because states, even if run by wholly self-interested persons, partly reflect the balance of power, including rural–urban and intra-urban power. There is no reason to believe that this balance of power should in theory, or does in practice, produce systematically more UB when mediated through a strong state and weakened markets, than through strong markets and a weak state; or through state power, than through market power.

If UB is not attributable mainly to the self-interest of state agents – and if it is not necessary (power aside) to finance that self-interest by 'taxing' the villages – then UB will seldom be cured by making the state smaller, as the World Bank in the early 1980s appeared to believe. There is no principle of politics to tell us whether a balance of power that favours the urban alliance will, in general, express itself more, less, or equally effectively through a strong state, or through market power or extra-economic coercion in the presence of a weak state. The dwindling outreach of many States in less developed countries during fiscal crisis and 'structural adjustment' accompanied not only a fall in price-based UB, but also – and I believe in direct correspondence – a steady fall in agriculture's share of central government expenditure. In LDCs as a whole (excluding oil exporters), that share fell every year, from 7.9 per cent in 1975 to 4.5 per cent in 1988 [*Lipton, 1991: 232*].[4] This is consistent with a model in which the relative power of various competing groups remains roughly constant. Then the state, compelled by fiscal crisis, 'conditionality' or other necessity to reduce UB in some respects, bows to the (largely unchanged) facts of internal power by increasing it in others.

Rational-choice theorists rightly claim that the state's agents, that is, administrators and politicians, are more autonomous, and more self-interested, than the above interpretation suggests. However, this claim is pushed much too far by attempts to locate UB in 'the state' – rather than in the power balance as the various classes and groups use (and perhaps change) the institutions of state, market, *and* civil society. Moreoever, such attempts lead to unwarranted expectations that UB can be cured by weakening the State, or by reducing its scope. A weak, fiscally starved state cannot even 'hold the ring' – cannot guarantee the Hobbesian prerequisites for a tolerably non-violent Hegelian civil society. Such a society may well increase the *absolute* capacity of all groups to change policy in their interests. On balance, however, it is likely to help the *relative* capacity of rural interest-groups to organise freely, to apply peaceful pressure, and to exploit the possibilities of advancing their interests by less urban-biased outcomes that also increase the GNP – the value of the variable-sum game.

V

'The core of the rational-choice model lies in the proposition that the shift to high agricultural protection in Korea and Taiwan was caused by the increasing capacity of farm interests to influence government policy' (Moore, p.96). This 'capacity' *vis-à-vis* that of urban interests and of State agents – together with the particular outcomes for which these interests see UB (or RB) as important to them;[5] and with the costs and gains, to the members of alternative coalitions that might be formed, of forming and managing each such coalition *to achieve a particular outcome* – determine, according to rational-choice theory, the path of UB during development *with respect to the various outcomes* (prices, medical service allocations, etc.) that may reflect sectoral bias. Thus Moore (p.87) shows how the interest-group model on its own appears to 'predict [less UB for] cash crops than for food crops'; that this prediction 'is clearly violated in . . . sub-Saharan Africa'; but that the violation is largely explained by 'institutional and logistic contrasts between food and cash-crop markets', that is, by the greater economic and political ease (lower cost) of extracting surpluses in the latter, especially by inducing State agents to undertake non-transparent trade and forex manipulation.

At the level of abstract reasoning, this is persuasive. What is now needed is evidence, preferably with numbers, that the calculus of self-interest, organisational costs, and perception of the importance of outcomes to the well-being of members of coalitions (see, for instance, Moore, note 6) in fact works out that way. In another field of research, Leonard [*1977*] has successfully quantified the impact of organisational forms upon the behaviour and performance of extension workers in Kenya. However, choice-theoretic explanations of outcomes in respect of different areas of UB (food prices, export-crop prices, roads, schools, etc.) remain largely at the level of suggestive but untested hypothesis. One of the few pieces of empirical analysis remains [*Herring and Edwards, 1983*], showing that Maharashtra's Employment Guarantee Scheme was financed in ways that recirculated urban income to rural areas and examining the power relations involved; but such financing only partly offset many indicators of UB that are not treated by Herring.

I have seen no empirical account of the costs, benefits, and results of alternative coalitions, seeking to influence particular and initially biased urban–rural outcomes. In such fields as medical resources, roads, or civil-service postings and pay, such an account for a particular province (or even nation) would be of great interest. Several excellent analyses of rural institutions do provide materials for putting outcome-specific flesh on the bones of choice-theoretic explanations of UB and its evolution, but the materials do not seem to get used for that purpose. For example, large corrupt payments to their superiors by irrigation managers, receiving postings to canals in Andhra Pradesh, India, in the early 1980s, had to be recouped by illegal charges to farmers for water-related services. These payments moved by osmosis up the system, certainly to senior irrigation authorities in the state capital, perhaps to even more senior party and government officials [*Wade, 1982*]. The process is a minutely observed instance of resources funnelled from rural periphery to urban centres, but it is not analysed in that framework.

For rational-choice theory to contribute substantially to empirically based generalisations about how specific UB outcomes are realised, it will surely have to explain why sets of people, especially powerful rural people, choose to enter into one sort of coalitions rather than another. Both game-theoretic and (Olsonian) coalition-cost explanations, at present, seem little more than ingenious reformulations of statements that people enter the coalition that best implements their perceived self-interest. However, coalitions are not as bloodless as this truism suggests. People's political action tends to cohere around concerns that they perceive as fairly durable, central to well-being, and threatened by other people; in view of the costs (and unpleasantness, for most people) of political action, it will seldom be effectively mobilised for lesser concerns. Such conditions of coherence are *additional* to the subscription enforcement costs emphasised by Olson, and to the dominance conditions emphasised by game theorists, but are at least as important in determining which coalitions emerge and are effective – especially whether (and when) various groups of rural rich ally themselves with (some) rural poor or with (some) urban rich. Oddly given the history of political theory, it is the coherence conditions that are the most neglected by researchers.

Rational-choice theory will have limited success in explaining particular UB processes unless it (a) engages with empirical and quantified examples (of the processes, not just their outcomes), and (b) develops a testable theory of the formation and durability of coalitions with which to account in general for such examples. Such a theory is likely to be a class theory. 'Class' will be something much more than a logical construct of set theory (a class of left-handed persons is less interesting for UB analysis than one of big landlords). But 'class' will not be, in most cases, a Marxian construct defined by relationship to the means of production. Too many agents affected by UB or its changes, in deciding which coalitions to join, are affected by multiple or fast-changing relations to the means of production: the *bricoleur* is exemplified not only by the multipurpose peasant–labourer–herder–cobbler, but also by the part-time farmer–commuter–employee of Sri Lanka or Korea. Also, the coalitions likely to form in order to affect the rural–urban allocation of key infrastructures (schools, clinics, roads, and much else) depend on coherent sector-cum-class relations quite outside the narrow means-of-production sense of 'class'. An approach via the conditions for non-exploitative group membership and rights of withdrawal [*Roemer, 1985*] will have usefulness, in this context, well beyond Roemer's concerns with exploitation in the context of analytical Marxism.

VI

What do the coalitions, contesting outcomes that may feature UB, care about? What do their members gain from? It seems to me clearly false that in Indonesia 'the debate over UB and rural power, to the extent that it is quantitative at all, is primarily concerned with changes in the real price of [major crops] to the domestic economy' (Timmer, p.161); or that in India (even in conjunction with the growing proportion of MPs who call themselves farmers) the increase in advocacy by political parties of higher farm output prices, and in farmer representation on the Agricultural Costs and Prices Commission, indicates that 'rural power has unambiguously increased' (Varshney, p.184).

In fact, price bias against farmers – whether caused by domestic controls and procurement, by effective protection (negative for farmers' output, positive for their purchases), by overvaluation of the domestic currency, or otherwise – is usually a small component of the impact of urban-biased outcomes on rural welfare and on rural-to-urban transfer and extraction. This is because most rural people can usually escape most price bias. Sometimes they can eat the price-repressed output instead of marketing it.[6] Sometimes they shift production towards crops such as cassava, with characteristics (for example, de facto non-tradeability) that impede price repression. Sometimes rural activity is switched from agriculture towards services or industry, where price repression is almost impossible without harming urban producers as well. All these switches have costs for rural people – and efficiency costs for GNP – but the costs are much smaller than the 'tax on agriculture' that would arise, if rural people were unable to respond to price repression by these and other methods of effective avoidance or evasion.

While price repression is often readily thus escaped – though at substantial cost, especially if the repressed products tie up a lot of capital (livestock, tree crops) – expenditure repression is not. 'Where the state gives agriculture a real drubbing is on the expenditure side'

248

(Colburn, p.66). This is not only because, as he points out, inflationary finance of selectively urban social security and infrastructure is a 'tax' proportionate to *spending*, and therefore an especially heavy burden, relative to *income*, upon rural people, who being typically poorer than townspeople have a higher spending/income ratio. The 'drubbing' arises also because rural people, even at the same level of private income as urban people, are denied remotely equal access to health, education, roads, and other infrastructures not only of production and marketing but also of consumption.

Expenditure UB in public services and infrastructures (see Oi, p.139) not only produces a directly urban-biased outcome, in that it would in almost all LDCs be more cost-effective as well as more just to raise rural areas' share of (say) health outlays or road outlays. There are also four indirectly urban-biased outcomes.

The first is to worsen the impact on rural people of price repression, because urban products, with prices already biased upwards, are filtered through narrow transport and market channels that raise costs, probabilities of non-competitive supply, surplus profits, and hence prices to final rural buyers. The second effect is the heavy concentration of the multiplier benefits of public outlays – not just subsidies – on the towns (Colburn, pp.66–7); the process was memorably described by Kautsky [*Lipton, 1977: 117–19*] in the context of Austria in the 1890s. Third, the relatively better urban life created by expenditure bias towards the cities, especially for middle-income groups, attracts enterprise and skills, that is, savings embodied in human capital, away from the countryside; parallel to this, extra flows of cash savings are moved away, especially to buy houses or further education. Fourth, bias in public outlay to provide, or subsidise, infrastructures towards the cities improves their prospects, relative to rural areas, of being chosen by private entrepreneurs for industrial expansion; that choice is right and proper when it rests upon genuine economies of scope or agglomeration, but the outcome is urban-biased if such economies were and continue to be artificial consequences of expenditure bias.

It is essential to look at price and public expenditure components of UB jointly, so as to avoid misleading statements that overall UB has declined when it has merely changed its manifestation from price outcomes to expenditure outcomes. Oi (p.138) documents this sequence for China in 1988–89. More generally, the concentration of structural adjustment lenders in the 1980s upon price-correction led, given the power structure of most developing countries, to an offsetting intensification of expenditure UB (see above). In the longer term, the inconsistency between price-correction, farmers' price response, and the industrialisation imperative for rural wage-goods (food, fuel, fibres) for the cities (Varshney, p. 7) also creates pressures away from price bias,[7] and therefore – if the power constellations leading to UB remain much the same – towards UB based, rather, upon expenditure allocations. Only as rural people become more powerful, coherent, and able (given the ground-rules of civil society) to enforce their interests, is it likely that UB will decline, or even be reversed, in price and expenditure modes at the same time.

Given these realities of classes and coalitions, it is important to avoid reducing UB to price-bias, and measuring it accordingly. There are also technical reasons why attempting to measure change in UB in this way requires special caution. It is extremely difficult to assess what parts of price movements, or of their consequences, are due to government-induced or monopolistic distortions, and what part of such distortions can properly be categorised as a UB outcome. Lipton [*1977: 208, 304–7; 1984: 145–7*], at the cost of rejecting some potential evidence apparently supportive of his general argument, warned against attempts to equate 'worsening' barter terms of trade for agriculture with increasing price bias against rural people, or even against agriculture. The view of some Indian commentators, as reported by Varshney (p.190), that a worsening of the ratio between average costs and average prices for a crop indicates some sort of systemic bias against it, is even less defensible.

Obviously, movements in the domestic agricultural terms of trade, and even more in cost-price ratios, can have many causes in the sphere of real domestic or foreign production or distribution costs, of taste changes, or of market liberalisation or organisation. Only a fraction of such movements can be attributed to changes in domestic UB. Furthermore, it is perfectly feasible for farmers' real incomes to be increasing – and/or for urban incomes to be decreasing – while farmers' *barter* terms of trade are worsening. Even if farmers' average cost–price ratios are rising for every farm output, they might be getting better off, if their total output were rising fast enough, or if their output-mix were shifting towards products with more favourable cost–price ratios; such a set of events, too, is perfectly consistent with a falling ratio of non-farm to farm incomes (and *a fortiori* of urban to rural incomes). For analogous reasons, improvement in farmers' domestic terms of trade or cost–price ratios provides, on its own, no evidence that UB – or even price bias against farmers – has lessened.

A standard, and in my view correct, technique for measuring *price* bias against *agriculture* in any year is due to Lewis [*1970*]. The question asked is: if farmers were permitted to sell their products, and to buy their purchases of inputs and consumables, at world prices – allowing for transport costs – by what proportion would their net farm income rise (indicating anti-farm price bias before the permission was granted) or fall (indicating previous pro-farm price bias)? This question implicitly assumes that price UB deters neither farm production nor its distribution between marketing and self-consumption, so that the answer tends to underestimate UB in any given year; but that can be allowed for, as can the impact of exchange-rate interventions. The S.P. Lewis method allows us to estimate levels and changes in price bias against agriculture.

Changes in the farm–non-farm terms of trade, as Timmer again shows, are an amalgam of changes in domestic and foreign costs, tastes, and conditions of demand and supply. Timmer adds observations suggesting that, in most of South-east Asia, changes in the domestic *relative to the international* purchasing power of rice – that is, on the S.P. Lewis model price biases against rice – are, in fact, frequently the result of Governmental efforts to stabilise domestic rice prices to producers, consumers or both, in face of international price changes; Timmer denies that this can be interpreted as (changing) price UB. Timmer's efforts to decompose such changes, (in effect) into stabilisation effects and changed-bias effects, do the best job possible. However, the task may not be feasible conceptually.

First, after a given (or changed) price intervention, its impact in changing farm or non-farm income, as compared with their levels with neutral (or unchanged) interventions – that is, the impact on the bias of the *outcome* – is the same, whether the intervention (or the change) was motivated by a wish to stabilise income for farmers or consumers, or to modify the intersectoral transfer in an urban-biased or rural-biased direction. Second, further problems are created if, as through most of the period in question, the authorities (namely BULOG) – if they sought to stabilise – had to do so about a trend of incomes, a trend generated by transactions in rice at international prices themselves on a steady and generally underestimated downward path. Suppose that BULOG characteristically intervenes, in part, with the intention of compensating farmers for what it perceives as downward fluctuations about a world rice price trend; but that in fact there are much smaller downward fluctuations than BULOG (or anyone else) believes, but a considerably sharper downtrend in world prices. Then the outcome of BULOG's interventions – but not their intention – is to reduce rice price bias against farmers (or to increase it in their favour). In short, Timmer may be applying econometrics to a problem soluble only by clairvoyance: to the discovery of the relative roles of stabilising and resource-transferring *motives* in BULOG's rice price sequence. The obverse point is made (though in a context where the equilibrium rice price is largely determined by domestic harvests, not world markets) by Oi's analysis (p.137) of how a would-be extractive policy of rice pricing in China turned out in 1983–84 to be stabilising *ex post*.

A third problem is that, to isolate the effect of stabilisation, Timmer has to assume (p.163) that 'variations in the real domestic price of rice' comprise the correct upper bound – neither too high nor too low – for the impact of policy changes in price bias for or against rice. However, it is true of this price, as of the ratio of farm-gate to domestic prices (Widner, p. 29; my italics), that 'the degree to which [it] reflects strong UB depends on [*inter alia*] the *reason for the difference in prices* and the ultimate destination of the government's share of the funds extracted'.

Especially in Africa, that reason often is very high transport costs (Widner, p. 37). It should be noted, however, that – while above-border prices of urban goods in rural areas due to high transport costs do not illustrate price bias against farmers – they may well, in large part, reflect past *non-price* (expenditure) UB, against transport infrastructure for rural areas. The effect in increasing rural prices of urban goods is higher than the effect in increasing urban prices of rural goods, because rural goods for urban areas tend to be produced close to such areas (especially where unit transport costs are high), whereas even remote rural areas must buy urban goods at prices reflecting inter-sectoral transport costs.

Let us sum up on the role of price UB and RB, as compared with the role of expenditure bias.

* Price bias is in most cases much more readily (though not costlessly) avoidable than non-price bias by the populations it harms.
* Price bias normally affects output of economic sectors, such as agriculture, whether rural or urban (commonly 10–15 per cent of urban people in LDCs are mainly dependent on agriculture and 25–35 per cent of rural people's non-household income is generated outside agriculture); most expenditure bias, on the other hand, affects all sectors in a particular set of localities or regions.
* Price UB is therefore likely in most cases to do less net damage to rural populations than comparable[8] non-price UB.
* Price UB, unlike expenditure UB, is almost certain to focus its effects largely on marketed outputs; both incentive and financing consequences of price UB are therefore much likelier than are those of expenditure UB to reduce substantially, in the longer term, the flows – including the extractive flows attributable to UB – of farm surpluses, both of food and of savings, to urban areas.
* Given the structures of power and of preferences, reductions in price UB that shift welfare from urban to rural areas are liable to be offset

by increases in expenditure UB; the few available data suggest that
this offset has happened in many LDCs since the late 1970s.

* In the special but important case of repression of staple food prices,
  short-run gains are likely to accrue to net food buyers, even rural
  ones; but almost all rural persons are likely to lose from expenditure
  UB.

* Since the rural rich are major losers from price UB – whereas many
  forms of expenditure UB focus on the rural poor – the secondary
  rural effects of expenditure bias are larger relative to primary effects
  than is the case with price bias (assuming that poor rural people
  spend a larger proportion of extra *income* on rural products than do
  rich rural people [*Harriss, 1987*]).

All these factors militate against efforts to judge the scale, or impact,
of levels or time-paths of overall UB outcomes by examining indicators
of price bias. Moreoever, most such indicators are seriously misleading,
for three reasons. First, farm/non-farm price ratios (and their movements) reflect many other things than domestic, relative urban and
rural, policy and/or market power (and their changes). Second, even if
farm/non-farm price ratios are (say) declining towards the border price
ratios, this may indicate not UB but a reduction in earlier farm protection. Third, such ratios are seldom clearly related to farm/non-farm
welfare distributions.

Farm/non-farm price ratios and their changes, therefore, cannot *suffice* to answer the key questions about UB. To what extent are urban–
rural resource allocations, including but not only relative prices, ineffi-
ciently, inequitably, or unsustainably skewed towards town or country?
How are changes or even reversals in such skewing related to changes in
the balance of power and self-interest – in particular to the coalition-
forming preferences of the powerful rural groups?

VII

This latter question relates to the various issues about the rural–urban
'border', and those who cross it, that many critics have rightly seen as
tests of the usefulness of UB as an analytical concept. The 'border'
applies to *people* – the rural rich and powerful, the urban poor and
weak. It applies to *places* – small rural towns of, say, 3,000–15,000
persons. It applies to *change options* – UB can be self-correcting if
enough of its victims vote with their feet, and if returns tend to decrease
at the margin to extra urban activity, and increase at the margin to

correspondingly reduced rural activity. Several of the contributions cast light on these matters.

First, what of the alleged border between powerful urban and less-powerful rural *people*? In my earlier work, I have, as Moore suggests, been too prone to see the rural rich as crypto-townspeople, and the urban poor as temporarily sojourning countryfolk. Yet the rural rich do often live and spend in cities, transfer their rural surpluses there, and ally themselves with the urban sector. Richer farmers obtain directed credit, debt forgiveness (Varshney, p.183), and subsidies for inputs and outputs largely specific to themselves as surplus producers of items critical to the cities. In return, those more powerful farmers agitate rather little for better rural schools, clinics, and similar services, partly because the rural rich are much less likely to use them than are the rural poor. As for the urban poor, there are growing numbers of more or less permanent urban residents who are by any standards poor, and who lose (as do the rural poor) proportionately more than the rich when reduced UB brings rises in staple food prices (Timmer, p.154). It remains an empirical question, however, whether the urban poor, even slum-dwellers, are deprived of clean water and sanitation, primary school access, or famine relief to the same extent as the rural poor; whether, if so, they really do not return to their villages of origin; and whether, if not, their capacity to riot (and to infect) does not impose a constraint upon neglect that is absent among the distant, dispersed rural poor.

Second, what of borderline *places*? The studies in this collection do not discuss the urban–rural borderline, except for Oi's observation (pp. 142–3) that the industrialisation of the countryside renders that border-line problematic after the mid-1980s. I wish we could agree on, say, contiguous residence in places of under 5,000 inhabitants, of whom at least half depend on agriculture, as a definition of rurality. This approxi-mates roughly to the definitions used in most of Asia; elsewhere, definitions usually rest upon administrative questions, for example, forms of local government. In Africa and Latin America, it is common for the urban–rural border to be set in official data at 2000 – far too low to exclude many places both remote and mainly dependent directly on farm incomes. It is an empirical fact that, in the dozen or so developing countries with data for contiguous communities by size of populations, it is very unusual for more than 15 per cent of people to reside in places with between 5,000 and 20,000 residents [*Lipton and Ravallion, 1993*]. Hence a rural–urban dichotomy could, it seems, reasonably be based principally on population size of settlement, perhaps supplemented with a '50 per cent of workforce in agriculture' requirement for rurality. Is UB on the main important outcomes less, or (as I suspect) more, when urban populations and/or power are dispersed over many potentially extractive towns of 20–100,000 each with a rural hinterland – rather than concentrated into a megalopolis where central leaders may be compelled to consider the national interest? Evidence is wholly absent.

Third, what about rural–urban migration? Little is said about this topic in these contributions. Probably this is because the authors recognise four facts [*Connell et al., 1976; Lipton, 1977; 1982a; 1984; Preston, 1975; Williamson, 1991*] First, in *low-income* countries the true net flow of rural-to-urban migrants is small, both as a proportion of rural people and as a share of urban growth. Second, the poorest are usually constrained from joining this flow. Third, even if they do, they and their rural families seldom derive substantial benefit. Fourth, urbanisation, while generally helping both the migrant and the economy, does not tend to reduce UB, in part because the villages are drained of skills and often of leaders. The evidence for these statements has been widely rehearsed, and never seriously challenged. Perhaps, therefore, other analysts will follow the precedent of this collection, and spare us academic journalism about the rising tide of migration-led urban poverty – except in the middle-income countries, where indeed such a tide is not a mirage.

Finally, what has changed since the late 1970s, as regards (a) my view of UB in the light of new research and evidence, (b) more important, the role of UB in the world? What research agenda is now implied?

(1) In 1977, I underestimated the political, administrative and fiscal *unsustainability* of UB – the extent to which many of its manifestations contained the seeds of their own destruction. I emphasised that this seldom happened automatically by equilibriating processes of individual decision-taking (for example, as rural-to-urban migrants voted with their feet). The dual in 'price space' of this non-automation is that price corrections, whether due to supply-and-demand or to political decisions to reduce distortions, seldom suffice to end UB, as they tend to be countervailed by increases in its non-price manifestations.

However, the fiscal, administrative, and in some cases environmental costs of UB create strong pressures to reduce it. Such pressures do not seem to have sufficed in most of Africa, despite that continent's exceptionally high degree of UB, and despite the fact that it is in Africa that the fiscal (and often environmental) unsustainability of UB seems clearest. This is partly because of unduly exclusive emphasis by aid donors on price corrections. Such corrections, while themselves desirable, are usually less important than corrections of the less avoidable, and hence more harmful, biases against expenditure on rural services and infrastructure. The latter corrections, however, are harder under fiscal difficulties; yet it is these very difficulties (severest in Africa) that permit powerful pressure by donors. Africa's relative failure to correct UB is also in part due to its general, though diminishing, lack of open political systems and of well-articulated, competitive institutions in civil society. However, experience in Asia and Latin America suggests that these factors disguise, rather than overcome, the difficulty of sustaining extreme UB.

(2) In 1977, I failed to distinguish sharply enough between UB affecting *transfer or extraction* of rural outputs, incomes, or surpluses for urban use, and UB that reduced (below efficient, equitable and sustainable levels) the rural sector's share in the *recirculation* of resources, extracted on current account, for private-sector or public-sector investment in physical or human capital.

(3) In 1977, I tended to list, demonstrate, and assess the consequences of each manifestation of UB in turn – price, overt tax, educational provisions, and so on. These distinct UB outcomes, however, need not all exist in the same time and place. Especially in open or democractic polities, 'concessions' to rural people on some dimensions may be needed to render UB on others politically sustainable. To understand how UB changes over time, and varies among places, more attention should be paid to the different (as it were) *composition* of UB as between different countries.

(4) This collection of studies demonstrates that, in 1977, I paid insufficient attention to establishing 'exceptions to UB'. Indeed, the alleged exceptions I listed, while politically diverse, included some countries that are now rightly regarded as manifestations of rather extreme UB on *some* outcomes (for example, China, Tanzania).

(5) On two counts, I plead 'not guilty'. At no time did I suggest that UB was principally caused by, or could be largely corrected by reducing, (a) anti-agricultural price bias, *vis-à-vis* border prices at 'correct' exchange rates; (b) the size and power of the state. To my own surprise, I found that (with some striking exceptions) 'price twists', though harmful and significant, were usually avoidable and minor as compared to expenditure bias. Furthermore, on admittedly very crude measures, I found no correlation between indicators of state size or power and UB – and only weak correlations between economic 'openness' and absence of UB. In the early 1980s I restated

these findings, because I was alarmed by attempts to recruit my work to the flag of Reaganomic characterisations of 'the State', and of price 'distortions' for which it was alleged to bear sole and independent responsibility, as (i) unique causes of UB, and (ii) exogenous and operable cancers on an otherwise healthy Third World body politic [*Lipton, 1977: Chs.3, 13; 1981*]. It is not my fault that the expression 'urban bias'[9] is still persistently misused as part of the polemic of pricism and state minimalism.

(6) These contributions show that useful progress is being made on the macro-political and macro-economic research agenda of UB and RB. Unfortunately, the micro-politics and micro-economics are far less advanced. Studies such as Urwick [*1983*] are rare. The gap between urban and rural indicators (and provision) of health, education, mobility, shelter, and much else, remains striking in many LDCs; in some, the gap or the ratio is increasing; also the effect on different groups (women and men, young and old, poor and rich, etc.) varies greatly as between city and village. The facts are only beginning to be explored. The economics and politics, explaining why such dimension-specific urban–rural disparities exist – and to what extent they are, or are not, inefficient, inequitable, unsustainable, or usefully identifiable with UB – have hardly begun to emerge. The recent flowering of work on the rural non-farm sector, and the first stirrings of a corresponding recognition of the role of urban agriculture especially in the incomes of women and the poor, should be seen in this context.

NOTES

1. Awkwardness with regard to households, (male?) 'heads of households', and gender is inherent in this mode of generalisation.
2. 'But what are the simple constituent parts of which reality is composed? – What are the simple constituent parts of a chair? – The bits of wood of which it is made? Or the molecules, or the atoms? – "Simple" means "not composite". And here is the point: in what sense "composite"? It makes no sense at all to speak absolutely of the "simple parts of a chair" ' [*Wittgenstein, 1958: 21e. para. 1.47*].
3. It was largely because of this prior recirculation (into irrigation and agricultural research in particular) that Asian agriculture – in marked contrast to sub-Saharan Africa – showed considerable aggregate supply elasticity, even in the fairly short term, to the price adjustments.
4. Only a small part of this fall can be explained by the rising share of government expenditure swallowed up by interest payments. The remaining fall is very much faster than the fall in agriculture's share of GNP or employment. (Both the earlier and the later figure would increase somewhat, if the expenditures of government authorities below the central level could be allowed for.)

5. At the centre of the UB model is the hypothesis that many big farmers initially see themselves as *benefiting* from the UB package, and hence join the urban alliance.

6. For this reason, the Valdès and Schiff [*1992*: 6] estimates of negative effective protection relative to total farm output are too high, as an indicator of 'tax' rates on agriculture, if much of this output is self-consumed.

7. These pressures are weaker to the extent that, as indicated above, rural producers can evade or avoid price bias. If that happens, however, extraction based on UB also has to look to other channels than price manipulation, so that a shift towards increasing expenditure-based UB remains likely.

8. For example, 10 per cent repression of farm output prices, relative to border levels allowing for transport costs, might be compared to ten per cent reduction in rural public expenditures, relative to the level that (given the cash constraint on total public expenditure) would maximise expected GNP.

9. Probably this expression was used well before [*Lipton, 1968*]. I certainly have no claims of copyright!

REFERENCES

Anderson, K. and Y. Hayami, 1986, *The Political Economy of Agricultural Protection*, Sydney: Allen & Unwin.

Axelrod, R., 1984, *The Evolution of Cooperation*, Estouer, Plymouth: Basic Books.

Connell, J. *et al.*, 1976, *Migration from Rural Areas: The Evidence from Village Studies*, Oxford: Oxford University Press.

Dumont, R., 1962, *False Start in Africa*, London: Andre Deutsch.

Glewwe, P. and J. van der Gaag, 1992, *Confronting Poverty in Developing Countries: Definitions, information and policies*, LSMS Working Paper No. 48, Washington, DC: World Bank.

Harriss, B., 1987, 'Regional Growth Linkages from Agriculture' (Discussion), *Journal of Development Studies*, Vol. 23, No. 2.

Herring, J. and Edwards, R.M., 1983, 'Guaranteeing Employment to the Rural Poor: Social Functions and Class Interests in the Employment Guarantee Scheme in Western India', *World Development*, Vol.11, No.7.

Kakwani, N., 1993, 'Measuring Poverty: Definitions and Significant Tests with Application to Côte d'Ivoire', in M. Lipton, and J. van der Gaag (eds.), *Including the Poor*, Baltimore, MD: Johns Hopkins (forthcoming).

Leonard, D. 1977, *Reaching the Peasant Farmer: Organization Theory and Practice in Kenya*, Chicago, IL: University of Chicago Press.

Lewis, S.R. 1970, *Pakistan: Industrialization and Trade Policies*, Oxford: Oxford University Press.

Lipton, M., 1968, 'Urban Bias and Rural Planning', in P. Streeten, and M. Lipton (eds.), *The Crisis of Indian Planning*, Oxford: Oxford University Press.

Lipton, M., 1977, *Why Poor People Stay Poor: Urban Bias in World Development*, Cambridge, MA: Harvard University Press.

Lipton, M., 1981, 'Why Poor People Stay Poor', Sixth Vikram Sarabhai Memorial Lecture, Indian Institute of Management, Ahmedabad.

Lipton, M., 1982a, 'Rural Development and the Retention of the Rural Population in the Countryside of Developing Countries', *Canadian Journal of Development Studies*, Vol.III, No.1, pp.11–37.

Lipton, M., 1982b, 'Migration from Rural Areas of Poor Countries: The Impact on Rural Productivity and Income Distribution', in R. Sabot (ed.), *Migration and the Labour Market in Developing Countries*, Boulder, CO: Westview Press.

Lipton, M., 1984, 'Urban Bias Revisited', in J. Harriss, and M. Moore (eds.), *Development and the Rural–Urban Divide*, London: Frank Cass.

Lipton, M., 1987, *New Seeds and Poor People*, with Richard Longhurst, London: Unwin Hyman and Baltimore, MD: Johns Hopkins.

Lipton, M., 1991a, 'The State-Market Dilemma, Civil Society, and Structural Adjustment', *The Round Table*, Vol.317.

Lipton, M., 1991b, 'Agriculture, Rural People, the State and the Surplus in some Asian Countries: Thoughts on Some Implications of Three Recent Approaches in SocialScience', in J. Breman and S. Mundle (eds.), *Rural Transformation in Asia*, Oxford: Oxford University Press.

Lipton, M., 1992, 'Accelerated Resource Degradation by Third World Agriculture: Created in the Commons, in the West, or in Bed?', in S.A. Vosti, T. Reardon and W. von Urff (eds.), *Agricultural Sustainability, Growth and Poverty Alleviation: Issues and Policies*, Proceedings of the conference held 23–27 Sept. 1991, IFPRI/DSE/ZEL, Feldafing.

Lipton, M. and M. Ravallion, 1993, 'Poverty and Policy', in T.N. Srinivasan and J. Behrman (eds.), *Handbook of Development Economics*, Vol. III, Amsterdam: North Holland.

Olson, M., 1965, *The Logic of Collective Action*, Harvard, MA: Harvard University Press.

Olson, M., 1982, *The Rise and Decline of Nations*, New Haven, CT: Yale University Press.

Popper, K., 1934/59, 'Simplicity and Degree of Falsifiability', in *The Logic of Scientific Discovery*, London: Hutchinson.

Preston, S.H., 1975, 'The Changing Relationship between Mortality and Level of Economic Development', *Population Studies*, Vol.29, July.

Roemer, J. (ed.), 1985, *Analytical Marxism*, Cambridge: Cambridge University Press.

Ruzicka, L., 1982, 'Mortality in India', mimeo, British Society for Population Studies, Oxford Conference, Dec.

Urwick, J., 1983, 'Urban Bias in an African Educational System: The Case of Secondary Education in Sokoto State, Nigeria', D. Phil., University of Wisconsin.

Valdès, A. and M. Schiff, 1992, *The Plundering of Agriculture in Developing Countries*, Washington, DC: World Bank.

Wade, R., 1982, 'The System of Administrative and Political Corruption: Canal Irrigation in South India', *Journal of Development Studies*, Vol.18, No.3.

Williamson, J., 1991, 'Migration and Industrial Revolutions: Using History to Inform Contemporary Debate', paper presented to Nobel Jubilee Symposium on Population Economics, Lund, Sweden.

Wittgenstein, L, 1952, *Philosophical Investigations* (tr. G.E.M. Anscombe), Oxford: Blackwell.

World Bank, 1990, *World Development Report*, Washington, DC.

World Bank, 1991, *India: 1991 Country Economic Memorandum, Vol.II, Agriculture: Challenges and Opportunities*, Washington, DC.